W. PAUL COOK

The Wandering Life of a Yankee Printer

WITH SELECTED WRITINGS
BY AND ABOUT HIM

THE FIRST AND ONLY ISSUE OF COOK'S FAMOUS MAGAZINE.

W. PAUL COOK

The Wandering Life of a Yankee Printer

WITH SELECTED WRITINGS
BY AND ABOUT HIM

❧

Edited with an Introduction,
Bibliography and Notes
by Sean Donnelly

"For Love Only"

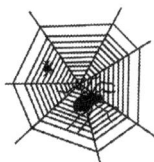

Hippocampus Press
New York

Published by Hippocampus Press
P.O. Box 641
New York, NY 10156
http://www.hippocampuspress.com

Cover art by Gale Mueller.
Cover design by Sean Donnelly and Ana Montalvo.
Hippocampus Press logo by Anastasia Damianakos.

First Edition

1 3 5 7 9 8 6 4 2

ISBN 0-9771734-6-1

CONTENTS

Extermination
Parasites
The Plan
Mission
Confidence
Boomerang
The Butt
Fealty
Vacation
Tabloid
"Not Molested"
Amusement
The Parting
Joy Street
Church

ILLUSTRATIONS

ॐ

Preface

W. Paul Cook is remembered most often as a friend of H. P. Lovecraft; and so he has lingered posthumously in the shadow of his famous friend. It is tempting to subtitle a book about him "Lovecraft's Friend" or something in that spirit, but it is contrary to my purpose. That purpose is to place Cook in his own light; to illuminate his own talents as a writer of fiction, essays, and poetry; as a publisher and printer; and as a sincere exponent of amateur journalism.

This book is a companion volume to *Willis T. Crossman's Vermont: Stories by W. Paul Cook* (University of Tampa Press, 2005) that I edited with Leland M. Hawes, Jr. I originally planned to produce one large book; a "Portable Cook," collecting prose and poetry, with works both by and about him, rounded out with a biography and bibliography. However, as materials were gathered and sorted it became apparent that one volume would not suffice. It was better to give Cook's alter-ego, Willis T. Crossman, his own exclusive forum in a book collecting what I think are the best of his "flat verse" or "staggered prose" tales of Vermont and her people. We hoped this would serve to garner belated attention for Cook as a regional writer deserving rediscovery.

On a personal note, it's been my pleasure to become better acquainted with Paul Cook over the past five years. I find myself drawn to and inspired by impractical people like him who are devoted to their loves and interests. They give so much more than they can ever expect to be repaid. His friends and colleagues recognized this in him and I marvel, as they did, time and again, at both the quantity and quality of his work. He deserves to be rememberd as more than just a footnote in another man's biography, and my desire to bring greater attention to his accomplishments has sustained the making of this book.

Sean Donnelly

Acknowledgments

First and foremost, I thank the gentlemen who read the book in manuscript and offered invaluable suggestions and corrections: Kenneth W. Faig, Jr., Leland M. Hawes, Jr., S. T. Joshi, and David E. Schultz. ᐤ Thanks also to the institutions who provided copies of W. Paul Cook manuscript letters in their collections: the John Hay Library, Brown University (with special thanks to Rosemary Cullen and Ann Stover Patrick); the Newberry Library; the Minnesota Historical Society; and the State Historical Society of Wisconsin. ᐤ For various courtesies I also thank Eugene Biancheri, son-in-law of the late Herman C. Koenig; Alistair Drurie (author of an online index of *The Vagrant*); Rollin Milroy of Heavenly Monkey Press; Angela Terry; Janine Awai and Paul E. Camp of the Special Collections Library, University of South Florida, Tampa; Richard Mathews; and Derrick Hussey for his faith and patience.

Special thanks to Gale Mueller of Spokane, Washington—artist, gentleman and fellow ajay—who produced the woodcut portrait of Paul Cook reproduced on the cover of this book. - *S.D.*

ABOUT W. PAUL COOK

Vrest Orton, Walter J. Coates, and W. Paul Cook.

W. Paul Cook: "An Ordinary Printer"

BY SEAN DONNELLY

He was elusive in life, and remains so in death. Even his closest friends could not say they knew Paul Cook well. Edward H. Cole, a friend of forty years, had to admit "now that he is gone, I am astonished to realize what large gaps there are in my knowledge. But it is all a part of the pattern of acquaintance with him: he opened the door of his life only so far to a friend; he closed it on much."[1]

In these pages we will re-open the door on the life of a modest man who styled himself "an ordinary printer," but whom friends called "The Colossus of the North" and a "sterling patron of weird literature." He was an amateur, in the true sense of the word, who labored with love for half a century as a printer, publisher, editor, and author in his native New England. The pleasure of the work itself was often the only reward for his labors.

YOUTH AND AMATEUR JOURNALISM (1880-1906)

By his own account, W. Paul Cook was born on August 31, 1881 (or 1882), to William and Alma Cook in Pittsford, Vermont. The only truth in that statement is that Vermont was the state of his birth. W. Paul Cook was actually born Arthur Garfield Cook on August 26, 1880, to George and Drisella Cook in Mt. Tabor, Vermont.[2]

Census data enumerated on June 3, 1880—several months before Paul Cook's birth—record only one Cook family residing in Mt. Tabor:

Horace, head of household, blacksmith, 50;
Marah (wife) 47;
Dellah (daughter) 16;
George (son) 28, married, blacksmith;
Willie (William Fitzroy) (son) 26, blacksmith;
Fred (son) 20, married, printer;
Allice (daughter-in-law) 18, married (to Fred);
Patience (mother) 78, widowed.

This may be identified with some certainty as the family of Paul Cook's father. Aside from a married son named George (the name of

3

Paul's father), the father (Horace) and another son (Willie) worked as blacksmiths. Paul is known to have had an uncle named William (who raised him) and a paternal grandfather named Horace, both of whom worked as blacksmiths; they ran a blacksmith and wheelwright shop in Marlborough, New Hampshire, in the 1890s.[3] Paul's other uncle, Fred, was a printer by trade, and he perhaps encouraged his nephew to pursue what eventually became his life-long vocation.

Though George Cook was married, his wife was not living with him. This raises questions that cannot be answered at this date, but one may speculate that Drisella went to live with her own family, away from the crowded Cook household, during her pregnancy. In June she would have been about seven months pregnant.

Two months later Drisella died during childbirth, and George—who census records show was 28 at the time—apparently felt incapable of raising Arthur alone. The boy was raised by his father's brother, William, and Alma LaBounty, who were married later in the year on December 1, 1880. The couple renamed the infant William Paul.

Cook's family had deep roots in America that stretched back to colonial times. Paul claimed descent from Benning Wentworth, royal governor of New Hampshire in the eighteenth century.[4] In an editorial Cook wrote in 1913 he shed more light on his genealogy by acknowledging Scottish, French, English, German, Dutch, and Iroquois ancestors. Cook further revealed that his grandfather Horace came from Scotland and that the family name was originally McCook.

Cook spent his youth in Vermont and New Hampshire. He attended schools in Readsboro, Chester, Center Rutland, and West Rutland, Vermont, and Marlborough and Claremont, New Hampshire, where he attended Stevens High School. According to his sister, Cora,[5] "Paul as a youth was very outgoing and he had many young friends. Paul and his crowd were a very mischievous group"[6] However, Paul also had a quiet, literary side to his personality which found expression when "his first published writing appeared in *The Echo*, of West Rutland grade school, in 1892,"[7] and later when he founded and edited Stevens High School's *The Red & Black*.

If his later passion for books is any indication, Cook was an avid reader from childhood. Like many boys of the day, he would have read story papers, novels by authors like Horatio Alger, Oliver Optic, and

Harry Castlemon, and popular juvenile magazines like *Golden Hours*, which published serials and short stories. "Correspondence circles were formed among the subscribers, and these led to clubs formed in all parts of the country."[8] The clubs issued papers that eventually numbered in the hundreds. One of those papers was *Tom Thumb*. Cook was living in Marlborough, N.H., when he "became associate editor of *Tom Thumb*, published at Elmwood, NH (now Chesham, NH), three miles from Marlborough. His associate was Harry J. Morse."[9] Cook was referring to *Tom Thumb* when he later wrote, "I printed papers before I knew that there was such a thing as organized amateur journalism."[10]

"Organized amateur journalism" meant the National and the United Amateur Press Associations, whose officers were elected at annual conventions, in contrast to the loose affiliations among the *Golden Hours* Clubs. The United actually had its origins in those clubs. "In 1895 one of these '*Golden Hours* Club' members was William H. Greenfield of Philadelphia. [. . .] He conceived the idea of a union of these scattered club papers and editors into one national organization, and with apparently no associated planners he announced the formation of the United Amateur Press Association."[11]

As a reader of *Golden Hours*, Cook inevitably learned about the association and "was introduced to organized amateur journalism through one of the branches of the United back in 1901."[12] A few years later he joined the venerable National (which was founded in 1876). It's not surprising that the teenaged Cook entered the ranks of amateur journalism, a hobby group for people who write for, publish, or print journals for free circulation among members of an association. His previous experience as an editor and writer made it a natural pastime, which dovetailed with his intention to pursue printing and editing professionally.

By 1901, Cook was in Hanover, NH, working at the Dartmouth Press. There he kept the presses and other machines, like the linotypes, running. "He made arrangements to be instructed in English literature three nights in the week by Prof. Charles Francis Richardson of Dartmouth College. [. . .] He had seen some of young Cook's compositions, or articles, and he volunteered to assist him. This was a wonderful compliment to Cook. Working days and studying nights for a year and a half, Cook got the full course of instruction in English literature."[13]

The press put first-class printing equipment at Cook's disposal. He took full advantage of his situation when he began to produce his first great amateur magazine, *Monadnock Monthly*. The premiere number, dated November 1901, is plain in appearance, but much superior in size and quality to the majority of the period's amateur publications. On the cover of that first issue is advertised a subscription rate of fifty cents per year. This was quickly discarded in favor of a motto that sheds light on most of Cook's subsequent activities as a printer, publisher, author, and editor: For Love Only; You Cannot Buy It. The second issue of the monthly was published on time, but it was two years before another saw print. Part of the reason for the delay lay in Cook's sometimes off-hand attitude: "It always interested me more to print a paper than to send it out. [. . .] If one gets a personal kick out of writing or printing something, what does it matter if anyone else sees it or not?"[14]

Over the next few years ever larger and more elaborate numbers of *Monadnock Monthly* were published, in editions as large as 700 copies. The size was usually 6 × 9 inches. Many were illustrated with plates reproducing tinted photographs with scenes of his beloved New England, which made it as handsome as some professional magazines of the period, like *Century*. Among the contents were poems, articles (including profiles Cook wrote of New England authors), editorials with news and reviews of the amateur press, and fiction.

Some of the short stories in *Monadnock* were by Willis Tete Crossman. This was in fact the *nom de plume* of Paul Cook. In all, more than a dozen Crossman stories saw print, in *Monadnock* and in other amateur papers like Anthony Wills's *Fiction*. Cook's authorship of the Crossman stories was not widely known. One friend remarked that "Cook likes to guard it."[15]

Crossman's real identity was revealed publicly in the July 1919 *National Amateur*.[16] But by then he had nearly stopped writing short stories, and he later disavowed them all: "Up to the age of about twenty, I had amused myself by writing short stories. They were probably the worst short stories ever written—puerile, even infantile, innocuous, ill-balanced, poorly constructed, and even worse written. Even when

I opened my eyes and stopped writing them, I had a few on hand which I suppose I was too lazy to destroy, and they found their way into amateur papers."[17] It's unfortunate that he thought so little of his fiction, for H. P. Lovecraft wrote to a correspondent: "Cook has written a most vivid & dramatic short story called 'The Ends of the Law,' about a Western Sheriff & his prisoner in the midst of a desert. The suspense, incidents, & development stamp Cook as a gifted fictionist."[18]

Besides his own publications and writings, Cook worked on cooperative amateur papers like the *Reflector*. In the August 1906 issue his co-editor, Louis N. Starring, announced: "We are sorry to have to report, that owing to poor health Mr. Paul Cook has had to give up his work at Hanover, New Hampshire".[19] With no family ties and perhaps no other prospects of work in New Hampshire, Cook moved to Athol, Massachusetts. He was living there in November 1906, when he and Vincent Haggerty issued the *Pilgrim*. Cook and Haggerty knew each other through the UAPA, but this paper was "devoted to the approaching election of the Atlantic Coast Amateur Press Association."[20] The association was only in its second year and apparently aimed at fostering amateur journalism in the East. Since the *Pilgrim* was a one-shot publication, it may be assumed the A.C.A.P.A., Cook's association with it, or both, were short-lived.

WANDERING YEARS (1907-1912)

Cook's move to Athol foreshadowed an unsettled time in his life. During the following six years he moved around the Northeast as an itinerant printer and editor. His membership in a typographical union would have given him the liberty to move easily from job to job. Between 1906 and 1912 he "engaged in newspaper work in Ansonia, Seymour, and Danbury, Connecticut"[21] and worked as a printer in Claremont, Manchester, and Hanover, New Hampshire; New London, Norwich and Waterbury, Connecticut; Portland and Belfast, Maine; New Rochelle and New York, New York; Camden, New Jersey; Erie, Pennsylvania; and Boston, Worcester, Springfield, Amesbury, and Athol, Massachusetts.

In the parlance of the day Cook was living the life of a "tramp printer." By the early 1900s tramp printing was in its fourth phase, "from the introduction of the Linotype in 1886 to the Great Depression of the 1930s."[22] John Edward Hicks described the life and those who lived it in his *Adventures of a Tramper Printer: 1880-1890*—

> The tramp printer, as a usual thing, did not marry early, but if married, he had things so arranged that he could make his departure from town without delay, and when things became disagreeable he left quickly, without even a good-by. As for home, home was where he happened to be, and a situation was merely a matter of convenience. He didn't own anything, never expected to, and wouldn't know what to do with it if he had.
>
> [. . .] Printers were not tramps of necessity, but from choice. When a printer had finished his term of apprenticeship, he was told to get out and and learn something. The style was different in each town and there was much to learn. He took to the road in order to broaden himself mentally and efficiently, or to see the country. In those days the trade afforded a good living to the itinerant printer. The tramp printer was a salty character, as interesting as he was salty. He was an individualist, sworn to personal freedom of action. He had an insatiable urge to be on the go. He could not be anchored to a regular job for long.[23]

What gave the tramp printer his freedom were the traveling cards issued by typographical unions. "The traveling card ensured geographic mobility. [. . .] If the printing establishment was experiencing a slow time, the tramps were given food money and the right to sleep in the office for the night."[24]

Despite Cook's unsettled life he tried to remain active in amateur journalism. At the 1907 UAPA convention he was voted Official Editor. That made him responsible for the publication of volume seven of the official organ, the *United Amateur*. He edited only one issue (dated September 1907), and the editorship passed to Homer P. Pickrell with the November 1907 number. In that number a brief note appeared in the "President's Message" by Edward F. Daas: "With great regret I announce the resignation from office, of W. Paul Cook. Mr. Cook's sudden illness which delayed the appearance of the September official organ, and his inability to publish the current number on time, caused him to tender his resignation, which I reluctantly accepted."[25]

Early in 1908 Cook moved from 244 Franklin St. in Norwich, CT, to 88 Spring St. in Keene, NH. This is recorded in the *United Amateur*, where his name appears on the membership list through the July 1908 issue. It is absent thereafter until September 1911, when he appears again as an Honorary Member living in Boston. During the interim Cook remained in touch with his ajay [amateur journalist] friends. Edith Miniter noted in the *Aftermath* that Cook attended a meeting in Boston on February, 22, 1909. "Good and clever boy, [Edward H.] Cole was with us in the space of time described as a jiffy, escorting Paul Cook."[26]

Cook was living in Danvers, Connecticut, in 1910 when he met Adeline "Addie" Emmeline Smith. She owned the boarding house where Cook lived. She had already been married and widowed twice, and had children, but the 32-year-old Cook was enamored. Paul and Adeline married in 1912.

SETTLED DOWN (1913-1925)

The newlyweds settled in Athol, Massachusetts, in January 1913. Paul described it unflatteringly as "a north central Massachusetts town which was the most absolutely devoid of historical, architectural, scenic, archaeological, or sentimental interest of any town I ever saw anywhere."[27] Cook took a job as foreman of the local newspaper, the *Transcript*. The equipment and personnel of the paper's printing office made it possible for Cook to again print amateur journals, and later books, for himself and his friends. The job paid well, allowing Cook to buy his first home and more books for his prized library. Most importantly, he forged lasting friendships with fellow amateur journalists and other like-minded literary people during this period. Altogether, the move to Athol marked the beginning of the most settled and productive period of his life.

After several years of inactivity, Cook returned to amateur journalism with an issue of the magazine that had first made him famous: "One of the most heartening aspects of 1912-1913 was the sudden unheralded return to activity of W. Paul Cook. [. . .] Cook issued one of his remarkable numbers of the *Monadnock Monthly* [*sic*], 76 pages, 7 x 10. Well did Maurice Moe write, 'I am struck speechless.'"[28] The issue was dedicated to his mother, Alma M. LaBounty Cook, and published on her birthday, May 12, 1913. Though Cook contemplated another issue of *Monadnock* as late as 1919, the May 1913 would be the final issue.[29]

Cook renewed acquaintances with old friends and met new amateurs when he attended a meeting in Boston on Labor Day, 1913:

> [T]he following enthusiastic amateur journalists gathered at 18 Gurney Street: Miss Hazel B. Pratt, of Brooklyn, N.Y., W. Paul Cook, of Athol, Mass., Miss Elinor Parker, a promising recruit, Chas. A. A. Parker, Edward H. Cole, George Kilpatrick, B. Edward Sawyer and Albert Sandusky. Visitors to *The Torpedo* print-shop improve each golden minute by sticking type, running the press, or folding the mailing papers and recruiting circulars. [. . .] Mr. Cook, fresh from his triumphs of issuing the most stupendous amateur paper in years, is an amateur we have been trying unsuccessfully to meet ever since we came to Boston, and we naturally were very glad he could be with us. Mr. Cook is very enthusiastic and before the year is out will give Amateur Journalism a number of surprises.[30]

One immediate surprise was the inauguration of Cook's "Typographical Criticism" column in the September *United Amateur.* The advice given in his practical criticisms of George A. Thomson's *Bay State Advocate* reveals his hands-on experience as a printer:

> The very first thing that Mr. Thomson has to do is to thoroughly clean his type. Every page, before it is distributed, should be given a thorough scrubbing with a brush and benzine or gasoline. A rag will positively never clean the type. A brush is absolutely essential. I would advise Mr. Thomson to set his cases right out and clean his type thoroughly before attempting another issue. This done, he would have more excuse for greater care in his presswork.
>
> In his presswork, Mr. Thomson must apply more impression to begin with. He cannot possibly produce decent results otherwise, and with clean type he can safely give a great deal

more "squeeze." Next, greater care should be taken in the distribution of his ink. In every case, when applying ink to the disc, remove the form from the press and thoroughly distribute the ink before taking an impression. This will prevent part of a page being a light unreadable gray and part of it a dark unreadable gob of ink,—as in the case in the copy before the critic.[31]

A couple of years later Cook introduced the *Vagrant,* the second of his three great amateur papers (between the *Monadnock* of the 1900s and *The Ghost* of the 1940s). It fit the profile of most amateur papers of the period: a mix of poetry, fiction, essays, and editorial matter (often gossipy and sometimes catty). From the slim 10-page inaugural issue, dated December 1915, the paper grew to 16, 24, 40, 92, and then 148 pages with the June 1918 number, but following issues were trimmed back to around 48 pages until the mammoth fifteenth and final issue of 312 pages issued in Spring 1927.

Among the new recruits to amateur journalism in 1914 was Howard Phillips Lovecraft (1890-1937) of Providence, Rhode Island. Though he and Cook lived fairly close to each other, three years passed before they met. On September 24, 1917, Lovecraft wrote to fellow amateur journalist Rheinhart Kleiner:

> Just a week ago I enjoyed the honour of a personal call from Mr. W. Paul Cook, amateur of eminence & editor of *The Vagrant.* I was rather surprised at his appearance, for he is rather more rustic & carelessly groomed than I had expected a man of his celebrity to be. In fact, his antique derby hat, unpressed garments, frayed cravat, yellowish collar, ill-brushed hair, & none too immaculate hands made me think of my old friend Sam Johnson; another great literary man who was somewhat negligent as to personal appearance & the like. But Cook's conversation makes up for whatever outward deficiencies he may possess. Though not overwhelmingly bookish, he has a keen mind, dry humour, & an infinite & quite encyclopaedic knowledge of the events & personages of amateur journalism past & present. I cannot see how one head can hold such a mass of amateur history & anecdote. He is opinionated to a considerable degree, & has scant love of any existing amateur

press association; but his love of the general cause is so great, that he is ever willing to oblige any amateur irrespective of associational affiliations. He is to print the September *United Amateur*, though he will not accept a regular appointment as official Publisher. His coming *Vagrant* promises to be an ample & notable issue, having, I believe, 56 pages. I think I shall have Cook print *The Conservative* in future, for he underbids all competitors. His low rates are a philanthropic favour to amateurdom, & are based upon a complete sacrifice of personal profit. He is so anxious to establish a revival of amateur journalism, that he is doing the work absolutely at cost. His rates are as follows:

> 300 copies 5 × 7—per page—$0.85
> 300 copies 6 × 9—per page—1.05
> 300 copies 7 × 10—per page—1.25

I was greatly pleased with Cook, for he is interesting, high-minded, and intellectual in tastes. He takes amateur journalism with phenomenal seriousness—it is his world, so to speak; and its history and institutions are sacred to him.[32]

The "coming *Vagrant*" was the fifth number (dated June 1917). It included Lovecraft's "To Templeton and Mount Monadnock." Cook couldn't resist the charms of this ode to the beauties of New England. The love they shared for their native New England was one foundation of their friendship. Before long Lovecraft also learned that Cook had an affinity for "weird" literature. On November 8, 1917, he wrote Rheinhart Kleiner, "I think I shall send this piece—'Nemesis'—to the *Vagrant*, since Cook seems fond of the unusual."[33] These were the first of a handful of notable poems and short stories—like "The Statement of Randolph Carter" and "Dagon"—that Cook published in the *Vagrant*.

The friendship between Cook and Lovecraft had a profound influence on both men. One need only read Cook's affecting memoir to know what Lovecraft meant to him after more than twenty years. As for Lovecraft, though he wrote no piece dedicated to Cook, his letters to Frank B. Long, Jr., Clark Ashton Smith, Donald Wandrei, and others contain various expressions of gratitude toward Cook for the crucial role Cook played in encouraging him to write fiction.

"I never encountered [anyone interested in the weird] till 1917, when I stumbled simultaneously on Cook & [Samuel] Loveman."[34] Cook "saw some of my old stuff & urged me to begin again" and then "egged me on to the point of actual production."[35] "I chanced to send Culinarius [HPL's playful Latinization of *Cook*] 'The Alchemist', and he immediately told me that fiction is my one and only province! Mildly amused, I sent him the 'Beast', which he snapped up as though it were worth printing. My stock of tales was now quite exhausted, but Cook kept urging me to improve my supposed gift for weird tales, so I decided to revive the old atmosphere. [. . .] I did—'The Tomb' and 'Dagon' being my first fresh attempts. Cook spoke so highly of these that I kept on."[36] Cook told Lovecraft that "The Tomb" "immeasurably surpassed all my juvenile attempts" and offered to print it. HPL likewise received a "glowing acknowledgment" from Cook for his "Psychopompos".

It is no wonder that Lovecraft told Frank B. Long, Jr., "If I ever have a book of tales I mean to dedicate it to [Cook]; for it is thro' his urging that I resumed the practice of fictional composition."[37] Thanks to Cook's *Vagrant*, Lovecraft had a regular and well-produced forum for his early work. And perhaps Lovecraft's work gave Cook an incentive to maintain a regular publication schedule. It may be no coincidence that Cook discontinued *The Vagrant* around the same time that Lovecraft graduated from amateur journalism to a professional career with the advent of *Weird Tales* in 1923.

Lovecraft's contributions to the *Vagrant* are the most notable, but also worth notice are the works of Elsa Gidlow and Roswell George Mills. Gidlow was a poet who published, with her friend Mills, the amateur paper *Les Mouches Fantastiques*; and the two made no secret of their homosexuality.[38] In 1923, Gidlow's *On a Grey Thread*, the first collection of lesbian poetry published in the United States, was issued by Will Ransom.[39] Works with homosexual themes were not common in the amateur, or even in the professional, press at that time, but Cook published some of their work in his *Vagrant*. Surely Cook was not ignorant of the subject matter even when it was not overt. But, as he explained in a letter to August W. Derleth, who had submitted a work with a gay theme to Cook for publication, he made a distinction between types of homosexual love:

I fear that I must subscribe to previous opinions as to the advisability of publishing "Rebirth." Relations between sexes are, and always have been, subjects for art. To a much lesser degree Lesbianism (if I may coin a word) as between females, may be used in an archaic, Alexandrian, or wine-crowned setting with an artistic interest. But relations (erotic) between males in a modern setting are too deeply and inherently abhorrent for any stage of decadence, or for successful handling in a convincingly artistic way. You have simply set for yourself in this sketch a subject that the very greatest masters of the art could not successfully handle. I have read it with considerable interest, but it left me cold.[40]

The years when Cook regularly issued the *Vagrant,* from 1915 to 1922, were the most active of his association with amateur journalism. Cook's own contributions to the magazine were mostly editorials. Lovecraft wrote of them: "I cannot but marvel at the patient accuracy with which he delves into the minutiae of amateur history. He chronicles the trivialities of a convention as faithfully as most men would record an historical assemblage of statesmen. [. . .] And yet, I suppose it is well to have a record of everything—so Cook is doubtless to be congratulated on his patience."[41] An exception to his routine editorials was a short essay titled "Howard P. Lovecraft's Fiction." It appeared with Lovecraft's "Dagon" in the November 1919 *Vagrant.* Here we have Lovecraft's first important work of supernatural fiction together with the first of innumerable essays and articles about his work. Cook wrote, "With 'Dagon', in this issue of the *Vagrant*, Mr. Lovecraft steps into his own as a writer of fiction," and he predicted, "He will never be as voluminous a fiction writer as a poet, but we may confidently expect to see him advance even beyond the high mark he has set in 'Dagon.'"[42]

During this period he also held official office again, for the first time since his editorship of the *United Amateur* in 1907. He was Official Editor of the UAPA in 1918-19. During the same time he was Official Editor of the NAPA, when Graeme Davis was president. In retrospect, it was judged that his volume "ranks top and lives to support the thesis that W. Paul Cook was one of the most efficient and thoroughly genuine amateurs of our time."[43] Amidst the success of his amateur activities there was one sad note: Cook's adoptive father, William, passed away in September 1918.

Early the next year amateur journalism lost one of its most active members when Helene Hoffman Cole died so suddenly and so young after a minor outpatient surgery went awry. She was a leading figure in the U.A.P.A. in which Cook (and Lovecraft) were active. Cook wrote immediately to her husband, Edward Cole, to express his condolences:

> It is a seeming mockery at times like this to attempt to pen words of sympathy—what is needed is the silent hand-clasp that speaks louder than any words or than reams of written condolence.
>
> Allow me to say that you are bereft, but that your bereavement leaves a void in Amateur Journalism which can not be filled any more than can the place at your fireside. In these drear days such an one can be sorely spared. But she leaves you Sherman to work for and to watch over—and this is a priceless legacy, her memory and her son.[44]

Following immediately on the heels of his editorship, Cook was elected president of the National for 1919-20 at the 1919 convention. He had hitherto avoided holding any of the overtly "political" offices in ajay. His retiring and stand-offish attitude was not suited to the quarrelsome game that office-holding could be. Early in his term he sent an encouraging letter to the membership that read, in part,

> The President will himself be active, will be heard from frequently, and he urges all members to follow his example—or, better still, set an example for him to follow.
>
> Activity! More papers! More Laureate entries! More of every element that goes to make up Amateur Journalism.
>
> Fraternally yours,
>
> W. Paul Cook[45]

Anthony F. Moitoret was elected Official Editor, but Cook took over that responsibility in January 1920, when Moitoret moved from Cleveland to California, to avoid confusion and the expense of a change in post-office registration. By the end of his term Cook could boast that the National had 275 members, 3000 membership applications were distributed, the association was out of debt, and 96 papers were issued during the year. Cook capped off his presidency of the National by publishing William C. Alhauser's *Our Ex-Presidents* (1919), a handsome clothbound book illustrated with photographs, with Cook himself as the last entry. His fellow ajays in the National were grateful to him for his service and the handsome book, but the same couldn't be said for the ajays in the United:

> The United is bound for trouble again, this time because of the idiotic way some members have been nagging Cook about the lateness of the official organ. They ought to know that he is practically giving them this de luxe thing as an act of charity— but they don't; and instead of being grateful they ask for more! Such is mankind. [. . .] Cook has just sent me the rough draft of his resignation, as he means to forward it to Miss D. and Mrs. R. DAMNATION! Kin ya imagine the result? The year's programme ruined, and that nasty wretch Dowdell gloating and triumphant! I have written Culinarius a note of ultimate appeal, imploring him for the sake of old and hallowed memories not to desert the flag in time of need. Will he heed? I hope so! If not, back to Ericson—higher rates, less intelligent work, and just as much delay after all.[46]

Trouble was stirring in the National as well. The administration of Anthony Moitoret, who succeeded Cook as president, was a difficult one. The association found itself in a poor financial situation, owing at least partly to a general slump in the post-World War I economy. Political games were another cause, and they would drive Cook away from the position he'd taken on the official board.

In the latter part of the Moitoret administration, George Houtain [President, 1915-16] began again to awake from his slumbers. [. . .] Histrionics were his by-line. Having moved up to Massachusetts and into the orbit of a woman from those parts, he thrust that fair damsel's best hat into the ring for N.A.P.A. Prexy to follow Anthony F. Moitoret.

Mrs. E. Dorothy McLaughlin was unknown outside the Boston area. She had no legitimate claim to any office in the association. Her name appeared for the first time on a membership list in the March 1921 *National Amateur*. She was shortly, however, to become Mrs. George Julian Houtain, which was apparently enough to elect her, since she possessed no claims of her own. [. . .] The McLaughlin campaign was about as turbulent as any amateur journalism ever recorded. Houtain master-minded it but he used youngsters like John Milton Heins to publish his personal attacks, the youngster taking the beating while George chuckled somewhere in the background. This mud-slinging, directed not against political issues but against personalities, lost to amateur journalism many worth-while members, some of whom have never returned.[47]

In the aftermath, Cook resigned from the official board. Some said he was removed because of inactivity, which was ridiculous in light of his great efforts on behalf of amateur journalism. Edith Miniter suggested jealousy was the reason. "Mr. Cook seems to have been allowed to resign because it is never wise to keep on the establishment an underling whose achievements overshadow the head of the house."[48]

Despite these troubles Cook attended the NAPA convention in July 1921. It was the first he'd ever attended, though he'd been an amateur journalist for more than two decades.

The dramatic moment was when Edward H. Cole, at the close of an address on quite another subject, fished a silver loving cup of severely simple design from under the head table, and presented it to W. Paul Cook, who had been carefully located with his back to said head table. It was inscribed: "Presented to | W. Paul Cook | National Amateur Press Association | President 1919-1920 | A tribute of appreciation for 25 years' service | in the cause of Amateur Journalism." One of Mr. Cook's friends related that a few weeks before the convention Cook was heard to remark that he was glad nothing had been done to revive the loving cup scheme which Cleveland had side-stepped. He is said to have added that anyhow he "wouldn't want to receive any such gift in Boston." He'd "prefer to receive it in an enemy city." Well, no city would seem to be that to Paul Cook!. [. . .] [H]e has more than once pulled the organization out of a slough, is indeed referred to as a veritable Messiah by his myriad admirers. [But] he hastily begs to be omitted [from consideration for office].[49]

While Paul Cook was thanking the delegates for the Loving Cup presented to him in recognition of his services to amateur journalism, Mrs. Paul Cook was packing and wrapping and tieing it up and [. . .] said "I still have something to say and no one shall see this cup until Mr. Cook buys me a home worthy of displaying it in."[50]

Cook returned to his irregular publishing activities with *In Memoriam: Jennie E. T. Dowe* in September 1921. Jennie Dowe was the mother of Edith Miniter. The booklet received some attention outside of amateur journalism when it was reviewed in the *Boston Transcript* by William Stanley Braithwaite. In 1921 Cook also published *Ring and Diamond* by William H. Greenfield, a collection of works by the founder of the United. The imprint on this book is "Cook Publishing Co.", in contrast to the use of his name alone on the Alhauser book he issued in 1919. One wonders if Cook was considering a regular publishing program at this time. As early as 1922, Lovecraft was trying to "induce Cook to publish a book of collected Loveman poetry."[51] For the time being, he printed Loveman's amateur journal the *Saturnian*.[52] The penultimate issue of his own *Vagrant* appeared the same year, dated March 1922, containing Lovecraft's "The Tomb."

Lovecraft also submitted "The Terrible Old Man" and "From Beyond" to Cook for publication, but Cook returned them with regrets. "Letting these stories go unpublished is the greatest penalty I am paying for allowing myself to fall into disastrous financial circumstances."[53] The exact nature of his financial setback is unknown, but he was working odd jobs to help pay the bills. The letter quoted above was written on letterhead for the Publication Office of "The Spirit of '98", a monthly published by Major Frank Keck Camp No. 53, United Spanish War Veterans, Department of New York. Cook is listed there as Managing Editor. Despite his financial worries, though, Cook did consider taking on a new project. "Regarding the book of Mr. Hoag's poetry of which you spoke in your letter of February 2. I think perhaps if you still wish, that I might undertake the matter, seeing that you are to handle it yourself."[54] The book, *The Poetical*

Works of Jonathan E. Hoag, was eventually published in 1923 with a preface by Lovecraft. The book lacks an imprint so there is a question surrounding the identity of the printer. But it seems unlikely that Cook printed it, as it does not compare well typographically with his other publications from this period.

Lovecraft continued to send his stories to Cook for appraisal. On January 10, 1923, Cook wrote to tell him, "I have enjoyed both the stories of course, and perhaps 'The Unnamable' is salable, but I doubt if even *Weird Tales* would use 'The Festival.'"[55] The first issue of *Weird Tales*, a pulp magazine that would have an enormous influence on American weird fiction, was soon published in March 1923. Lovecraft became a regular contributor of fiction, poetry, and letters to the editor. One of those letters inspired a neighbor of Cook's in Athol, Massachusetts, to contribute to the magazine too. In December of 1924 Cook wrote to tell Lovecraft:

> I have recently become acquainted with a young fellow in town, Harold W. Munn, a nephew of a one-time well known Charles Clark Munn. Young Munn is steeped in the weird and supernatural, has read all numbers of *Weird Tales*, is in love with your own work, and has from your suggestion in an early number of *Weird Tales* written a 15,000 work yarn, the autobiography of a were-wolf (his first story), which has been accepted by *Weird Tales*!!![56]

Enthusiasts of weird fiction were so rare that it is no surprise that the discovery of Munn in his little town of Athol thrilled him.

THE RECLUSE PRESS (1925-1929)
"A Declaration of Independence"

By the mid-1920s Cook had produced a variety of miscellaneous books and magazines related to amateur journalism. But in 1926 he decided to inaugurate a publishing program with a distinctive new imprint: The Recluse Press. Amateur journalism had rewarded Cook with friendship and camaraderie, but he was disappointed with what he had achieved in the hobby. The energies he'd put into amateur journalism would be rechanneled into his modest ambition to publish works of genuine literary quality.

Discussions of similar ambitions, which no doubt encouraged his own intentions, took place in Vermont in the summer of 1925, when Cook, Walter John Coates, and Vrest Orton gathered at Orton's home in North Calais. Walter John Coates (1880–1941) was a Universalist minister, author, and occasional publisher. Like Cook, he'd issued miscellaneous booklets, beginning in 1906, then founded The Driftwind Press. Between 1918 and 1928 the press issued ten publications, all of them bound in wraps and less than about 50 pages in length; the majority were works by Coates himself. He owned a general store that also served as his press office in North Montpelier, Vermont, where he lived with his wife, Nettie, and daughter, Flora. Vrest Orton (1897-1986) was, like Cook and Coates, a Vermont native, who lived for a time in his youth in Athol, Massachusetts. He enjoyed a successful career in publishing until settling in his native state and founding The Vermont Country Store in 1946 with his wife, Ellen.

What first brought the three men together was a collection of Coates's poems, *Mood Songs*, published at the Solitarian Press.[57] The publishers were two brothers, J. Howard Flower and Donald Flower. Their books remind one of those produced by the Roycrofters, and Howard himself dressed and grew his hair as Roycrofters founder Elbert Hubbard did.

Of Vrest Orton, Cook wrote: "I number Orton as one of my dearest friends. [. . .] I envy him his energy and his resurgent power to dream and make his dreams come true."[58] Orton likewise held Cook in high regard. According to Lovecraft, Orton considered Cook "one of the finest & most extraordinary characters he ever met—a man of high intellect & keen taste despite the rusticity which poverty for two or three generations behind him has imparted to his speech, dress, & manners."[59]

Coates and Orton both wrote accounts of the 1925 meeting in North Calais. Orton recalled: "I was that summer occupying an old three-story brick house, which had been, a hundred years ago, a post-road tavern. Surrounded by what we liked to believe the spirits of our ancestors, we talked of bringing them to life again—all, that is, who had written anything worth remembering. We were happily optimistic. The garden was shaded by a butternut tree and cooled by high stone walls—there was plenty of fine tobacco—some cider, I think—and the talk was good."[60]

Coates's account is in the same mood: "Dreamy laziness was the method; literature was the menu; utopian visions were the dessert. We smoked, of course. We built castles. We talked. Individuality ran rampant—for each had literary loves, literary aversions. But on one subject all were agreed: something must be done to stimulate more widespread and unified literary activity in Vermont—to encourage nascent writers and promote keener appreciation for their work. Both they and their local reading public were suffering from a self-imposed inferiority complex."[61]

Out of this meeting a literary magazine was born: *Driftwind*, first published in April 1926. It was described as an amateur magazine done for love only, echoing Cook's own motto. Appropriately, years later, Cook was called upon after Coates's death to keep the magazine going, and he did so until his own death.

Around the time he was encouraging Coates to publish *Driftwind*, Cook made a dramatic decision about his ties to amateur journalism and the future course of his own publishing activities. Though the announcement did not appear in print until the final issue of the *Vagrant* was published in Spring 1927, his friends were aware of his intentions in 1925:

> The intent of this issue of the *Vagrant* is plain. During the last years of active amateur publishing, I at various times accepted for publication and promised to publish a great deal of matter which was not used when my activity ceased. It is to redeem these promises only that I have issued this *Vagrant*. To relieve its monotony I have inserted some things which please me.
>
> This does not end my non-professional publishing, but it ends my amateur publishing in the sense of any connection with organized amateur journalism. I shall have a non-professional magazine in time which will be circulated among book lovers and those interested in literary effort. This will mean that some amateur journalists will receive it, along with many who are not amateur journalists.[62]

By the fall of 1925 rumors of "Cook's coming magazine" began to circulate among the Lovecraft circle.[63] In the late summer of that year Cook had proposed that Lovecraft write an article "on the element of terror & weirdness in literature."[64] Cook also wanted fiction and poetry for the magazine. Lovecraft promised "The Outsider" and another story for publication, but "The Outsider" appeared instead in *Weird Tales* and the other story would have a strange fate.[65]

> My "Shunned House" will be published next spring in W. Paul Cook's proposed magazine, *The Recluse*, which he may or may not try to launch professionally. Cook, after cancelling all his obligations toward amateurdom by the issuance of a 312-page *Vagrant*, (the largest publication to appear in the entire history of amateur journalism) will commence a experiment in book publishing; handling first a volume of Belknap's poems & next a volume of Loveman's. He will try to market the books through regular channels, & gain for himself & quiet Athol a reputation in the literary field. He may visit New-York in the winter or spring, in which case the gang will take pleasure in shewing him the sights & directing him to all the rare book emporia. It seems likely, from various chance remarks of his, that he possesses the finest private library of any person ever connected with amateur journalism—a thing one would hardly suspect upon beholding his slight, malaria-racked, & obviously rustic form faltering hesitantly & bewilderedly along the crowded & engulfing streets of a city."[66]

The number and rarity of the books that Cook lent to Lovecraft as he prepared his essay on supernatural literature does indeed suggest that Cook owned a fine library. He later estimated it numbered 3,000 volumes.[67] In early January of 1926 Lovecraft wrote, "My own favourite pastime lately has been writing that weird tale article for Cook, and doing the incidental reading essential thereto. [. . .] Culinarius will greatly lament that sentence of his—'there is absolutely no limit as to length.'"[68] Cook had encouraged Lovecraft's reading of weird fiction since the beginning of their friendship by suggesting authors and loaned hard-to-find works. In 1919 Cook was trying to get him to read Guy de Maupassant and Gustave Flaubert.[69] The next year, Cook was "outlining a reading course in Haggard [and] I have just finished Stoker's *Jewel of Seven Stars*, lent me by Cook."[70] A few years later Cook lent him Lucius Sargent's *Dealings with the Dead*,[71] another of Stoker's novels, *The Lair of the White Worm*, and M. P. Shiel's *The Pale Ape and Other Pulses*. The Shiel volume included "The House of Sounds," which "both Cook and I solemnly declare to be a peerless masterpiece—the finest horror-story of the generation."⁷² In a letter Cook wrote on Memorial Day, 1923, he advised Lovecraft to read Radcliffe's *Mysteries of Udolpho*, which he found "quite worth while, if one can smother the usual disgust at the passages depicting the weak-minded and sorrowing and clinging-vine 'females.'"⁷³ As for other fiction, Cook recommended he not "bother with any of my Stokeriana," and mentioned that he was collecting first English editions of Jules Verne and works by Arthur Machen. On the subject of Machen, Cook wrote:

> I am cursorily familiar with Arthur Machen, and have taken it for granted that you were. In fact, some two weeks ago I ordered *The Terror* as a beginning for collecting him. I have not seen *The House of Souls*, but I have read *The Bowmen and other Legends*, *The Great God Pan*, *The Secret Glory*, *The Shining Pyramid*, *Far Off Things*, *Things Near and Far*, *The Hill of Dreams*. If you have an opportunity to get hold of *The Fortunate Lovers*, *The Hill of Dreams*, or Machen's translation of *The Heptameron* at a reasonable price, sieze them at once. Most of his stuff is held at prohibitive prices.⁷⁴

Cook also lent him Shiel's *The Purple Cloud* and Radcliffe's *The Italian*, and in 1927 Lovecraft borrowed two classic works that impressed him greatly: Robert W. Chambers's *The King in Yellow* and E. R. Eddison's *The Worm Ouroboros*. After reading the former, Lovecraft wrote, "With Cook I agree that it's an eternal pity for Chambers ever to have been sidetracked from his early tendency."⁷⁵ Of Eddison's novel he said, "Never shall I cease to thank Cook for forcing me to read this book."⁷⁶ After he finished the supernatural literature essay, Lovecraft continued to borrow books from Cook. "I have also gone through several weird books lent me by Cook—the best of which are Eino Railo's *Haunted Castle*, (a history of the Gothick novel by an Anglicised Finn professor), Pemberton's *The Weird O' It*, (mediocre horror tales) and Vernon Knowles's *Street of Strange Houses* and *Here and Otherwise* [*sic*]."⁷⁷

The references in Lovecraft's and Cook's correspondence give a tantalizing picture of Cook's library. In Cook's own letters there is further evidence of the depth and quality of his collection of weird literature, and his broad knowledge of the field. There are also hints of the strange lengths a collector will go to to acquire a desideratum. For example, Cook was collecting Conrad Aiken when he began corresponding with Donald Wandrei (1908-1987), the poet and supernatural fiction writer who later co-founded Arkham House. Wandrei lent him his university library's copy of Aiken's *The Charnel Rose* to read. Cook read and returned it, but asked Wandrei, "What will it cost to lose that copy and pay the library for it?"[78] Wandrei did "lose" the book and mailed it to Cook. Cook declared "I want Aiken complete" and *The Charnel Rose* brought his Aiken collection to seven volumes.[79]

Cook was also acquiring books through more conventional channels, and wrote to Wandrei in late November 1927 that he'd recently acquired *The Italian* and *Romance of the Forest* by Mrs. Radcliffe, *The Old English Baron* by Clara Reeve, *Uncanny Tales* by F. Marion Crawford, *Wagner the Wehr-Wolf* by G. W. M. Reynolds, *As It Was In the Beginning* by Philip Verrill Mighels, *Out of the Past* by Spurrill, *Ghost Stories* by Michael Arlen, *Tongues of Fire* by Algernon Blackwood, *The Haunted Castle* by Railo, *The Galleon of Torbay* by E. E. Speight, *Weird O' the Pool* by Stuart, *Strange Story of Falconer Thring* and *Wisdom of the Serpent* by Constantine Ralli, *Tolla the Courtesan* by Rodoconachi, *Priestess of Isis* by Edouard Schure, *Spotted Panther* by James F. Dwyer, *Shrine of Sebesh* by Phayre, *The She Wolf* by Formont, and *Marvelous Experiences of John Rydale* by Scott. This list, though rather random, shows that Cook was beyond pursuing the common and well-known works in the field. Cook may have been right when he told Wandrei, "I thought that I had seen every book of an outré character published in the [18]90s."[80] Besides Lovecraft and Wandrei, Cook was also in touch with author August W. Derleth, who later co-founded Arkham House with Donald Wandrei. On August 9th, 1926, Cook wrote him:

> I have your letter of the 5th about M. P. Shiel's *Pale Ape and Other Stories* [*sic*], and especially his wonderful short story, "The House of Sounds."
>
> I am collecting first editions of [M. P. Shiel] and have obtained most of my copies from England. [. . .]
>
> As English booksellers, I recommend W. & G. Foyle, Ltd.

The story in question was first published under the title "Vaila" in a volume called *Shapes in the Fire*, published by John Lane in 1896. In [1911] it was published much revised (and vastly improved) by T. Werner Laurie in *The Pale Ape and Other Pulses*.

Do not accept anything but *The Pale Ape*, where the story appears as "The House of Sounds."[81]

In addition to the magazine, work on the first book to carry the Recluse Press imprint, *The Man from Genoa and Other Poems* by Frank B. Long, Jr., was under way. It was being readied by Cook in November.[82] Within a year, the Recluse Press imprint appeared for the second time on Samuel Loveman's *The Hermaphrodite*. Lovecraft lamented that though he read proofs of the book five times, a typo still made its way into the text, which he blamed on "James Joseph Moloney of the Culinary type force."[83] Moloney was a co-worker at the *Transcript* who Cook employed after-hours to typeset the Recluse Press books on the newspaper's linotype machines.[84] Cook also published that year *Out of the Past,* a collection of works by old-time amateur journalist Charles H. Fowle. No doubt he did this merely as a favor to an old friend.

These several titles marked the beginnings of the Recluse Press, and Cook was eager to publish more. "Cook has a vague and as yet unformed idea of publishing my longish short story 'The Shunned House' as a thin book uniform with Long's poems and Loveman's *Hermaphrodite* and coming *Sphinx*."[85] Cook intended to issue Loveman's *Sphinx* with a drawing by Clark Ashton Smith, but rather than as a separate Recluse Press book it was issued years later in the third issue of Cook's magazine the *Ghost*.[86]

As a publishing program began to develop, Lovecraft wrote to Donald Wandrei in February and asked, "Have you thought of writing Cook, who published the Long & Loveman books? He does excellent work, & you could discuss arrangements at length. Long's aunt financed his book, but Cook himself assumed the responsibility for Loveman's."[87] Lovecraft also suggested that Wandrei submit work to Cook for publication in the *Recluse* and gave him Cook's address.[88] Wandrei did so immediately. In reply, Cook acknowledged that "Mr. Lovecraft has written to me about your interest in the weird," thanked him for the opportunity to see his work, and chose "The Twilight of Time," "On the Threshold of Eternity," and "A Legend of

Yesterday."[89] However, Wandrei informed Cook a few days later that *Weird Tales* editor Farnsworth Wright had just accepted "The Twilight of Time" (published as "The Red Brain" in the October 1927 issue). Cook returned all three items because he felt the other two "would hardly go without the first."[90] As substitutes for those stories Wandrei submitted "A Fragment of Dream," which was accepted, and Cook already had it in type for the coming *Recluse* when he wrote again on April 21st. In the same letter Cook responded to Wandrei's suggestion that Cook publish his first book of poems. Cook told him that "when I adopted the Recluse Press imprint I made up my mind that nothing but real literature should go out with its stamp" and "your work apparently lies along the lines which I am following." The cost of the book would be the same of Long's and Loveman's (300 copies of a 32-page, clothbound book for $130.00). "I am obliged to ask half in advance on this work, as I am able to save money over ordinary costs, by paying for each process in the making of a book as I go along, and I have not the capital to finance many ventures."[91]

The year 1927 continued to be a busy year for Cook. In March, he had decided definitely to publish *The Shunned House*. "Cook [. . .] means to publish my *Shunned House* sooner than he thought. He has asked Long to write a preface, though I tell him that a preface to a short story is absurd."[92] And by May, Lovecraft's "Supernatural Horror in Literature" had been put in type.[93]

Cook and H. Warner Munn took a trip to Providence to visit Lovecraft in late July 1927. "Cook brought with him the book of Goodenough's poems [*Songs of Four Decades*] which he has just printed, as well as an unfinished copy of his coming *Recluse*."[94] While there, the three connoisseurs of the weird and outré made a nocturnal visit to St. John's churchyard. Later in August, Lovecraft went to Athol, and from there he and Cook traveled to Brattleboro, Vt., to visit Arthur Goodenough and deliver copies of his book in person. Lovecraft's stay in Athol elicited the remark that Cook had "a wife who certainly lives up to her name."[95] This, unfortunately, is one of only several recorded accounts of Addie Cook.

Cook didn't let himself rest after finishing the Goodenough book. His decision to issue *White Fire,* a memorial collection of poems by an amateur poet, John Ravenor Bullen, who had recently died, meant more work. "I shall have a good deal of business with Cook during the coming months, for that man in Chicago [Archibald Freer] is in deadly earnest about the Bullen book. When I quoted him Cook's price he said it was too small, & sent a cheque for $500.00 with a request that we use it up in increasing the luxurious appearance of the volume!"[96] With the Bullen book only in the planning stages, Cook found spare time to turn his attention to the book by Donald Wandrei. In August a final agreement was reached and in late September Wandrei delivered the manuscript and a check. It may not have been for much money, because the final bill that Wandrei received from Cook totalled $161.00. "Your matter will be put into type at once and you will see first proofs ere long. Do not plan on it by the middle of November, as I do not believe it can be done."[97] Wandrei asked for purple cloth, and Cook promised to attend to the copyright. Within a week he was setting the type.

Work progressed on his anticipated magazine as well. "*The Recluse* is now in process of binding, and I have put your name on my list so that you will duly receive a copy. It will itself explain better than I can what it is. If you have out of the ordinary MSS. which you cannot get printed elsewhere I shall be glad to see them. Frequency of issue of the *Recluse* depends entirely on the collection of suitable MSS."[98] In a letter to Frank B. Long, Jr., Lovecraft wrote of it, "there is something of yours in *The Recluse*—the St. Anthony poem—tho' I wish there were more. Too bad you recalled the story you had contributed!"[99]

Despite the pressures of work at the newspaper and his own press, Cook found time for his favorite pursuit. "Cook has been down twice this autumn—once on the 15th and 16th of October, and again last Sunday. On each occasion we have made trips to [Arthur E.] Eddy's Book Store—Cook nearly buying the old fellow out. [. . .] I am now trying to complete my family file of *Old Farmer's Almanack,* and have got Cook doing the same thing."[100] Cook later described Eddy's with a true bibliophile's passion:

> An immense store lined from floor to ceiling with shelves packed with books classified by authors or subjects. Tables through the center piled with books. The floor heaped with books over which you sometimes had to scramble. Large drawers filled with books. A mezzanine floor choked by books. The stairs to

the basement cluttered with books. All these upstairs books had been gone over and priced—very moderately priced. Then the basement, to which few were admitted. A huge room with cords of books—and that is the way to describe them. Here the books were brought in trucks and deposited in the regular truckman's manner. Heaps, piles, a heterogeneous mixture of everything under the sun. When there was a vacant place upstairs, a few armfuls were brought up, inspected, and priced. Books from the show windows in front to the basement doors in the rear. [. . .] I seldom passed through Providence without filling the back seat of the car and wondering if the springs would stand it.[101]

Nearly a month after Cook and Wandrei last discussed *Ecstasy*, Cook wrote with a belated update. "I must report on progress or your impatience will get beyond control, probably. [. . .] *Ecstasy* is mostly in type, but I am having a great deal of it set over, and these first page proofs I do not want you to see. I shall send you the second set, after I have myself looked over the first set."[102]

One cause for delay was the mailing of the *Recluse*. In his letter to Wandrei, Cook admitted that "*The Recluse* is not all mailed yet." But before year's end it was. Alongside Lovecraft's "Supernatural Horror Literature," for which the magazine is justly famous, are to be found Walter J. Coates's "Early Vermont Minstrelsy," poems by Clark Ashton Smith, Frank B. Long, Jr., and Vrest Orton, a translation of Baudelaire by Smith, works by Donald Wandrei and H. Warner Munn, a literary essay by Samuel Loveman, and a checklist of George Sterling's first editions, prepared for Cook by Sterling himself. It is worth noting that Lovecraft's famous early story, "The Outsider," was meant to be published in *The Recluse,* but it appeared in *Weird Tales* instead. At the end of the magazine, the reader finds the following statement by Cook:

INTENTIONS

During the course of a long (too long) and misspent life, the writer has been guilty of publishing a number of papers and magazines of a non-professional character and various degrees of inanity. These have largely contained matter inserted to please others, rather than the publisher.

THE RECLUSE is the realization of a dream, long cherished, of the publication of a magazine to please the producer only. This foreword may be considered, therefore, as a declaration of independence. This magazine will contain only material pleasing to the publisher. If he takes a notion to publish an issue so "sophisticated" (overused word), as to be barred from the mails, he will do so even if he has to borrow a flivver to distribute the small edition. If he chooses to fill an issue with Methodist hymns he will do so. And all the gamut between. Be assured that everything in THE RECLUSE has met the approval of the editor for one reason of another.

Its frequency of issue depends also upon the whim of the editor and the securing of material. Nothing will be paid for contributions, and the magazine will, as have former efforts, be issued as an amateur and money cannot buy it.

W. Paul Cook

The magazine received a generally positive reception. Lovecraft observed that the *Recluse* "seems to have made a very decided hit wherever it has gone."[103] A copy was sent to Arthur Machen, whom Donald Wandrei said reacted well to it. Copies were mailed to other authors whose work had been treated in Lovecraft's essay, including Algernon Blackwood and M. R. James.

The magazine did not make a "decided hit" on James. In a letter dated January 12, 1928, to Nicholas (Nico) Llewelyn Davies, he noted "a funny American thing which was sent me the other day. A periodical, apparently, 'The Recluse, issued by W. Paul Cook for His Own Amusement—this being the First Number'. In it is a disquisition of nearly 40 pages of double columns on Supernatural Horror in Literature by one H. P. Lovecraft, whose style is of the most offensive. He uses the word cosmic about 24 times. But he has taken pains to search about & treats the subject from its beginnings to MRJ, to whom he devotes several columns. No doubt this is why I am favoured with a copy."[104]

On a more positive note, Cook later recalled, "when I published 'Supernatural Horror in Literature' in the *Recluse*, Meredith Janvier, the old-book dealer in Baltimore, wrote congratulating me on my *nom de plume*, characterizing it as 'perfect'."[105] Cook's point here is that

Lovecraft's name was too good to be true; but this anecdote tells us something else: A bookseller who knew Cook well thought he was capable of writing the essay, which remains a landmark in the field.

Even before the first issue was bound, Cook announced, "I am now beginning to collect material for the next issue."[106] Another issue never appeared, but some material for it was set in type, and there are clues to what its contents would have been. For one, Cook wanted to follow up Lovecraft's "Supernatural Horror in Literature" with complementary articles. "I have asked Munn to write his impressions of his lesser known favorites. I have [also] pointed out to Lovecraft the desirability of your handling a *third* article. I think you are more conversant with a wider range of better stuff than he is, and can sort of coordinate Lovecraft and Munn."[107] Lovecraft gave further details, in a letter to Vincent Starrett, about the projected "very informal paper on popular fantastic tales (of the *All-Story, Argosy*, or *Weird Tales* grade) by H. Warner Munn, who has had the patience to search out endless & arid reams of that sort of thing; & subsequently the less-known corners of the more standard field will be explored & recorded by Donald Wandrei [...] an encyclopaedic bibliography of all sorts of weird writing, good & bad."[108] Cook also asked Wandrei for "a poem and some prose. [. . .] One may be a grave one and one erotic, if you wish. Or both cosmic. Would prefer one grave."[109]

With the *Recluse* out of the way, Cook could turn to other Recluse Press projects. On November 27, a month since his last update, he was able to write Wandrei:

> Yesterday I mailed you a set of proofs of *Ecstasy*. I have hugely enjoyed doing the preliminary reading of the MS. and proofs. I have had a great deal of it set twice and some of it three times in an endeavor to determine correct indentures and appearance. I am confronted with a large number of run-over lines even yet, but we can do no better without enlarging the page size too much for a thin volume. [. . .] Now would you care to have Lovecraft look over the page proofs on this? You are the BOSS, you know, and what you say goes. A few weeks ago I was in Providence and took your MS. with me and he read it over. He made a few suggestions which are embodied in hand-writing on your MS. You may accept or reject any or all of these, but

I consider them all as improvements which in no way detract from your original idea but increase its effectiveness. The irregularity of your lines and modernity of of your verse does not lend itself to Lovecraft's impeccable rhythmical standards of revision, and therefore he made few suggestions. He has seen no proofs as yet, and I will leave it to you as to whether, in page form, you want him to see it.

How do you like the headings? I was never satisfied with the heads in Long's book, because they are of a slightly lighter shade than the text. I do not care for Goodenough's heads because they are too dark. So I have this time used Caps of the body letter.[110]

Reading this letter, one is impressed by the amount of care Cook was taking. He charged only the cost of production, with no compensation for the time and expertise he contributed. His personal investment in a book could be considerable, especially if typographic errors crept in. That was the case with the Bullen book, which spurred Lovecraft to write to Wandrei: "The Bullen misprinting has cost Cook much cash, me much labour, & you much delay in your book! Vae nobis omnibus! (Woe to us all!) We can just about get the de luxe copies to Freer by Christmas—the bulk of the edition can't make it. Your own volume is all in type, but Cook is sparing you the trouble by reading the earlier proofs—with the grosser errors—himself. You'll get the page proofs shortly."[111]

The problems with the Bullen book didn't interfere too seriously with other projects. Cook mailed proofs of Wandrei's *Ecstasy* on December 29. He made a few suggestions and told Wandrei of alterations he had to make for typographic reasons: "You will note I have made slight changes in the pagination and order of the poems in the first half of the book. It is practically essential that a long poem, occupying two or more pages, begin on the odd or right hand page. You figured on almost all of your long poems starting on the even or left hand page. Some rearrangement was necessary to overcome this difficulty."[112]

Plans for a second *Recluse* were also in the works. Among the submissions he accepted were poems by Wandrei. "Because it is your own favorite among your poetic fantasies, I am keeping 'The Woman at the Window' for the *Recluse*, and because I had marked it when choosing the cosmic dust trilogy which had been preempted. I have had no easy task selecting from among the poetry, as I liked them all, but I have finally settled on 'Mystical Quest', after having in turn taken every one!"[113] In addition to the poems Cook was interested in Wandrei's review of the famous gothic novel, *The Monk* by Matthew G. Lewis, as well as an article on gothic novelist Mrs. Radcliffe:[114] "If you have no market for these, I can use one in the *Recluse*. I hope you have used the *Monk* gently for my sake, because I think Lewis is more underrated than overrated, and that his influence in this literature was the most potent single force of any period in bringing together all the good points as well as all the clap trap of the romance of horror. As to Mrs. Radcliffe, you can't say anything much too caustic. She simply bores me to sickness."[115]

In the midst of making enthusiastic plans for *The Recluse* the Bullen book was finished. Lovecraft was thoroughly pleased with it.

> The Bullen book, despite all troubles, came out magnificently; & Cook has reluctantly agreed to attend to the marketing & distribution. It will cost $2.00 at retail & $1.50 wholesale—cloth of soft grey colour, paper labels, 86 pp 6 × 9 on art paper, with genuine photographic frontispiece in sepia on impressed panel. So far as I can see, there are absolutely no typographical errors. I am helping Cook send out the complementary & review copies, & shall try to place it in a few bookstalls—& have Kirk & Loveman list it in their catalogues. The special leather gift edition—dark green stamped with gold—is a veritable bibliophile's dream of austere sumptuousness! I shall pass my duplicate around among the gang, so that you'll see it eventually. Each copy cost Cook $6.50 at wholesale for the binding alone, so that it's really a $10.00 or $15.00 item."[116]

After several months Wandrei's book was selling so well that a second edition was a possibility.[117] Money was advanced to Cook for it, but it never appeared, although the entire book was typeset and proofs were prepared.

The unexpected extra work on the Bullen book had a negative effect on Cook's health. This slowed down his schedule and delayed the production of Wandrei's book. While Wandrei was concerned about his publisher's health, he couldn't help but feel anxious about the delays. In a letter dated March 22, 1928, Cook revealed:

> For the last six weeks I have been as near kicking in as I shall ever be. For two weeks I kept on my feet while Mrs. C[ook] was pretty bad, but finally had to give up. I cannot as yet go to business and it may be several days before the M.D. allows me to go to the office to even oversee things. He allows me two letters today.
>
> Your book has of course been printed a long time. It had not gone to the bindery as the finishing touches—the labels, folding, assembling, etc., I want to either oversee or do myself.
>
> If this delay is going to be too great a trial for you, if it will hurt the sale of the books—you need never pay me the balance due on delivery.[118]

After taking a break from all work to recover his health, Cook reported to Wandrei on April 2:

> Your books have been in the bindery some days now and there isn't the slightest doubt that you will have them long before the 20th.
>
> I am back on the job, for a time at least, and am getting things in general straightened out so that I hope to spend most of the summer out of the office, visiting it only to keep things moving.
>
> I have Lovecraft's *Shunned House* in type, and am now reading the first proof. This will follow *Ecstasy* very closely.
>
> I sincerely hope that when *Ecstasy* is out that you will not be disappointed in it in any way. As I have said before, it pleases me more than any book I have as yet issued.[119]

True to his word, the finished edition of 322 copies was mailed on April 10, with a bill for $161.00—Cook's net cost. Cook would later say of Wandrei's *Ecstasy and Other Poems*, "I regard this book as the outstanding publication of the Recluse Press—and the one I shall show with the most pride."[120]

Cook may not have felt as much pride in another book he published around this time: *Old World Footprints,* a travel book by Cassie Doty Symmes. She was a wealthy aunt of Frank B. Long, Jr., who financed the production of his *A Man from Genoa and Other Poems,* and no doubt paid to have her travel book printed, too. It is likely that Cook took on the project only for the profit he would make from the production fee paid by Mrs. Symmes.

By the summer Cook was in good health and visiting again with his friends. Lovecraft stayed with Cook for several days in June. They passed one evening at H. Warner Munn's home looking over his library of weird fiction.[121] Cook's love of weird literature inspired plans to publish Lovecraft's essay on "Supernatural Horror in Literature" as a book. It was also suggested to Cook that he produce a new edition of *The Monk & the Hangman's Daughter* by Ambrose Bierce and Adolphe de Castro "with additional matter translated from Voss's original, & with the plates which appeared in the first edition."[122] But these would all have to wait as Cook worked slowly to produce what promised to be his most notable book. "Cook is now printing *The Shunned House*—I saw the presses working on it last night when I called at the *Transcript* office,"[123] Lovecraft reported to Wandrei, to whom he sent a sample sheet.

Later in the summer, while Lovecraft was staying with Vrest Orton near Brattleboro, Vermont, Cook drove up twice to visit. On Sunday, June 17, a group gathered at Goodenough's home. Lovecraft later wrote to Zelia Bishop that Cook "kidnapped" "[me] for a week's visit to Athol, where I had the honour of seeing him send to press, with his own hands, the sheets of my story *The Shunned House,* which when published will form my first cloth-bound book."[124]

In July 1928 Cook received an inquiring letter from Will Ransom, the famed printer who co-founded The Village Press with Frederic W. Goudy. Vrest Orton had recently told him of The Recluse Press. Ransom was making final preparations for his monumental *Private Presses and Their Books* (Bowker, 1929) and needed details about the press as soon as possible for inclusion in the book. Cook's side of the exchange reveals much about himself, most especially how self-conscious and self-effacing he was about his work.

Ransom first wrote to Cook on July 18, and Cook promptly replied on July 21:

Perhaps I should be represented in your list, but my work thus far has been in its entirety too unsatisfactory for me to take a great deal of pride in it, or wish it widely advertised.

I am sending you four Recluse Press books which will indicate to you clearly where I have not succeeded in my ideals.

The Hermaphrodite comes the nearest to my conception. I wish to emphasize extreme plainness of typography, without ornamentation of any kind; readable to the last degree; with proper margins; sedate, substantial, dignified bindings; the paper of the best quality, heavy weight.

The contents I hope to make eventually to consist wholly of an outstanding character—perhaps like *Ecstasy*—not necessarily erotic; but bearing a stamp of the unusual.

I am now taking up the matter of typography seriously, and perhaps in the future may show something worthy of note.

At present, I hardly think the Recluse Press worthy of being included in your list. I have no desire to make an entirely commercial project of it. In fact, up to the present I have not made one cent and have lost money on all my ventures. I am playing with it because I enjoy the work! It is most clearly an amateur venture with certain professional ear marks.

I thank you for your interest.[125]

Cook's modesty is characteristic of the man. But Ransom wouldn't be put off so easily. He replied to Cook on August 28, restating his original request, and assuring Cook: "Of course you should be represented in the book. That you are not yet satisfied with results is the best possible viewpoint—Heaven send you never do become satisfied, no matter how much more you may accomplish."[126]

Despite Ransom's encouraging words, Cook did not immediately respond. Ransom had to write him again, on October 31, asking Cook to send the requested information so the book could be finished. Cook replied on November 14:

[. . .] I am still of the belief that the product of my efforts to date is not of a quality to warrant its entry into a bibliography of "Private Presses." But since you insist I have jotted on another sheet the list of books to date. I presume you do not need further detail.

I have to thank you for your interest in my negligible and quite unworthy undertaking.[127]

The list gave title, author, number of copies, and availability. *The Shunned House* was "now in binding." Ransom replied briefly on November 25 to thank Cook, but followed that two days later with another request for details, including month and year of publication of the books and information about the *Recluse* magazine, which Ransom had just learned about from a catalog issued by Meredith Janvier, a rare book dealer in Baltimore, Md., with whom Cook had done business. Cook wrote on the 29th:

> In reply to yours of the 27th, I am enclosing a list which is apparently what you desire.
>
> I hope you will excuse me for my laxity in preparing this information for you, but I did not know that you were going to give such complete accounts—and I rather shrank from having the Recluse Press included in such a bibliography, because of the unsatisfactory charcter of my productions to date.
>
> Regarding the *Recluse* magazine: It is practically unobtainable now. I am sending you one of my few remaining copies. From my "Intentions" you will see my sole aim in publishing it. There was no issue in 1928 because the only man [H. Warner Munn?] capable of preparing the leading article did not, and has not even yet, completed his work on it. I plan it now for summer of 1929.
>
> I am in some doubt about as to the ethics of Janvier cataloguing and offering for sale the copy of the *Recluse* I sent him with my compliments. I do not know whether to be more annoyed at the unethical procedure, or flattered at the *Recluse* becoming so quickly a collector's item![128]

What followed was a list of books, including the *Recluse*, in order of publication. It's worth noting what Cook recorded here about the availability of each at that time:

A Man from Genoa: a few available
The Hermaphrodite: unobtainable
Songs of Four Decades: available
Out of the Past: available
White Fire: full leather de luxe, not for sale; ordinary (clothbound) available

Ecstasy: few remaining copies suppressed by author
Old World Footprints: not for sale
Land of Allen and Other Verse: available
The Shunned House: To be published January, 1929
The Recluse—An Occasional Magazine: never for sale[129]

Here at last, in late November, was the descriptive list of publications with all the information Ransom had been asking for since July. We may well guess that Ransom was not a little exasperated, but he remained cordial throughout their correspondence. Perhaps he was used to the eccentricity of bookmen. Cook did not hear again from Ransom, who'd been sick during the winter, until March 19, 1929. He had one last question for Cook, regarding the details of production. He wanted to know if Cook was involved in the actual printing of the books, or whether he was only the publisher. In reply, Cook wrote on March 22:

> To atone for past delinquincies I am answering your letter of the 19th a few minutes after its receipt!
>
> You may put me down as my own printer, the circumstances being as follows:—I am an employed printer, foreman of a printing plant here [Athol, Mass.]. My work is done where I am employed. If I should change my place of employment, my work goes with me.[130]

By the time Cook had written to Ransom in November 1928, Wandrei had withdrawn *Ecstasy* from circulation. Perhaps there'd been trouble, after all, with the morality police. The publisher and author shared some concern about running afoul of authorities like the post office, fearing that the title of the book would give the impression that it was indecent.

> I really think there is a danger from various pure food laws. That danger will be acute at two different times. First, when copyright is applied for and a statement must be sworn that it has been publicly distributed. Second, when put on sale in a bookstore or openly displayed. I would recommend that express be used for sending copies out, or that you go to your postmaster and get from him a statement as to its mailability. We must take our chances on the copyright.[131]

Cook shared those concerns with Wandrei in January 1928. By May, there had been no crisis. "I have not heard any explosion from the P.O. department yet. Have you?"[132] Though the exact reasons for the book's ultimate suppression are not known, it may be surmised that it was done in anticipation of a planned expurgated edition that was not published.[133]

Wandrei's poems appealed so much to Cook that he contemplated another volume. "I have a very great mind to offer to bring out a volume of your poems with about six drawings by your brother [Howard] provided you do not find a publisher by the first of the year. Of course there would not be as much money in it for you as there would be if you financed it yourself, as I would be compelled to offer you about the usual rates even if you guaranteed a sale of 500 copies. This would mean 15% or 18% for you. If the book was as good as Ecstasy and longer, and illustrated, we could get $3.00 a copy. If you would sell it yourself and leave the bookseller out of it you could have their 33 1/3%. This would give you $1.00 a copy and me $2.00. What do you think of this?"[134]

He thought otherwise, especially as he could see that Cook was having trouble with his Recluse Press obligations. The collection of poems they discussed, *Dark Odyssey*, was published by Webb Publishing Co. in 1931 in an edition of 400 signed copies, with illustrations by his brother Howard.

Wandrei had coped with the various problems that delayed the publication of *Ecstasy*, and now Lovecraft was feeling a bit impatient for the same reason. "About the 'Shunned House'—Cook is the guy to ask, not me! He bought a [170-acre] farm east of Athol this autumn, & began moving out to it; but found that he couldn't get the heating installed in time for cold weather. Therefore he has had to take rooms in Athol for the winter. All this moving turmoil has played havoc with his schedule."[135] A "hall bedroom and kitchette next to the engine house where [H. Warner Munn] rooms" is how Cook described his rooms.[136]

During the winter his friends lost touch with Cook. "None of us hears anything from Cook, & we are beginning to be somewhat worried about him—though inexplicable silences are not altogether novel phenomena on his part."[137] By the end of May 1929, Lovecraft's worries were erased by a visit he made to Athol: "Cook was a good host—my anxiety about his silence having been unfounded. Mere pressure of business was responsible, as I learned from a letter whilst re-crossing through NY City. He took me out at once to his new farm near the town—a place which most unfortunately must soon sell because his wife's health requires the comforts of urban life." Cook's place was one of the "sparsely scattered white farmhouses" "set on high ground with one of the most magnificent rural landscape effects conceivable—both foreground and far horizon of hills beyond hills. At one point a blue lakelet glistens among tall pines. No other house is in sight—just stone walls, green fields, distant hills, & the scattered buildings of the venerable farm. Here I stayed some time; occasionally taken on motor trips by Cook or by our young friend H. Warner Munn. [. . .] Once we went up to Vermont to see the poet Arthur Goodenough.[. . .] Another time we visited Westminster. [. . .] [I] had Cook bring me down to Providence in his car."[138]

Cook reciprocated the visit with a trip to Providence in early June, when he filled up his car with books at Eddy's.[139] The visit no doubt took his mind off concerns about the new home outside Athol. The matter of having the place heated properly had still not been dealt with, and since the home couldn't be lived in in winter without heating, Cook decided it'd be best to sell it. His wife, Addie, could not live there because of her poor health. By September Lovecraft reported that Cook was "very anxious to sell it." He surely echoed Cook's own feelings when he wrote, "It's really a pity to let it go," especially when one remembers Lovecraft's rhapsodic descriptions of the home and its views.[140]

Cook heard one last time from Will Ransom, who wrote on October 20, 1929, to tell Cook that the monumental *Private Presses and Their Books* was at last published. Along with thanks for Cook's cooperation he asked to be informed of any further publications from the Recluse Press.

Thanks to Ransom's persistence, details about Cook's short-lived press were preserved. They otherwise would surely have been lost. Besides the standard entry, Cook was singled out for special mention, along with his friends Walter J. Coates and J. Howard Flower, in the book's introduction:

In Vermont, including one just over the line in Massachusetts, are three presses fundamentally committed to literature of the section, though the equipment is used for a certain amount of commercial work. The Driftwind Press of Walter J. Coates, J. Howard Flower's Solitarian, and the Recluse of W. Paul Cook are united in a friendly community of local interest. Typography, unfortunately, seems to be of secondary importance in their scheme of things, though Mr. Cook announces creditable ambitions.[141]

Alas, Cook's entry in the book marked an end. It recorded the history of a press whose imprint would never appear on another publication. Ransom's hopes and good wishes would prove fruitless.

UPROOTED (1930-1940)

This productive period drew to a tragic end for Cook. Adeline, his wife of sixteen years, died in January of 1930, following a long illness. In the aftermath Cook's life came undone; he was apparently unable to cope with the loss. By his own account: "I suddenly found myself struck down from a comfortable condition of life with an income of about $5000 to a grade of no income and in debt about $1000. I have discarded everything; have given away or thrown away everything, including my job, my real estate, my household furnishings, and my library."[142]

As the Great Depression set in, Cook fell into a deep personal depression. He couldn't even summon the energy to finish half-done projects, like binding up the sheets of *The Shunned House* by his old friend Lovecraft or publishing another *Recluse*.

There was no second issue of the *Recluse*. When in 1930 I took my release from that town [Athol], I had nearly a hundred pages in type and about forty printed on another number. It was to have been well over two hundred pages. I had the printed pages thoroughly destroyed. In type was Lovecraft's 'The Strange High House in the Mist'. [. . .] When I abandoned the *Recluse* I also abandoned, and for the same reason, 'The Shunned House,' which was all printed and in the bindery. This should have been issued in 1928, and I think was marked for copyright that year.

It would have been a Lovecraft first edition of unique interest. But I could do no more. I was definitely through. Another phase of my life was ended.[143]

For most of the next decade he would have no regular job or residence. He drifted around, living with Vrest Orton in Clarendon, Vermont; alone in Boston; with friends in East St. Louis, Illinois; and with Walter Coates in North Montpelier, Vermont. He also lived at times with his sister, Cora Calkins, in Sunapee, NH. She is listed in the 1920 census as thirty-five years old, divorced, with a five-year-old daughter, Myrtle, and employed as a manager in a telephone office.

On January 14, 1930, Lovecraft wrote to a friend: "Cook is now feeling the strain of the autumn and winter—the long illness and eventual loss—so keenly that he says he must get away to a different milieu for a few days, and is planning a motor trip through the icy waste of Northern Vermont to visit steady, consoling old Walter J. Coates. He has asked me to come to Athol and accompany him, but I have had to refuse as a matter of sheer physiological imperative."[144]

It is not surprising that Paul Cook turned to Coates during that difficult time. Coates too had lost a wife (his first wife, Florence, died in 1906); and his background as a Universalist minister may indeed have made him a "consoling" influence. But the stay in Vermont did not improve his health, as Lovecraft noted in mid-1930.

I enjoyed my Athol sojourn immensely, though sorry to note Cook's poor health. The death of his wife last January, after a long illness, precipitated him into a severe nervous breakdown, from which he is recovering only slowly. Added to this is his chronic appendicitis, which gave him a great deal of trouble this month. He ought to have his appendix out, but refrains because of a morbid dread of the surgeon's knife. He is now boarding with one of his printers at his office—who lives on a farm about 2 miles from the village. The place is rather squalid & depressing, but Cook does not seem to mind such things.[145]

Before the year was over, Cook had "left Athol for good amidst a general nervous, physical, & financial breakdown."[146] His personal possessions, especially books and manuscripts, were entrusted to the care of friends and family. Things were left with his sister, others with Walter Coates, and some with Edith Miniter. Miniter was living with an elderly friend named Evanore Beebe during her final years, and following the deaths of Miniter and Beebe, Cook was unable to retrieve what he'd left there. By 1935 he gave them up as lost after Beebe's family refused him permission to search the home.[147]

In one of Lovecraft's letters from late 1930 one is given a picture of Cook's wanderings as he stays with friends and family:

> Orton has just purchased (or leased, I don't know which) a house [in Clarendon, Vt.]. The idea is for the two of them to found "The Parsonage Press" there, but Orton is so slow in getting the plan under way that Cook may not settle down until a press is actually purchased. At the moment I think Cook is visiting his sister at Lake Sunapee, N.H., but by the time a letter could reach him he will have moved on—either to Clarendon or to Walter J. Coates's at North Montpelier, Vt. Amidst all this uncertainty, Clarendon is the best permanent forwarding address to use. If Cook & Orton get together in this new press venture, they could do your coming book full justice typographically—for as you doubtless realize, Orton is more of a connoisseur of the aesthetic side of printing than Cook.[148]

Cook's typographic sensibilities were more evenly matched by those of Walter J. Coates. The modest publications issued by his Driftwind Press, and the complementary poetry magazine *Driftwind*, remind one of Cook's Recluse Press books. The typesetting for both of their publications was done on a linotype machine, which gives their work the look of conscientious but plain job printing. Will Ransom recognized the aesthetic affinity between their presses and remarked on it in his *Private Presses and Their Books.* The third publisher whom Ransom linked with them geographically and aesthetically was the Solitarian Press of J. Howard Flower. The three men were also drawn together by liberal political sympathies that are reflected in some of their publications, like Cook's *Protest Stuff* and *Contradictions,* Driftwind's *Christ in the Breadline* and *Ballad of Gene Debs,* and Solitarian's *Highly Respectable Murder: Poems in Remembrance of Sacco and Vanzetti* and *Red Songs of a Romantic Radical.*[149]

Coates gave Cook the opportunity to work as a printer—at his own pace and on his own projects. Cook could do what he loved without responsibilities, and in return Coates had his friend's expert assistance. The bibliography of the Driftwind Press reveals that while the press issued only several books in 1929 and 1930, its productivity leaped with Cook's arrival in late 1930. He reported in August the following year:

> All last winter and a greater part of this year to date I have been here with Walter J. Coates, who has a small printing outfit and a country store here. He issues a bi-monthly magazine, *Driftwind*, and when I came last December he got more type and we have printed five or six books for authors, and several items of a Vermont poetical and historical nature. However, I am now looking earnestly for a job and shall be moving on.[150]

One for which Cook received credit in print was *The Chestnut Tree* (1931) by Royall Tyler, a handsome booklet that Cook and Coates designed and typeset by hand. Among the other books they printed were Ella Warner Fisher's *Castles in Memory,* Florence E. Boyce's *Sunshine and Cheer from Vermont,* Coates's *Double Thirteen,* George Henry Coffin's *Earth Hunger,* Henry C. Taylor's *Adjustments,* and Doric Smith Stoddard's *Geography of Vermont.*

Mindful of his own poor circumstances, Cook looked for more gainful employment. In his letters from the early 1930s, he regularly hinted at efforts to find work in Boston and New York. He even considered moving to Oklahoma; in early 1931 his old amateur friend Paul J. Campbell had offered to find him work there in the oil industry.[151] One gathers from some his letters, though, that Cook wasn't all that eager to find employment.

> I am waiting the time when some one will come along and offer me a good job, but am in no great hurry for that to happen.[152]

He did take a job in September 1931 in Boston. First he moved to 17 Chambers Street, and soon thereafter to 7 Hancock Street, both on Beacon Hill. After months of wandering he made an effort to settle down and salvage his old life. This return to his familiar old life included visiting Lovecraft in Providence. The two hadn't seen each other since July 1930. Cook stayed with him for several days. The friends surely needed more than one day to catch up.[153]

One thing Lovecraft didn't bring up in conversation was the fate of his half-finished *Shunned House.* His correspondence with other friends reveals he was anxious about it—referring to its "probable loss"—but he knew there was little Cook could do. "I haven't had the heart to tackle Cook about that 'Shunned House' matter—for I don't like to bring up topics reminding him of his ill-fortune. If the whole thing goes up in smoke, the loss will not be beyond the world's limit of endurance."[154] The sheets of the book lay in limbo at a Boston bindery because nobody could afford the cost of binding it.[155]

In November Cook explored more of Massachusetts with Lovecraft when the two visited Portsmouth and Newburyport. (The following August they returned to the latter to view a total solar eclipse.)[156] Then in January 1932 Lovecraft spent a week with Cook in Boston. Lovecraft may have been in a wandering mood, or he was trying to distract Cook from his troubles. In any case the travelling and visiting helped boost Cook's poor spirits. Lovecraft noted, "His physical improvement over last year is astonishing, & I think he is close to getting back on his feet in every way—unless swamped by handicaps."[157]

In early 1932 the first and only issue of a new journal circulated among amateurs. The *Nomadnock* was obviously meant to remind readers of Cook's *Monadnock*. Paul Cook himself is actually listed as editor/publisher of the journal, which contains only a four-page editorial titled "The Rush-ian Rebel." But this anti-Communist diatribe against Roger Rush, editor of the *Rebel*, and a candidate for president of the National, was soon revealed to be the work of Rush himself. Rush's reasons for crediting *Nomadnock* to Cook are unknown—Cook himself was probably baffled by the attribution—but if Rush was looking for publicity, he achieved it. Cook's friend Jim Morton, a long-time amateur journalist, came to his defense with an article in the June 1932 issue of the *Garden State Amateur:*

> By the appearance of 'The Nomadnock,' Roger Rush, the editor of 'The Rebel," has suddenly been thrust into the limelight of amateur affairs. Mr. Rush's pleas for Communism will meet with few echoes in our circle; but his right to express his honest convictions, without being made the victim of proscription, is another matter. Just why the violent effusion from Boston should be dishonestly fathered by its anonymous editor on Paul Cook is very hard to say. Mr. Cook himself looks on it as a work of petty spite; but the sheet reads as if it were sincere in its

views. [. . .] He has a right to his opinions, wrong as they are, and should not have been so base a coward as to hide behind a mask. There are times when anonymous writing is entirely necessary, but not when it consists of personal attacks.[158]

In his straitened circumstances Cook couldn't afford to buy gifts for Christmas in 1932. But he was able to surprise one friend with something he'd long wanted. Lovecraft wrote to more than one correspondent to share the news of the gift—"nothing less than that famous & now out-of-print Gothic novel by Charles Robert Maturin, *Melmoth, the Wanderer*, in 3 volumes. I had been trying to get hold of this item for years, & you can imagine how Cook's gift virtually bowled me over!"[159] It was a book "for which I have been pining since 1919."[160]

The following year was difficult. By March Cook had lost his job when the company closed.[161] With time on his hands he turned his attention to old business. He left no record of his thoughts on the matter, but he no doubt felt some guilt over the unfinished *Shunned House*. He tracked down the unbound sheets and arranged to have it bound and marketed by Walter J. Coates.[162] At Coates's request, Lovecraft wrote to Farnsworth Wright, editor of *Weird Tales*, to inquire about the cost of an ad.[163] Such publicity would have reached the ideal audience for the book.

After a hiatus of nearly ten years, Cook also renewed acquaintances with amateur journalism when he attended the National's convention in July 1933 in New York City. He was back in Boston briefly in September when Lovecraft stopped by on his way to Quebec, but he didn't stay long.[164] In need of a change, he went to stay again with Walter Coates in North Montpelier, Vt. In a letter he wrote from there to Donald Wandrei he admitted—

I am now fed up with this place and want to get back to a city, and a big one this time. [. . .] I want a very small job, one without any responsibility and requiring no brains, and am willing to work for little money on such a job. Perhaps $25.00. I will do anything in a printing office but run a linotype or monotype. Will not touch those machines under any consideration. Prefer to work as job pressman, but will go on job composition or make-up. [. . .] I do not want to go back to Boston and do not want to stay in the country.[165]

A reason for his discontent in Vermont was expressed in a revealing letter to Lovecraft: "[T]he country is the most mentally unhealthy of all places in which to choose to live. One broods, and one is subject to moods, and from these brooding moods there is no escape."[166] Cook was apparently aware of his inclination to brood and found relief in a bustling urban setting like Boston or New York. He had decided on going to New York in early 1934 but ultimately remained in Boston.[167]

The coincidence of the loss of his wife, job, and home with the depths of the Great Depression gave Cook little relief from worry. The government's inability to cope effectively with the terrible social and economic problems suffered by millions of Americans led some to question the nation's democractic and capitalist foundations. The disenchanted looked to Communism, Socialism, and other radical programs for hope and solutions. Cook was among them. In one letter to Lovecraft, he expressed a wish "to live for two years in New York below 14th St. and mix up with the crowd of radicals."[168] The worst manifest ills of the period provoked his anger and inspired a revival of his Willis T. Crossman *nom de plume*. While living in Boston he wrote two booklets, *A Day in the Life of Willis T. Crossman* and *Protest Stuff*, circulated privately in 1934. *A Day* is a long prose piece that paints a grim picture of Cook's day-to-day existence, from his dingy boarding-house room to his job sorting potatoes in an underground warehouse. Cook blurs the line between fiction and nonfiction as he draws on his experiences and blends them with invented characters and incidents consistent with what he knew first-hand. Only Cook could tell us which details are true and which fictional. We would hope that his life was not as desperate as *A Day* would lead us to believe, but in the copy of the booklet that he gave to J. Howard Flower he wrote, "not all as fantastic as it might appear."[169]

While *A Day* was written in a journalistic style, the staggered prose pieces published in *Protest Stuff* are bold and unequivocal statements. Cook framed them between contemporary quotes from *The Boston Post* about the homeless and others living on the margins eating out of garbage cans, sleeping on park benches, and being molested by police. Pieces like "Paternalism," "The Root," and "Extermination" include pronoucements like "I would like to see a Soviet / In the United States / For one reason only— / To put the parasites to work" and "The workers have paid and paid and paid / For the criminal greed of the capitalist."

When he later wrote about what Lovecraft found appealing in the New Deal he revealed his own disenchantment with it:

> The New Deal was a decided move toward what he could and did believe in—an aristocracy of intellect, the rule of the intellectuals, a paternalistic government, a dictatorship of the intelligentsia instead of a dictatorship of the proletariat. Its leaders had not emerged from the masses of the people, but by birth were of a class fitted to rule. Its leader was the Squire of Hyde Park, and its inner circle was what Franklin Adams[170] ineptly but catchily called the "Brain Trust." It was incumbent upon the higher classes to rule and to take care of the masses. It was their duty to see that the lower classes were sheltered, fed, and given as much opportunity for literacy as was good for them. I doubt that if he had lived and seen the thing develop into a one-man dictatorship, he would have changed his mind except to differ in details. The suppression of minority parties and the final extinction of the untrammeled free speech which had been a feature of the American polity would not have altered his basic attitude. He would not have considered it a trend in the wrong direction to see the fostering of a class consciousness and the sudden emergence of a proletariat for the first time in the history of this country. I am sure it would not have displeased him at all to witness the pitiful spectacle of a delegation from Congress (representatives of "The Peepul") cooling its heels in an anteroom while waiting for admission into the executive Presence to be informed what legislation it would be allowed to pass or what fait accompli it would be permitted to put its "O.K." on.[171]

August brought another visit from Lovecraft. The friends toured Boston and went on to Nantucket. The visit was cut short by what Lovecraft, who witnessed it, described as a "nervous collapse."[172] Though being away from the city brought on brooding moods he fled to Vermont to recover. Within a month or so Cook was "rather better, though not feeling rather energetic."[173]

A group of Cook's friends, including Lovecraft and Edward H. Cole, met him in Boston in November. They travelled to Medford and "explored the ancient Royall mansion (1737), which Cook had never entered before."[174]

The story of the ill-starred *Shunned House* took another turn in 1934. Plans for the book's binding by Walter Coates fell through. He'd delayed so long that Cook took the sheets away from him. R. H. Barlow offered to take up the challenge and Cook agreed to have all the sheets stored at his sister's home shipped to Barlow in DeLand, Florida.[175] Lovecraft was visiting Barlow there when the shipment arrived from New Hampshire. Only 115 sets of sheets were found at first, but another box was eventually discovered.[176]

> This is the best set of sheets we can assemble out of the 115 copies—just arrived from Cook—which have survived from an original edition of 250. Not much of a story, but a pretty fair piece of printing. Barlow plans to issue the thing gradually—a "limited signed edition," a "general trade edition," & all that. [. . .] I wonder whether the bulk of it will ever be issued? Barlow is confident that it will. [. . .] But so was Cook![177]

Cook soon became involved in a small adventure related to amateur journalism and his old friend Edith Miniter. Cook learned that the ashes of Miniter's mother, Jennie Dowe, were in the possession of an undertaker named Briggs. Cook wrote to Lovecraft with a plan of action: "It would be a magnificent thing, and quite in keeping with the undoubtedly crazy nature of amateur journalism, to get those ashes and when a favorable time comes go to North Wilbraham [Mass.] and scatter them under the rose bushes."[178] Being unable to attend to the matter quickly, Cook suggested that Edward Cole be enlisted, since he lived closer. Cole did assume responsibility for them and the ashes were finally scattered in Wilbraham on September 28, 1935.[179]

By the summer of 1935 plans took shape for a radical decision. Cook's old friend from amateur journalism, Paul J. Campbell, offered Cook a job on a weekly newspaper he was publishing in East St. Louis, Illinois. Cook was ready for the changes the job promised.

> Well, I shall probably go to St. Louis by the 15th of July. I expect a small windfall July 1 which will enable me to pay my

own expenses out. There is no chance of Campbell ever paying them. He cannot get any passes. Perhaps I am a fool, but I want to get away from New England so bad that I am going to take a chance.[180]

As plans took shape for Cook's move he tied up loose ends. One was the question of what to do with the remains of his once impressive library. Barlow's ambitious offer to bind *The Shunned House,* and Lovecraft's high regard for him, convinced Cook that Barlow would give his cherished books a good home. "Yesterday I actually got the express shipment for Barlow away, so it will be there about the same time as this note. I have included in this shipment all the books in Sunapee that I thought might fit into Barlow's collection."[181]

Cook also sought to repay Vrest Orton for past kindnesses by helping him set up the printing operation they'd once planned together. "I expect Orton to come after me tomorrow and I shall spend the next two or three weeks in Weston [Vermont] getting his printing business laid out for him. He claims he now has the money to buy his machinery. Notice the way I put that!"[182]

By July 11 Cook was back with his sister in Sunapee, N.H., where he wrote to Lovecraft to report on Orton's venture and his plans to move.

Nothing would induce me to stay there [Weston, VT]. It is not for publication, but I regard Orton's enterprise as doomed to failure. I only hope he will be able to get out of the affair in the end without personal loss of prestige and legal complications of a bad nature. I may be crazy, but there is consolation in the fact that there are worse than I (I mean worse mental cases!).[183]

Cook's pessimistic predictions surely stem from the failures and misfortunes that dogged his Recluse Press.

I am not being quite as crazy as I may seem about the Campbell business, however. I have asked certain guarantees of him, including the closing of a $1500 contract, which is now under way, and I am waiting for a wire from him. I shall have my bus fare when it is needed, but can't get it before! I was hoping that it would not be too late to send you some money for your return trip north [Lovecraft was staying with Barlow in DeLand, Fla., at the time], which you will doubtless need. Predictions of dire disaster for my East St. Louis venture are universal! I am so used to 'dire disaster,' however, that the most it can do to me is to cause me to choose the Mississippi River rather than Sunapee Lake or our well known Atlantic Ocean.[184]

With time on his hands, as he waited for the green light from Campbell, Cook "spent time working on my *Vermont Gazetteer*, and in making tentative plans and laying out some work along the line of weird fiction. My ambition is to write a series of tales dealing with lycanthropy, vampirism, etc., in a matter-of-fact manner, without dramatics except as naturally occur, accepting superstitions as fact, (as natural fact), and making of them a simple narrative of events. A la Elliott O'Donnell in his ghost stuff, but I hope not as naïve and unconvincing as O'Donnell's childish efforts."[185] This revelation is surprising and one regrets that Cook never developed his plans so far as actually drafting those weird stories.

Cook also held out hope for his projected memorial of Edith Miniter. He sent Lovecraft a copy of a story by Miniter, "Dead Houses," that he wanted to feature in the memorial. Lovecraft was still at Barlow's when he received it, and showed it to Barlow, who expressed an interest in publishing it himself. Lovecraft apparently told Cook of Barlow's interest, and Cook replied, "Tell Bobby to please lay off 'Dead Houses' until it is assured that the Miniter Memorial will *not* be published. I am very confident that I shall want to use that piece as the leading specimen of prose. The way that countryside is ripped to pieces is thoroughly typical of Mrs. Miniter's genius."[186]

As the date for the move west approached, Cook asked Lovecraft not to publicize the matter. The reason had to do with Campbell's "sinking other people's money in various wildcat schemes" like an oil well. Fellow amateur journalists were among those Campbell had been convincing to part with their money over the previous ten years. "Not all these people are good losers."[187] It makes one wonder why Cook had any faith in Campbell's business proposition when he knew all the details of Campbell's past schemes, but, as he explained to Lovecraft, Campbell "is working his head off and has gone as far as he can alone. He has issued 45 numbers of a weekly paper on which he must have help if it is ever to become more prosperous. I realize that I am taking a chance, but I want to get out of New England, to completely break with the past so far as business goes, and I shall take that chance provided Campbell does come across with a livable personal promise."[188]

On the same day Cook heard that Jennie Dowe's remains had been scattered in Massachusetts, he received word from Campbell that everything was ready for his move to East St. Louis. He travelled by train, stopping along the way in Boston and New York City, where he was met by Vincent Haggerty, Frank B. Long, Jr., and Samuel Loveman. When he reached East St. Louis he stayed with Campbell and his family in a small bungalow. Cook filled several positions at the newspaper, the *Canteen Village News,* as printer, associate editor, and feature writer.[189] "Cook is doing pretty well out west. The paper he is on has improved 200% since his advent, & he has a bungalow all to himself—with a separate press shed in the back yard, & a view of the prehistoric Cahokia Indian mounds in the background!"[190]

Within a year the newspaper failed. Cook found a new home at 1305 Missouri Ave. in East St. Louis and a new job as a printer. Lovecraft sent him the *Old Farmer's Almanack* for 1937 as a reminder of his native New England.[191] He probably wished he was back home in familiar soundings and among his few close friends. But before he could recover from the failure of the paper—his best hope for a new beginning—he learned that H. P. Lovecraft, his friend of twenty years, had died on March 15, 1937, at the age of 46. Cook left a candid account of his reaction to the news in his justly famous memoir, *In Memoriam: Howard Phillips Lovecraft. Recollections, Appreciations, Estimates* (1941):

> When Howard Lovecraft died I was a great many miles from New England, my address was not widely known, and it was some time after the funeral when I received the news from several sources in one mail. Reaching into the pigeon-hole of unanswered letters, I pulled out not one, but three, from Lovecraft. Spreading the letters out before me, I went into a black spell of self-recrimination. It made no difference in my feelings that there was nothing in the letters requiring immediate reply. I had shown, to say the least, an unpardonable discourtesy to one of the truest gentlemen and staunchest friends I had ever known.[192]

HOMECOMING (1938-1948)

Before the end of 1937 Cook was home again in New England. He lost some of the restlessness that had plagued him since the death of his wife. Lovecraft's sudden death seemed to restore his old bearings and the drive to write and publish again. This led to the renewal of old acquaintances, especially with Donald Wandrei and August Derleth.

> Mrs. Gamwell has written me of your possession of the *Old Farmer's Almanacks* and the use you were making of them. This is perfectly all right with me, and you may retain possession of them until you have copied such data as you need. Of course you will for natural phenomena allow for the difference between New England and Sac Prairie [Wisconsin].
>
> It may perhaps be well to tell you that Howard wanted me to have his collection because we made our collections together and travelled a lot together for the purpose, and had many arguments, each trying to force the other to take some especially desirable item. He knew that the collections put together would probably be the most complete in private hands in the country; and we had agreed that whoever died first the other should have his almanacs. I never for a moment thought I would be the heir!
>
> If my own collection was easily available I would ship it to you for your use, but it is stored far away and not until I have a settled home can I get it. I had a list of Lovecraft's wants and he had a list of mine. Both of our collections were formed around our grandfather's copies.
>
> I had heard that you and Wandrei were putting an immense amount of work into the editing of Howard's remains, but I had not known that you were personally financing the proposition. It is a splendid thing that you are able and willing to do this. I only wish I could help.
>
> When I first knew of *Weird Tales* using "Psychopompos," I did not like the idea at all—because Howard was violently opposed to that particular thing receiving added publicity. I printed it long ago in the *Vagrant*,[193] and Howard was always sorry he allowed it printed at all. But I believe now that you did

right in using it. As he grew in stature in many ways I always thought that in certain things Howard went too far in growing away from the natural inclinations of his early efforts. In an honest collection of his Remains his first work must be used.

I haven't a line of the extensive correspondence with Howard of over 23 years. When I broke up my home it went with most other collected stuff.

Like yourself, Howard's death was the greatest shock I ever suffered. I have been compelled to plead inability to write of him. One publisher wanted an article of 10,000 words. I would have liked to do it, but couldn't.

I know of no one whose death would leave such a void.

I shall be here for a short time recuperating from a strenuous and fruitless two years in the middle west. I shall go to New York for five or six weeks, and then go to Coates and print a book[194] which I have nearly ready.

Always good to hear from you.[195]

Cook lived with his sister in Sunapee, NH, when he returned from East St. Louis, and he also spent time regularly at the Driftwind Press office in North Montpelier, VT. Walter Coates could always use an extra, expert hand to help with the printing of *Driftwind* and the steady stream of books issued by the press. By the late 1930s, Coates had published more than fifty regional literary titles, most of which were probably subsidized by their authors.

Cook wrote again to Derleth from North Montpelier on February 13, 1938, thanking him for the return of some of the almanacs Derleth had borrowed. "I have also seen the statement of your administration of Lovecraft's literary remains. You deserve much credit. I shall be here for some time yet. I am printing a book for myself which will take some weeks."[196] A month later he wrote to say he'd found some manuscripts among his papers, including Lovecraft's Dunsanian fantasy, "The Quest of Iranon." Cook asked, "Have you this? If not, I will send it to you. If you have it, I shall destroy the copy I have."[197] No doubt Derleth asked him not to destroy it.

The book that Cook worked on through the summer at the Driftwind Press was *Told in Vermont* (1938), the first of two books—the second was *Heard in Vermont* (1939)—collecting stories he wrote under his old pen name, Willis T. Crossman. Some were first published separately as small, charming booklets that Cook printed occasionally at the Driftwind Press, but most saw print for the first time in the two books.[198] Cook began writing them in the mid-1930s. They are entirely different from the social protest pieces of the early 1930s. The works of this third and final incarnation of Crossman celebrate the author's native Vermont. They are humorous, wise, and nostalgic stories about people Cook knew or heard of from family and friends. Some first appeared in *Driftwind* magazine and in newspapers like the *Rutland Herald*, whose editor, Howard L. Hindley, championed Vermont's poets in his daily feature, "Peregrinations"; but most had never been published before they appeared in the two books.[199] New stories by Crossman would appear occasionally in *Driftwind*, amateur journals, and as privately printed booklets through the early 1940s, but the majority of them were produced in that great burst of creativity in 1938-39.

While Cook's publications exhibit little typographic excellence, he did take extra care with the handful of Crossman booklets. All were printed by hand in Cook's spare hours at the Driftwind Press. Each had its own individual look—some square, others oblong, one illustrated, and another oriented sideways. The size and shape of each depended on the paper he could get hold of when preparing to print. He claimed to have used scrap left over from other jobs at the press. The most intriguing parts of these booklets—aside from the stories—are the colophons. A typical example is the colophon found in "Fiction": "done in the woodshed, by early candlelight (before breakfast), in the dead of a Vermont winter, on a contraption so ancient its makers have forgotten they ever committed the crime. I was very energetic, so I guess there'll be almost seventy of 'em."

One thing a reader will note immediately about the Vermont stories is the names. The people brought to life in them have names like Gabbatha Gough, Volumnia Voobury, Shearjashub Shedd, and Phalaris Pocock. They defy belief, and yet Cook vouched for their authenticity. One of his letters to Lovecraft gives proof of just how methodical Cook was in gathering genuine names:

{L}et me explain how I have gotten my collection of Vermont names. Lists of graduates of most of the colleges of the state prior to 1840, and some of them to 1870 and some to date. Lists of teachers in those colleges. Lists of ministers of various churches. In these we of course have the learning. Then there is 'Walton's Register,' started back in the 1820's, I think. This gives all town officials, postmasters, merchants, etc. I have had copies of that for much of the period of its existence. It gives lawyers, doctors, etc., a high class of people there, either intellectually or in a business way. Then I have explored all available grave yards. I have copies names from signs and made a note of those I heard. If I ever have a chance, I am going to go over the old court records.[200]

The other peculiar feature of the stories is their format. They don't even look like stories at first glance. With their short broken lines and stanza arrangements they appear to be verse. But they are really prose pieces set in creative typography. Cook's innovation had a practical purpose: to make brief texts more substantial on the printed page. Another, more subtle, purpose is to provide visual clues for reading the stories, like what to emphasize, or where to pause. They suggest unobtrusively how best to read them.

Cook finished printing the sheets of the second Crossman book, *Heard in Vermont,* in November 1939.[201] It was left unbound for years because it required a cloth binding, which couldn't be accomplished at the Driftwind Press offices.

Cook had been planning to publish an Edith Miniter memorial volume since her death in 1934. As her literary executor (with Lovecraft) he had access to the material needed for it. But he'd been discouraged because, as he told Edward Cole, "I could not get two or three articles I considered essential to it. The crowning point was when Barlow grabbed the chance as soon as Lovecraft died and issued 'Dead Houses' in his mimeographed paper [*Leaves*]. I had given strict orders that he should not do so, as I considered it another essential to the Memorial—reflecting, as I thought it did, the very essence of her work."[202] "[H]e got Edkins to finance a horrible mimeographed edition of 50 copies and did what I had expressly forbidden."[203] Despite this excuse, he acknowledged, "I was financially unable, of course, to swing the Memorial, anyway."[204] Kenneth W. Faig, Jr., has also pointed out that "Barlow's amateur magazine probably reached fewer than sixty persons."[205] Barlow's actions seem especially ungracious when one remembers that Cook gave him valuable books from his library, as well as the sheets of *The Shunned House.*

Cook's issues with Barlow didn't end with the Miniter memorial. He was apparently unaware of the document Lovecraft wrote shortly before his death appointing Barlow his literary executor. Therefore Cook, like other friends of the late writer, thought Barlow acted improperly when he took possession of Lovecraft's books and papers. Cook wrote in no uncertain terms, "Knowing as I do Lovecraft's opinion of Barlow's unreliability, no one can make me believe that he ever left word for Barlow to be his literary executor. It is the last thing he would do."[206] He revealed in another letter, "Before I left Athol, and before Mrs. Clark died, she had orders not to allow a soul in Howard's study if he died except me and *everything* was to be turned over to me. He was so anxious about his study and had so often expressed distrust of Barlow's stability, that it is difficult for me to understand if he really did want Barlow notified. But I had been out of personal touch with him for over two years. The last I knew he wanted Derleth."[207] Barlow may have deserved Cook's ire over the publication of the Miniter story, but there's no doubt that Barlow was the best choice Lovecraft could have made from among his friends for his literary executor. Cook clearly could not have done as fine a job.

Cook gave the materials for the Miniter memorial to amateur journalist Hyman Bradofsky, who dedicated the Spring 1938 issue of his journal, the *Californian,* to Edith Miniter. It printed the tributes Cook solicited from friends like Ernest A. Edkins, Arthur H. Goodenough, Sam S. Stinson, Edwin B. Swift, and Lovecraft himself. Bradofsky acknowledged Cook's role in realizing the memorial: "The editor would be lacking in gratitude if he did not make acknowledgement of his obligation to Mr. W. Paul Cook, without whom these several tributes could not have been written."[208]

Besides the unrealized Miniter memorial there were memoirs of other friends—Will Murphy, Arthur H. Goodenough, Leonard E. Tilden, Doc Swift, and Lovecraft—to be done, but Cook despaired of ever writing them. "Tilden was my oldest friend, dating nearly forty years. I probably knew Goodenough better than anyone. And I saw as much or more of Lovecraft than anyone else. But I have simply been unable to write of them. [. . .] I hope you are able to bring out an adequate Lovecraft memorial."[209]

Cole did indeed make plans for a Lovecraft memorial in the form of a special issue of his amateur journal, the *Olympian*. In the fall of 1940 Cole asked Cook to contribute a piece on the "personal side" of Lovecraft. The request found Cook at a low point. On October 3 he wrote, "It is now six years since I had a job, and three since I returned from the unfortunate venture in St. Louis with Campbell. I can kill time and relieve incredible boredom by doing awful junk like *Told in Vermont*, etc., but I can't do anything I should. Without a certain degree of 'social security,' I cannot bring back the old days." Despite this protest, Cook closed the letter with a promise. "Tomorrow I shall make an attempt at some words on Lovecraft. If you do not hear from me in a week, consider it a total loss."[210] Before long, Cook had an article ready to send Cole.

> Here it is, and I hope it meets with your approval. This is my first contribution to an amateur paper in over twenty years.
>
> On your own head be it if you get me enthused over amateur journalism and I break loose and do some crazy stunt to issue a paper!
>
> In the last few years I have been badgered in the attempt to get me so viate that I would renew activity and other stunts have been used without effect, but today I feel a gentle glow which is, alas, familiar from of old!
>
> In this Lovecraft piece, not only on account of there being so much to say, but because L. has relatives yet alive, there are many things I have not told. There is my first meeting with him, of which you speak. There is his first night away from home. There is the regrettable joke (as we thought) when Mrs. Miniter, Joe Lynch and I plunked Lovecraft on the sofa with Sonia—the first time they met. As so on. But the enclosed as it is runs to more length than you wanted.[211]

The story about his first meeting with Lovecraft did eventually find its way into print, but Cook chose not to broadcast his part in introducing Sonia Greene to Lovecraft. Cook obviously considered their brief marriage an unfortunate mistake for which he shared a little blame.

All Lovecraft fans and scholars must be thankful to Cole for encouraging Cook to put pen to paper after procrastinating for so long. The short piece titled "H. P. Lovecraft" saw print in the August 1940 issue of the *Olympian*. This effort fired Cook's memory and enthusiasm, and he was soon at work on a longer tribute. By February 1941 it was nearly done.

> I have my monograph on Howard practically ready to print. It runs to an immense length, nearly twenty thousand words. I have just finished typing it from my notes. Present plans are that I shall go to North Montpelier at the coming of warm weather and print the thing. It will take a long time, as I doubt if I can set more than three pages with the material available, and it will have to be printed one page at a time. At least three months, as I figure it. I *must* put it in type myself to do some revising, or Coates would linotype it for me.
>
> I shall not print over one hundred copies. It is for Lovecraft's personal friends only. I have told a lot, only omitting all mention of his marriage. I have gone so far as not to entirely forgive his mother the way she treated him. [. . .]
>
> I hope you and yours are well. I am myself distressingly healthy.[212]

Ten days later Cook followed up with a letter touching on the recent death of Lovecraft's aunt, Annie Gamwell.

> It so happens that Mrs. Gamwell's death will make no difference in my article on Lovecraft. I have said all that I have decided is best to say. The story of Howard's marriage, the influence of his aunts on him, the characters of his mother and the aunts (Mrs. Gamwell was the nearest approach to normal), all of which would help explain him psychologically, I have practically not touched upon.[213]

The change in tone from the previous year is almost miraculous. The work of remembering and writing gave Cook the relief he needed to keep from dwelling on his own problems, past and present. He printed the Lovecraft memorial—*In Memorian: Howard Phillips Lovecraft*—at the Driftwind Press between April and June, 1941, in an edition of 94 copies. It might have come out earlier than June, but he reported to Edward Cole on June 19, 1941, "I have been held up for three weeks on the Lovecraft memorial for lack of [paper] stock. This morning some came which doesn't match but I must finish it."[214]

Before the end of June Cook finished the memoir, his best and longest work in prose, and the best example of his skill as a printer and typographer. Edwin B. Hill, the respected publisher and fine printer, praised the memorial in the March 1942 *National Amateur:* "Mr. Cook's brochure is a monument to friendship. It will endure in amateur history for all time."[215]

Those who knew Lovecraft responded well to it, too. Cook was gratified by the enthusiasm of August Derleth, who had an idea for bringing the memoir to a wider audience.

> When writing again address me at Sunapee, N.H., as with the completion of the Lovecraft memoir my work here is done for a few months.
>
> I am of course glad that you like the Lovecraft memoir, but think you are wrong in thinking it fit to be used in a Lovecraft book. It is too informal and could not in the circumstances be as accurate as I would wish. In any event, I would want to go over it and correct some blunders, smooth out some grammar, and make it more accurate. I would want to consult a file of the *Vagrant* and get that right.
>
> You are absolutely right about Baird![216] I could not remember Baird's name! That section will have to be straightened out.
>
> About the New Deal, I think my estimate of that is right. I was myself a New Dealer until after the 1936 election, had many personal talks with Howard in 1933 and 1934, and the reasons I state are the very ones I advanced to him as arguments! I doubt if all that all of us told him finally influenced him except as a little shove in the right direction. The breakdown of both the Republican and Democratic parties and the hopes and trend of the new party, the New Deal, were his real meat.[217]

Cook was also in regular touch again with Donald Wandrei, Derleth's partner in the founding of Arkham House. They had recently issued the first collection of stories by Lovecraft, *The Outsider and Others,* which Cook couldn't afford at $5.00 a copy.

No, of course I have not been able to buy a copy of *The Outsider and Others*, as I am lucky to be getting something to eat, and if Coates had not had a copy here I would not have seen it. Your offer of a copy is very generous and I appreciate it. I *would* like both your and Derleth's signatures.[218]

Wandrei and Derleth both signed and warmly inscribed his copy:

> For W. Paul Cook — / who, as author, printer, / and publisher, has done an / equal service to the memory / of a mutual friend — /
> Donald Wandrei / August Derleth[219]

In a letter to Wandrei, Cook raised the issue of publishing his memoir in the second Lovecraft collection planned by Arkham House, *Beyond the Wall of Sleep*.

> Derleth has written that you and he had some thought of using the Memoir as an introduction to one of the Lovecraft volumes. It is a high compliment but my first reaction was unfavorable. I do not want to put anything in the way of you fellows in your splendid work for the perpetuation of Lovecraft's name, and therefore I shall not say 'no,' but I had a lot of fun doing that memoir, I purposely used a colloquial, informal style; it contains as much about myself as about Lovecraft; no one is interested in me; and I do not want it chopped up and edited. Whatever its value or attractions may be, they lie in any personality I may have injected into it. If any other edition of it was issued, I should want to correct a few errors in grammar (like the use of the objective case, which I did deliberately) and make some minor corrections which would not mean castration. I trust you see my point of view.[220]

On July 25, 1941, writing from Sunapee, Cook reported to Derleth on the inquiries he made (apparently at Derleth's request) about Lovecraft manuscripts at the John Hay Library, Brown University. In particular, he was searching for "The Dream-Quest of Unknown Kadath." He also wrote: "I am accepting the judgment of you and Wandrei that my Lovecraft memoir is fit for use in the next Lovecraft omnibus. I shall shortly make the necessary corrections [. . .] I am thinking of publishing one number of a paper something like the *Recluse*. What could you contribute to it. Bookish or macabre."[221] The paper Cook had in mind became the *Ghost,* the last of his three major amateur journals. But its debut would have to wait. Cook wasn't in Sunapee for long before he received startling news on July 29: "This evening I have a telephone call from [Coates's] son-in-law saying that Coates died from a heart attack while out in his car this afternoon."[222]

> I was up to Coates' funeral yesterday and promised Mrs. Coates to go up tomorrow and take over and finish uncompleted work there and carry on for awhile. I had just got settled and prepared to do something for myself and had my accumulated mail looked over and I am again uprooted. I may find it necessary to take over Coates' business. [. . .] North Montpelier is about the last place in the universe where I would want to stay for long periods. The jumping-off place.[223]

As he predicted, Cook did not find the Vermont capitol to his liking.

> I cannot say I am happy here. It costs me about five dollars a week, which of course I can't afford, besides being stuck in this God-forsaken hole. I have cleared up what stuff Coates had on hand, but have taken on no new work. I am merely printing *Driftwind.* I shall consider my duty to Coates done when the November *Driftwind* is out, but probably am stuck here for the winter. If a book should come along to print I might take it on.[224]

To August Derleth he wrote on August 15, 1941:

> I am back again in Vermont before having time to unpack in Sunapee. When Coates died they [Nettie and Flora Coates] came down after me and I am fulfilling a promise to him to look after his business for a time at least.
>
> I wrote and inserted the extra sheet in the current *Driftwind,*[225] which you have seen. Mrs. Coates wants me to thank you for your letter which she received today. She appreciates it highly, and may use it in the memorial issue, which we have tentatively planned for November.
>
> I have laid all wires, and more than one person will investigate the Lovecraft stuff in the John Hay Library in the next few months. I will sort all results.

Before long I shall have in your hands the corrected Lovecraft memoir. Am going over it as time permits.

I have had various requests for this Lovecraft monograph which I cannot fill, and I have told them all it will appear in full in the second volume of the Works.

Also I have given several the address of the Arkham House who had not previously known of the books. Hope this will help it along. [. . .][226]

The supplement that Cook wrote for the July-August 1941 issue of *Driftwind* notified the magazine's many friends and supporters of its founding editor's passing.

This, the first number of the sixteenth yearly volume of *Driftwind*, was ready for the mails when Dr. Walter John Coates, its founder, publisher, editor and printer, died suddenly from a heart trouble on July 29, while driving his car. His heart had given trouble for many years, but he valiantly carried on to the last moment. The last words he ever put into type for *Driftwind* are in this issue—"Happy landings."

In keeping with his wish, often expressed, his magazine will continue. He has left material selected by himself personally for at least two issues, and certain of his plans are known for several months to come.

Driftwind will continue to be published by Dr. Coates' family, and will be edited by Nettie Allen Coates (Mrs. Walter J. Coates), who has had a large share in the formation of policies and the selection of material for the magazine since its inception.

Various tributes to Dr. Coates will appear in future issues of *Driftwind,* and a memorial volume has been tentatively planned containing reactions of his friends to his life and work, as well as an authentic life, and estimates of his influence on the ideology of his generation.

Within a year of Coates's death ambitious plans were in the works for *Driftwind*. He wrote Edward Cole on July 15, 1942:

Next week I am compelled to make a trip to Littleton, Mass., for a conference with Percy MacKaye, Edgar Lee Masters, Seamus MacManus and possibly others in regard to some ideas *they* have, and which I sadly expect to have to spike. I shall be the guest of MacKaye, and hope to get the thing over in one evening.[227]

MacKaye, Masters, and MacManus were all well-known authors and "men of letters" at that time, and despite Cook's blasé tone, he must have been somewhat excited by the prospect of collaborating with them. But he never had to make a decision about whatever the men had in mind.

> I did not make the trip to Littleton in July. MacManus was sick in a hospital in New York, Masters did not get to Littleton, and MacKaye and I could not see the trouble involved in meeting at that time. So rather ambitious plans for *Driftwind* were deferred.[228]

Cook kept up a regular correspondence with Derleth during the next couple of years, and excerpts from that correspondence sheds light on Cook's activities as he took the reins of Driftwind Press and launched *The Ghost*.

> Yes, I am taking care of *Driftwind* for the present. I hope it won't be long, as I can't afford it!
>
> I am making corrections on the Lovecraft memoir as fast as scarcity of leisure will allow.
>
> All best wishes for the success of the Derleth book. I am sorry that, as a pauper, I can't subscribe. I haven't worked nor earned money for several years.[229]

> ———————

> As I told you a year or so ago, I contemplate issuing as soon as I can get my material, a publication as similar to the *Recluse* as I can. I am now starting in earnest to build up a number around an authoritative article by Mrs. Farnsworth Wright and E. Hoffmann Price on Farnsworth Wright. I have comparatively little up to date that fits such a number. I do not like to ask authors for material that might be salable, for I know that they are all having a tough time. Wandrei was going to hunt me up something, but you say he is in the army.
>
> I didn't know but that you had written something at some time that was too horrible for sale! In that case, it will be right down my alley. Things too good (or too bad) for sale is just what I want.

Of course the magazine will not be sold, will be a fairly limited edition (probably 200) and is designed to be rare. Any suggestions?[230]

<hr>

I have no recollection of ever having, or having seen, your thesis on "The Weird Tale in English since 1890." It sounds just like what I want. I don't care how long it is, the longer the better, so it will not be necessary to excerpt from it.[231]

<hr>

My projected paper is progressing slowly, as I have a hard job here getting out *Driftwind* and at the same time doing enough printing to use my ration cards, but I am planning two issues of a very large paper (larger than the *Recluse*) and the second issue is to be entirely weird matter.

Do you care to renew your subscription to *Driftwind* with a copy of the Clark Ashton Smith book? Credit for a year and a half. We have very little money to spare![232]

On July 27, 1943, Cook acknowledged receipt of Smith's *Out of Space and Time* and the manuscript of Derleth's essay, "The Weird Tale in English Since 1890," which Derleth wrote as his honors thesis at the University of Wisconsin (1930). "It will be used in an amateur magazine called *The Ghost*—somewhat similar in format to the *Recluse*. I plan two numbers, of which the first is slowly being printed, as I can get the time. The first is a miscellany. The second will be largely weird. This then is for the second."[233]

The first issue of the *Ghost* appeared soon after, with the optimistic date of Spring 1943. It lived up to Cook's promise that it would be a miscellany. The contents are a hodge-podge of prose and poetry by old-time amateur journalists like Ernest Edkins, Edwin B. Hill, Rheinhart Kleiner, and others whose names are scarcely remembered today. The most memorable contribution came from Dorothy C. Walter. Her short reminiscence, "Lovecraft and Benefit Street," was also published by Cook as a separate booklet following its appearance in the *Ghost*.

When Cook wrote to Derleth a year later, on June 29, 1944, the letter was datelined Sunapee, N.H., where Cook was on his "first vacation in two years," which lasted abour two weeks. In the same letter Cook answered questions about Lovecraft's early appearances in amateur papers, identifying place of publication of stories like "The Alchemist," "The Street," and "The Picture in the House," which he published in the July 1919 *National Amateur*.[234]

Cook had spent so much time reminiscing about his active years in amateur journalism that he apparently felt the urge to reconnect with the hobby and old friends. One step in this direction was his attending the National Amateur Press Association's convention in Boston in 1944. While there he went to a party at C.A.A. Parker's home[235] and fended off an attempt to nominate him for office. As he told Edward Cole, "[Burton] Crane nominates me for Judge, I see. Of course, I shall not accept the nomination. Have written him to squelch it. I have held all the offices in the National that I ever shall."[236] He did agree, however, to having his name listed in *The National Amateur* in the Panel of Experts as a contact for anyone seeking advice on the publication of "Vanity" magazines.[237] One of his conversations from the convention even made its way into the gossipy amateur journal of Helen Crane Heins:

> On the last day of the Convention, you could have knocked me over with a feather as Paul Cook sidled up to me and plaintively queried: 'Is it true Helen, that you hen-peck Charlie Heins?' And then it all came out, how tempter Cook had suggested to my spouse, to sneak from my protective side early in the morning to partake a couple of 'snifters' in the bar room. Charlie had adroitly side-stepped it with the pious declaration that I was the early riser. That I watched his every move, and kept him on the narrow path. Well! What next, I wondered. 'Look!' I said to Cook: 'You know Charlie for many years; see how he gambols around here and it's supposed to be his good behavior. Honestly Cook what do you really think?' Cook mulled this over, sadly shook his head. 'That's what I thought!' he said dubiously, then left me to figure that out.[238]

In the aftermath of the convention, a group photo of the attendees appeared in the September 1944 *National Amateur,* and Cook can be seen in the last row with an impish grin on his face as he looks sideways at his old stone-faced friend, Tim Thrift. Thrift published an issue of his journal the *Lucky Dog* earlier that year with an "Amateur

Dictionary" that included an entry for Cook: "COOK—Symbol of quantity, quality and quaintness in amateur publishing. Alter Ego—Willis T. Crossman."[239]

A perfect example of those qualities would be the *Ghost*. In the summer of 1944 he published the second issue, which is most notable for the first of a series of memoirs titled "The Book of the Dead" by veteran pulp writer E. Hoffmann Price. The first installment was dedicated to Farnsworth Wright, the editor of *Weird Tales* during its heyday from the mid 1920s to the late 1930s. This issue also gave Cook the chance to keep a promise he'd made in the 1920s: to publish *The Sphinx* by Samuel Loveman, which was also issued separately as a pamphlet.

The third issue was already being planned as Cook solicited material from Herman C. Koenig, the noted book collector and amateur publisher who also knew H. P. Lovecraft. At the time Koenig was doing his best to revive interest in the work of the British writer William Hope Hodgson.

You have done a good job for Hodgson in the *Reader and Collector*. It needed to be done. A work like that would be welcomed by the *Ghost*. Why not do an article on some important figure for it?

I see Derleth announces the Charleston item[240] for the third Lovecraft book. So that stops its being used in the *Ghost*.[241]

Back from a vacation on August 5th, Cook wrote to Derleth, announcing the imminent release of the second *Ghost* and to discuss Derleth's contribution to the next issue.

Number 2 of the *Ghost* has been ready to mail since the first of June. I put off sending it out until I returned from my vacation, as I did not want to take care of the correspondence involved. I am sure you will find it interesting.

Your "Weird Tale in English Since 1890" is to be the feature of No. 3. I have all the first part in type with the exception of the smaller type for the quotations, which I shall put into type at once. I have the Bibliography set up to Henry James, and have stopped there. Have you a carbon copy of this Bibliography? If not, I will send you this copy, for there are unquestionably many errors in the dates—doubtless due to the stenographer going haywire. I had suspected some of the dates as I went along, but could do nothing about it. But I finally came to Rider Haggard, whose first editions I have here. Your copy says: *She*, 1907; *Ayesha*, 1895. This is pretty bad. *She* was 1886; *Ayesha*, 1905. I cannot help but think that some of the other dates are as badly off as this.

Will you have your copy checked over or shall I send this copy for your corrections?

Sorry to bother you with this thing, but I regard this as a most important article for which the *Ghost* will be treasured, and I no less than you want it right.[242]

Derleth replied quickly to Cook's questions and concerns.

Yours of the 7th received and I have made the corrections indicated in the MS.

I agree with you that there should be an explanatory letter from you to go with the MS. You have an introductory note, but I think it would be a good thing to have a note explaining that the dates given are not necessarily first editions, and telling how the dates were obtained. [. . .] I am now putting into type the eight-point quotations, and may print the first part of the article any time. This does not mean that you have to hurry with your note of explanation, as I can never tell just when and how much I can work on my own playthings.[243]

Cook didn't wait long to issue the third *Ghost* in the spring of 1945. It carried a second installment of "The Book of Dead," this one about Robert E. Howard, the author of incomparable stories best-known as the creator of Conan. The memoir dominates the issue, but a reader would also notice, tucked away near the end of the magazine, a short essay by Cook titled "A Plea for Lovecraft." He gave a candid appraisal of the growing Lovecraft cult in passages like these:

Irreparable harm is being done to Lovecraft by indiscriminate and even unintelligent praise, by lack of unbiased and intelligent criticism, and by a warped sense of what is due him in the way of publication of his works. [. . .]

Arkham House can not be blamed for cashing in on the present Lovecraft furore. With great faith, courage, personal sacrifice and hard work they published the first omnibus volume,

The Outsider and Others, and for several years held the bag before they got back their cash expenditure on it. Strange to say, it was the publication of the second omnibus (which should never have been published) that put Lovecraft over with a bang, and made the publishing of other weird books a lucrative business.

August Derleth is mentioned by name and gently chided for his literary judgment, and occasional lack thereof. One might wonder if Cook was jealous of the success of Arkham House, in light of the failure of his Recluse Press and the stillborn *Shunned House*. He had also been the first person to encourage and publish Lovecraft at the beginning of his career as a fiction writer. But the criticisms have a sincere ring to them. At least one friend, Herman C. Koenig, voiced his support. In a letter dated April 25, 1945, he admitted, "I wish I had the courage to write paragraphs you did in the article."[244]

Koenig may have felt caught in the middle. He agreed with some of Cook's opinions, but he wanted to stay on good terms with Derleth as they worked on the Hodgson omnibus that Arkham House would publish. He wrote a diplomatically phrased letter to Derleth in the wake of the article's publication. "I can well appreciate your reaction to Cook's article in the latest *Ghost*. On the other hand; I am somewhat in sympathy with some of Cokk's [*sic*] expressions. [. . .] I'm not sure the inclusion of some of Howard's early stories in books intended for distribution will help to enhance his reputation as a writer."[245]

The controversy over Cook's article continued into the summer of 1945. In late July Koenig wrote to tell Cook that Derleth was making a public feud out of the matter.

> A few days ago I received the group of letters re the last issue of *Ghost,* that Derleth is circulating around the country. He certainly didn't pull his punches, did he? I dislike this sort of thing, and I sincerely hope that it isn't permitted to continue. At any rate, I'd appreciate it very much if you don't introduce me or my last letter to you into the controversy.[246]

Cook was aware of the trouble he'd stirred up, and he enjoyed it.

> Of course I am being bombarded. When you scratch the vanity and egotism of a little tin god it is interesting to see how far he can go into the vituperative gutter. He started by writing

a letter which he demanded be printed in *The Ghost*. I told him there would be no round-table discussion of the matter in *The Ghost* and that if I did use his letter I would also use some commendatory letters. I believe he is passing copies of this letter to me around. He did not want other letters used, but only his—of course. Then he started his vituperations. I have not answered any of his letters except the first one. Perhaps I may write first a note by and by to keep him at the boiling point. He is, in short, the victim of an uncontrollable rage.

As a matter of fact, I have said in *The Ghost* all I care to say about Derleth. I covered all the points I care to make. I have something more to say about the Lovecraft furor in general. There is a clear-cut and absolutely fake picture of him emerging. There will be no names mentioned this time, but I shall make two or three more enemies.[247]

The controversy over Lovecraft aside, Koenig and Cook continued discussions about a piece that Koenig was preparing for the *Ghost*. "In your last letter you rashly invited me to contribute to the GHOST on some phase of 'Weird Collecting.' I'm not quite sure what you had in mind, but what do you think of the enclosed 'Ramblings.' If it is the sort of stuff you'd care to publish, let me know how much longer you'd like to have it—and I'll try to complete it during the summer."[248] In November Koenig was still working on the essay. On the 7th he wrote: "I am enclosing a few more paragraphs for that 'Rambling' article of mine. Hope you can use them. I have a few more underway and will send them along in due course."[249]

Despite Derleth's hostile reaction to Cook's "A Plea for Lovecraft" and Derleth's attempts to make it a public debate, the two men remained on cordial terms. Derleth sent a complimentary copy of *Supernatural Horror in Literature,* published in hardcover in 1945 by Ben Abramson with a foreword by Derleth. "Just before I left North Montpelier I had a note from you that you were sending me a copy of 'Supernatural Horror.' It has doubtless arrived since I left, but as I shall not be back there for ten days or so yet, I feared you would think me churlish in not acknowledging it."[250]

Though much, or the best, of the material Cook published in the *Ghost* had a supernatural flavor, the magazine was first and foremost an amateur publication. He kept in touch with friends old and new during his years in Vermont, and continued to be charmed and pleased by the efforts of other amateurs. One enthusiastic young recruit to the hobby who impressed Cook was Helen Vivarrtas Wesson,[251] who also shared his love of supernatural literature—especially Lovecraft's work. Here is his reply to her request for a copy of his Lovecraft memoir.

By gum, if any real person really wants a copy of the Lovecraft memoir as badly as you seem to, they ought to have it! I am sending a copy by this mail. It is one of two copies which I have been trying to keep for myself. Enthusiasm such as yours is its own reward, but if anyone can help they should do so.

There is a standing offer of ten dollars a copy for this thing—but I know you won't be tempted!!

So you are going to Japan! Good! I wish I was. Oh, for new scenes and pictures green. But alas, there is no chance. When you get there, remember me to Burton.

I have enjoyed all your papers, with the hand colored drawings and their vivacity and freshness of contents. Thanks for pleasant moments.[252]

The winter 1945 issue of the *Aonian,* an amateur journal published by Tim Thrift and Ernest A. Edkins, featured a tribute to Cook's career from Edward H. Cole. "The Colossus of the North" is a warm appreciation of all that Cook had done in the cause of amateur journalism. Many of the journals he issued overshadow those produced by nearly all of his contemporaries in size and quality. Cook contributed "The Great What Is It" to the same issue, an essay that tries to explain the attractions of amateur journalism, the hobby to which he'd devoted so much effort since his teenage years.

The fourth issue of the *Ghost,* dated July 1946, featured "Burrowings of an Old Bookworm" by Rheinhart Kleiner. A year later the fifth and final issue was published. It was dominated by memoirs of James Ferdinand Morton, a long-time amateur journalist and a member of Lovecraft's circle of friends. The lead piece was the third of Price's "The Book of the Dead" series, followed by other memoirs of Morton by Cook, Cole, Kleiner, and Morton's widow, Pearl. Herman Koenig's article on collecting, "Ramblings of a Reader and Collector of the Weird and Fantastic," finally saw print. Cook closed the issue with a warning that was consistent with his credo, "For Love Only." It read: "May my curse follow him who ever offers a Ghost for sale."

In September 1947, Edward H. Cole and his wife stopped in North Montpelier while motoring through Vermont. "The Driftwind Press was much as of yore, except that Paul had taken down the sign—to discourage business. Linotype filled the racks and overflowed to every available space on the shelves. Another *Monadnock Monthly* is in process, but not far advanced as yet. We spent an hour or so in casual chat about amateur affairs and personalities, then went forth into the warm sunshine to behold Mrs. Coates's garden and flowers."[253]

The downed sign was ominous. Though Cook wrote around this time that "I am not one of those who will ever retire on a pension!" his health prevented him from maintaining his old hectic pace.[254] In the fall of 1947 he was sick with the flu and it settled in his bladder. This was discovered after an operation in early December. The doctors told him he would have to come back for another operation. According to his sister Cora's account:

> [H]e came back to No. Montpelier for a week to get things in shape. At this time he was under opiates every second. He went back to the hospital the fourth of January and went on a liquid diet and that last few days before the operation, just vein feeding. Twelve days after he went back he had the first operation, on a Friday. The next Sunday they sent for me. The wound had broken open and they performed an emergency operation, not thinking he would live through the day. He rallied during the evening and the doctors were encouraged again, but Tuesday he began to get steadily worse and peritonitis was found to have set in and spread very rapidly. He was kept under opiates and was fully conscious of what went on and what was said to him although he could not talk to be understood. [Cook died January 22, 1948.] He really suffered terribly. I know that the only reason he went through with it was because he thought for Mrs. Coates's sake he must take the chance if there was any at all. He knew that if anything happened to him she would have to give up. Which of course was true. [. . .] I feel that he was happy there at No. Montpelier as he was practically his own boss and had a chance to do a great deal of writing."[255]

Cook's friends in the community of amateur journalists were quick to note and lament his passing. Edward Cole mailed a broadside announcement, dated January 23, 1948, with the news of Cook's death that declared, "With his passing amateur journalism loses one of its most sincere and lavish servants." Edna Hyde McDonald wrote an obituary for the March 1948 *National Amateur* that shows how Cook's death effected even those who did not know him well. "He was not an aggressive member. His was a humble spirit. Little is known about him, and except for the intimate friends he had in the hobby, few knew him at all. But to meet him even once was memorable."[256] In the July 1949 issue of his *Churinga,* James Guinane wrote a perceptive appraisal of Cook's legacy.

> W. Paul Cook [. . .] printed much and wrote little. But could he by any exaggeration be called a man who was concerned only with the form of his printing and to whom it mattered not what he printed? Cook's later works—those five magnificent *Ghosts*—brought to amateur journalism some of the writings which later we will dig among for our literature.[257]

The finest of the tributes came from Edward Cole. It offers an intimate portrait of the man from a friend of nearly forty years.

> Of Paul Cook I cannot write easily or without emotion. He was a close friend; I cherished him deeply. I have known him since I was a boy, a novice in amateur journalism. There were large gaps in our acquaintanceship, years when we lost sight of each other; but those lapses served only to strengthen friendship as it was renewed. I know, too, that the passing of friends who were dear to us both—Howard Lovecraft, Tim Thrift—has brought us closer together in recent years, as we have realized how precious friendship is. To me he confided the fact of his illness and impending operations; he directed that in case of untoward event, I should be notified; and he and I knew that the outcome might mostly likely be as it was—fatal. [. . .]
>
> To me, a remarkable aspect of his career and his achievements is that during his long activity he was relatively aloof from his fellow amateur journalists. Rarely did he attend a convention; moreover, his personal contacts with his fellow amateur journalists

were comparatively few. Unquestionably, his friendship with Howard Lovecraft was his closest with any amateur journalist. This is understandable, for he was responsible for bringing Lovecraft from seclusion and leading him into the world about him. I have known Paul personally ever since he attended a Hub club conference in mid-winter, 1907 or 1908. A quality that struck me then remained characteristic of him through the years; he cared to participate in gatherings only to a point; when he had had enough, he left without farewell and went about pursuits that pleased him more. In just that way he faded out of the 1944 convention of the National, even though he had played a major part in the events behind the scenes determining the outcome of the meeting. I have known him to fail to keep an appointment even with Lovecraft and me when we had a dinner engagement at another amateur's home. It was a characteristic you had to recognize and overlook, for so long as he was with your, he was companionable and genial.[258]

Cook may have found peace during those final years in Vermont, or the contentment one finds in the work that best suits him. After the death of his wife, loss of his job and home, and an unsettled decade that coincided with the worst years of the Great Depression, he found his footing again and returned to his first loves: writing, printing, and publishing. Only love for the work can explain his productivity. Besides sixteen books and pamphlets of his own (published under the Willis T. Crossman pen name), Cook printed five large numbers of the *Ghost* and several related booklets, and he was also responsible (after Coates's death) for the monthly *Driftwind* magazine and more than twenty Driftwind Press books that he designed and printed.

When holding and reading the books and magazines he published, one feels the love of their maker. They are not ostentatious, which is befitting the work of a man who called himself "an ordinary printer." But there is the love of printing in them, and there is nothing ordinary about what is done with love. The printed word not only shaped Cook's work and legacy. It also gave him the enduring friendships—with H.P. Lovecraft, Walter J. Coates, Edward Cole, Vrest Orton, and so many others—that enrich one's life.

NOTES

Abbreviations used in the notes: AWD = August W. Derleth; DAW = Donald A. Wandrei; EHC = Edward H. Cole; HCK = Herman C. Koenig; HPL = H. P. Lovecraft; JHL = John Hay Library, Brown University; MHS = Minnesota Historical Society; NL = Newberry Library; SHSW = State Historical Society of Wisconsin; *SL* = H. P. Lovecraft, *Selected Letters* (Arkham House, 1965-1976; 5 vols.); WPC = W. Paul Cook; WR = Will Ransom.

1. EHC, "Footprints on the Sands of Time", *Interlude* (February 1948): 3.

2. Thanks are due to R. Alain Everts' research for some facts about Cook's life and family history.

3. R. Alain Everts, "W. Paul Cook and The Ghost", *Outsider International* (1995): 30.

4. "Cook is a lineal descendant of Gov. Benning Wentworth by his first wife; whilst another friend of mine—the novelist Mrs. Miniter of Wilbraham, Mass.—is descended from Benning & wife #2." HPL to Elizabeth Toldridge, March 8, 1929 in *SL* 2.319.

5. Cora, as the daughter of William and Alma Cook, was actually Cook's cousin.

6. Everts, 30.

7. *Bibliography of Vermont Poets,* ed. Walter John Coates (N. Montpelier: Driftwind Press, 1942), p. 91.

8. Truman J. Spencer, *The History of Amateur Journalism* (NY: The Fossils, 1957), p. 86. Greenfield organized the UAPA on September, 2, 1895.

9. Leonard E. Tilden, "*The Monadnock Monthly*; An Amateur Magazine, You Cannot Buy It", *The National Amateur* (July 1919): 329.

10. *Vagrant* (May 1920): 32.

11. Spencer, p. 86.

12. *Vagrant* (May 1920): 32-33.

13. Tilden, 329.

14. W. Paul Cook, "In Memoriam: Howard Phillips Lovecraft. Recollections, Appreciations, Estimates", in *Lovecraft Remembered,* ed. Peter Cannon (Sauk City: Arkham House, 1998), p. 149.

15. HPL to Rheinhart Kleiner, September 22, 1918 in *SL* 1.148-49.

16. Tilden, p. 330.

17. Cook, "In Memoriam", p. 136.

18. See note 15.

19. *Reflector* (August 1906): 4.

20. "Before and after the turn of the century, the regional associations were still very important. For instance, many in New England put loyalty to the NEAPA first and did not even join the NAPA. They also had single-state associations like the Massachusetts. Local clubs, where active, generally replaced state and regional associations as the 20th century progressed. But at one time regionals like the Atlantic were very important. There was a lot of politics in ajay and the abundance of local, state, and regional groups meant more offices for people to hold." (Letter from Kenneth W. Faig, Jr., to the author, April 1, 2007.)

21. *Bibliography of Vermont Poets,* pp. 91-92.

22. William S. Pretzer, "Tramp Printers: Craft Culture, Trade Unions, and Technology", *Printing History* 6:2 (1984): 14.

23. John Edward Hicks, *Adventures of a Tramper Printer: 1880-1890* (Kansas City: Midamericana Press, 1950), pp. 19-21.

24. Maggie Holtzberg-Call, *The Lost World of the Craft Printer* (Urbana: University of Illinois Press, 1992), p. 64.

25. *United Amateur* (November 1907): 33.

26. *Aftermath,* Random Number Issued on Account of the Good Times at the Boston Conference (February 22, 1909): 2.

27. WPC, "In Memoriam", p. 129.

28. Edward H. Cole, "Resignations Plagued NAPA in 1912-1913", quoted in Edith Miniter, *The Coast of Bohemia and Other Writings,* Edited with Introduction and Appendices by Kenneth W. Faig, Jr. (Glenview: The Moshassuck Press, 2000), p. 831.

29. HPL to Annie Gamwell, December 11, 1919, in *SL* 1.64.

30. *The Torpedo,* ed. Frank Austin Kendall (September, 1913): 19-20.

31. WPC, "Typographical Criticism", *United Amateur* (November 1913): 37-38.

32. HPL to Rheinhart Kleiner, September 24, 1917, in *H.P. Lovecraft: Letters to Rheinhart Kleiner,* eds. S.T. Joshi and David E. Schultz (NY: Hippocampus Press, 2005), p. 115-16.

33. Cook published "Nemesis" in the June 1918 issue of the *Vagrant.*

34. HPL to DAW, March 27, 1927, in *SL* 2.121.

35. HPL and DAW Jan 29, 1927 in *Mysteries of Time and Spirit: The Letters of H.P. Lovecraft and Donald Wandrei,* eds. S. T. Joshi and David E. Schultz (Portland: Night Shade Books), p. 17; see also HPL to CAS, Jan 11, 1923, in *SL* 1.202.

36. HPL to Bernard Austin Dwyer, March 3, 1927, in *SL* 2.110.

37. HPL to Frank B. Long, Jr., November 8, 1923, in *SL* 1.259.

38. For more about Gidlow and Mills, see Ken Faig Jr., "Lavender Ajays of the Red-Scare Period: 1917-1920", *Fossil* no. 329 (July 2006): 5-17.

39. Will Ransom (1878-1955), co-founder with Frederic W. Goudy of the Village Press, was later a member of The Fossils, the alumni association for amateur journalists, from 1949 until his death in 1955.

40. WPC to AWD, September 11, 1927 (ms., SHSW).

41. HPL to Rheinhart Kleiner, in *H.P. Lovecraft: Letters to Rheinhart Kleiner,* p. 115.

42. See pages 154-55 for Cook's "Howard P. Lovecraft's Fiction."

43. Edna Hyde McDonald, "The Years of the Locusts: 1915-1930", in *National Amateur* (March 1948): 37.

44. WPC to EHC, March 26, 1919 (ms., JHL).

45. WPC, letter in *Cleveland Sun* (August 1919): 2.

46. HPL to Alfred Galpin [April 1920], in *H. P. Lovecraft: Letters to Alfred Galpin,* eds. S. T. Joshi and David E. Schultz (NY: Hippocampus Press, 2003), p. 70.

47. McDonald, pp. 38-39.

48. Edith Miniter, editorial in *The Muffin Man* (April 1921) in Edith Miniter, *Going Home and Other Amateur Writings,* Edited with Notes and Bibliography by Kenneth W. Faig, Jr. (Glenview: The Moshassuck Press, 1995), p. 778

49. Edith Miniter, editorial in the *Aftermath* (November 1921) in *Going Home,* p. 802.

50. George Julian Houtain, "Three–Oh!–Three Veni! Vidi! Vici!", in *National Tribute,* August 1921, quoted in *The Coast of Bohemia,* p. 772.

51. HPL to Maurice Moe, May 18, 1922, in *SL* I.176.

52. "Samuel Loveman's new *Saturnian,* just emerging from the press of W. Paul Cook, is without a doubt the artistic event of the year. No magazine of even approximately equal aesthetic merit has appeared for many months. The exorcism against modern verse is a thing to remember, and the translations from Baudelaire and Verlaine are things to chant and admire." [HPL, "News Notes", *United Amateur* 21, 3 (1922): 32.]

53. WPC to HPL, March 11, 1921, (ms., JHL).

54. Ibid.

55. WPC to HPL, January 10, 1923, (ms., JHL).

56. Charles Clark Munn (1848-1917), author of popular novels like *Rockhaven* (1902), several of which were illustrated by Frank T. .Merrill. H. Warner Munn was inspired to write his first story, "The Werewolf of Ponkert" (1925) by a letter to the editor from HPL to *Weird Tales* suggesting that someone write a werewolf story from the werewolf's perspective.

57. See pages 89-92 for "The Birth of Driftwind" by Walter John Coates.

58. WPC to DAW, November 14, 1928 (ms., MHS).

59. HPL to Lillian D. Clark, December 23, 1925, in *H. P. Lovecraft: Letters from New York,* eds. S. T. Joshi and David E. Schultz (Portland: Night Shade Books, 2005), p. 259.

60. Vrest Orton, "Editorial", *Driftwind* (June 1927): [3]. The first issue was dated April 1926. Coates originally intended to issue *Driftwind* as a free amateur publication, inspired by the example of Cook's *Monadnock.* However, the costs soon proved too high. *Driftwind* became a bi-monthly—sold at $2.00 per yearly subscription—with the November 1927 issue.

61. *Driftwind* (July 1932): 5-8 (as "Pictorial Reminiscences by the Editor").

62. WPC, "The End", in *Vagrant* (Spring 1927): 311.

63. HPL to Clark Ashton Smith, circa September 1, 1925, in *SL* 2.25

64. HPL to Lillian D. Clark, November 19, 1925, in *Letters from New York,* p. 249.

65. HPL to Lillian D. Clark, October 9, 1925, in *Letters from New York,* p. 216.

66. HPL to Lillian D. Clark, December 2, 1925, in *Letters from New York,* p. 251.

67. WPC to Wilfred Townley Scott, April 26, 1944 (ms., JHL).

68. HPL to James F. Morton, January 5, 1926, in *SL* 2.36.

69. HPL to Alfred Galpin, September 30, 1919, in *H. P. Lovecraft: Letters to Alfred Galpin,* p. 54.

70. HPL to Rheinhart Kleiner, February 10, 1720 [1920], in *H.P. Lovecraft: Letters to Rheinhart Kleiner,* pp. 181-82.

71. HPL to Rheinhart Kleiner (March 12, 1722 [i.e. 1922]), *H.P. Lovecraft: Letters to Rheinhart Kleiner,* p. 221.

72. HPL to Frank B. Long, Jr., October 7, 1923, in *SL* 1.255.

73. WPC to HPL, Memorial Day, 1923 (ms., JHL).

74. Ibid.

75. HPL to DAW, June 2, 1927, in *Mysteries of Time and Spirit,* p. 111.

76. HPL to Frank B. Long, Jr., September 24, 1927, in *SL* 2.171.

77. HPL to Frank B. Long, Jr., November 1927, in *SL* 2.186. The books by Vernon Knowles are actually titled *The Street of Queer Houses and Other Tales* and *Here and Otherwhere.*

78. WPC to DAW, August 27, 1927 (ms., MHS). The Minnesota Historical Society in St. Paul houses the Wandrei family papers, which include a file of letters from Cook to Wandrei, dated 1928 to 1946.

79. WPC to DAW, September 17, 1927 (ms, MHS).

80. The book Cook hadn't seen before was *The Goddess of Atvatabar* by William R. Bradshaw. WPC to DAW, January 21, 1928 (ms., MHS).

81. WPC to AWD, August 9, 1926 (ms., WHS).

82. HPL to James F. Morton, November 22, 1925, in *SL* 2.30-31.

83. HPL to James F. Morton, November 17, 1926, in *SL* 2.91.

84. Cook's books were "printed direct from the linotype slugs." WPC to DAW, May 19, 1928 (ms., MHS).

85. HPL to Dwyer, March 3, 1927, in *SL* 2.106.

86. See also HPL to DAW, March 13, 1927, in *Mysteries of Time and Spirit,* p. 54.

87. HPL to DAW Feb. 10, 1927, in *Mysteries of Time and Spirit*, p.31.

88. HPL to DAW March 16, 1927, in *Mysteries of Time and Spirit,* p. 55.

89. WPC to DAW, March 29, 1927 (ms., MHS).

90. WPC to DAW, April 7, 1927, (ms., MHS).

91. WPC to DAW, April 21, 1927 (ms., MHS).

92. HPL to Clark Ashton Smith, March 24, 1927, in *SL* 2.114.

93. HPL to Clark Ashton Smith, May 12, 1927, in *SL* 2.127.

94. HPL to Maurice Moe, July 30, 1927, in *SL* 2.157-58.

95. HPL to DAW, July 31, 1927, in *Mysteries of Time and Spirit,* p. 137.

96. HPL to DAW, August 6, 1927, in *Mysteries of Time and Spirit,* p. 143.

97. WPC to DAW, September 25, 1927 (ms., MHS); DAW to HPL Oct 2, 1927, in *Mysteries of Time and Spirit,* p. 167.

98. WPC to AWD, September 11, 1927 (ms., SHSW).

99. HPL to Frank B. Long, Jr., September 24, 1927, in *SL* 2.171.

100. HPL to Frank B. Long, Jr., November 1927, in *SL* 2.185.

101. WPC, "In Memoriam", pp. 125-26.

102. WPC to DAW, Oct. 23, 1927 (ms., MHS).

103. HPL to DAW Oct 22, 1927, in *Mysteries of Time and Spirit,* p. 173.

104. "An M.R. James Letter, Introduced and Annotated by Jack Adrian", in *Ghosts & Scholars* 8 (1986). The letter was dated 12 January 1928.

105. WPC, "In Memoriam", pp. 137-38.

106. WPC to DAW, September 17, 1927 (ms., MHS).

107. WPC to DAW September 17, 1927 (ms., MHS).

108. HPL to Vincent Starrett, December 6, 1927, in *SL* 2.209.

109. WPC to DAW, October 23, 1927 (ms., MHS).

110. WPC to DAW, November 27, 1927 (ms., MHS).

111. HPL to DAW, November 25, 1927, in *Mysteries of Time and Spirit,* p. 188.

112. WPC to DAW, December 29, 1927 (ms., MHS).

113. Ibid.

114. The essay on Radcliffe was published in *A Donald Wandrei Miscellany* (2001).

115. WPC to DAW, January 1, 1928 (ms., MHS).

116. HPL to DAW, January 20, 1928, in *Mysteries of Time and Spirit*, pp. 210-12.

117. HPL to DAW, April 5, 1928, in *Mysteries of Time and Spirit*, p. 218.

118. WPC to DAW, March 22, 1928, (ms., MHS).

119. Cook to Wandrei, April 2, 1928, (ms., MHS).

120. WPC to DAW, April 19, 1928 (ms., MHS).

121. HPL to DAW, June 26, 1928, in *Mysteries of Time and Spirit*, p 221.

122. Ibid, p. 222.

123. Ibid.

124. HPL to Zelia Bishop, July 28, 1928, in *SL* 2.245.

125. WPC to WR, July 21, 1928 (ms., NL). The correspondence between WPC and Will Ransom is in the collection of the Newberry Library, Chicago.

126. WR to WPC, August 28, 1928 (ms., NL).

127. WPC to WR, November 14, 1928 (ms., NL).

128. WPC to WR, November 29, 1928 (ms., NL).

129. Ibid. See pages 107-32 for a complete bibliography of Cook's publications.

130. WPC to WR, March 22, 1929 (ms., NL).

131. WPC to DAW, January 21, 1928 (ms., MHS).

132. WPC to DAW, May 19, 1928 (ms., MHS).

133. "Cook tells me that you are planning an expurgated edition [of *Ecstasy*]." HPL to DAW, June 26, 1928, in *Mysteries of Time and Spirit*, p 221.

134. WPC to DAW November 18, 1928 (ms., MHS).

135. HPL to DAW November 23, 1928, in *Mysteries of Time and Spirit*, p 231.

136. WPC to DAW November 18, 1928 (ms., MHS).

137. HPL to Elizabeth Toldridge, May 4, 1929, in *SL* 2.335.

138. HPL to Elizabeth Toldridge, May 29, 1929, in *SL* 2.348.

139. HPL to Wildred B. Talman, June 8, 1929, in *SL* 2.349.

140. HPL to DAW Sept. 12, 1929, in *Mysteries of Time and Spirit*, p. 244.

141. Will Ransom, *Private Presses and Their Books* (NY: Bowker, 1929), p. 120.

142. WPC to DAW, August 23, 1931 (ms., MHS) and WPC, "In Memoriam", p 151. Cook did not dispense with his entire library at that time. Several years later he had some choice books stored at his sister's home that he gave to Robert Barlow and Lovecraft. Much of his library, and other personal items, were given to H. Warner Munn for safe-keeping. Cook made frustrated attempts in the mid 1930s to get some things back from Munn but it is not certain whether he was successful.

144. HPL to James F. Morton, January 14, 1930, in *SL* 3.110.

145. HPL to DAW June 30, 1930, in *Mysteries of Time and Spirit*, p. 253-54.

146. HPL to DAW Nov. 2, 1930, in *Mysteries of Time and Spirit*, p. 262.

147. WPC to HPL, July 28, 1935 (ms., JHL).

148. HPL to DAW, December 1, 1930, in *Mysteries of Time and Spirit*, pp. 268-69.

149. *Protest Stuff* by Willis T. Crossman (Driftwind Press, 1934); *Contradictions* by Willis T. Crossman (Driftwind Press, 1934); *Christ in the Breadline* (Driftwind Press, 1933); *Ballad of Gene Debs* by Sarah N. Cleghorn (Driftwind Press, 1928); *Highly Respectable Murder: Poems in Remembrance of Sacco and Vanzetti* by Donald M. and J. Howard Flower (Solitarian Press, 1928) and *Red Songs of a Romantic Radical* by J. Howard Flower (Solitarian Press, 1928).

150. WPC to DAW, August 23, 1931 (ms., MHS).

151. HPL to DAW, April 12, 1931, in *Mysteries of Time and Spirit*, p. 273.

152. WPC to DAW, July 29, 1931 (ms., MHS).

153. HPL to DAW Sept. 25, 1931. in *Mysteries of Time and Spirit*, p. 286.

154. HPL to DAW, April 12, 1931, in *Mysteries of Time and Spirit*, p. 273.

155. "'The Shunned House', which at last report was printed but not bound, is now at a bindery in Boston." HPL to DAW, June 30, 1930, in *Mysteries of Time and Spirit*, p. 253-54.

156. HPL to J. Vernon Shea, October 13, 1932, in *SL* 4.88.

157. HPL to DAW Oct. 24, 1931, in *Mysteries of Time and Spirit*, p. 289.

158. James F. Morton, "A False Issue", in *Garden State Amateur* (June 1932): 1.

159. HPL to J. Vernon Shea, January 28, 1933, in *SL* 4.144.

160. HPL to James F. Morton, January 12, 1933, in *SL* 4.130.

161. HPL to Annie Gamwell, March 24, 1933, in *H. P. Lovecraft: Letters from New York*, p. 178.

162. HPL to DAW, May 31, 1933, in *Mysteries of Time and Spirit*, p. 324.

163. HPL to Farnsworth Wright, June 18, 1933, in *SL* 4.214.

164. HPL to J. Vernon Shea, September 25, 1933, in *SL* 4.245.

165. WPC to DAW, November 20, 1933 (ms., MHS).

166. WPC to HPL, September 19, 1934 (ms., JHL).

167. WPC to DAW, January 6, 1934 (ms., MHS).

168. WPC to HPL, September 19, 1934 (ms., JHL).

169. Inscription to Flower in a copy of *A Day* owned by the editor.

170. Franklin Adams (1881-1960), was a prominent journalist who worked for New York papers like the *Tribune* and the *Post,* a member of the Algonquin Round Table, and a panelist on the radio show "Information, Please!"

171. WPC, "In Memoriam," p. 152.

172. HPL to Elizabeth Toldridge, August 31, 1934, in *SL* 5.23.

173. HPL to Elizabeth Toldridge, October 6, 1934, in *SL* 5.43.
174. HPL to J. Vernon Shea, February 10, 1935, in *SL* 5.105.
175. WPC to DAW, February 19, 1934 (ms., MHS).
176. "Cook writes that there is another box of the sheets stowed somewhere in his sister's cellar at Sunapee, although there is no immediate prospect of getting at them." HPL to DAW, May 26, 1934, in *Mysteries of Time and Spirit*, p. 345.
177. HPL to DAW May 17, 1934, in *Mysteries of Time and Spirit*, p. 341
178. WPC to HPL, February 8, 1935 (ms., JHL).
179. WPC to HPL, September 28, 1935 (ms., JHL).
180. WPC to HPL, June 16, 1935 (ms., JHL).
181. Ibid.
182. Ibid.
183. WPC to HPL, July 11, 1935 (ms., JHL).
184. Ibid.
185. Ibid.
186. WPC to HPL, July 28 [1935] (ms., JHL).
187. WPC to HPL, July 30, 1935 (ms., JHL).
188. Ibid.
189. HPL to R. H. Barlow, June 13, 1936, in *H. P. Lovecraft's Letters to R. H. Barlow,* eds. S. T. Joshi and David E. Schultz (Tampa: University of Tampa Press, 2007), p. 349.
190. HPL to DAW November 10, 1935, in *Mysteries of Time and Spirit,* p. 369.
191. HPL to DAW, December 20, 1936, in *Mysteries of Time and Spirit,* pp. 387-88.
192. WPC, "In Memoriam", p. 106.
193. Lovecraft's "Psychopompos" was published in the October 1919 *Vagrant.*
194. Cook printed *Told in Vermont* (Driftwind Press, 1938), published under his Willis T. Crossman pseudonym.
195. WPC to AWD, November 22, 1937 (ms., SHSW).
196. WPC to AWD, February 13, 1938 (ms., SHSW).
197. WPC to AWD, March 12, 1938 (ms., SHSW).
198. See also WPC to Cole, August 30, 1938 (ms., JHL).
199. Lillian M. Ainsworth, "Howard Lister Hindley", *Driftwind* (December 1936) p. 159-64.
200. WPC to HPL, February 6, [no year] (ms., JHL).
201. WPC to EHC, April 18, 1940 (ms., JHL).
202. WPC to EHC, August 30, 1938 (ms., JHL).
203. WPC to EHC, June 8, 1941 (ms., JHL).

204. WPC to EHC, August 30, 1938 (ms., JHL).
205. "Edith Miniter: Her Life and Work" by Kenneth W. Faig, Jr. in *Coast of Bohemia*, p. 902.
206. WPC to EHC, June 8, 1941 (ms., JHL).
207. WPC to EHC, June 19, 1941 (ms., JHL).
208. Hyman Bradofsky, editorial note in the *Californian* (Spring 1938) p. 20.
209. WPC to EHC, August 30, 1938 (ms., JHL).
210. Ibid.
211. WPC to EHC, [undated, late October 1940] (ms., JHL).
212. WPC to EHC, February 2, 1941 (ms., JHL).
213. WPC to EHC, February 12, 1941 (ms., JHL).
214. WPC to EHC, June 19, 1941 (ms., JHL).
215. Edwin B. Hill, "Cook Prints Tribute to H.P.L.", in *The National Amateur* (March 1942): 3-4.
216. Edwin Baird (1886-1957): the first editor of *Weird Tales* from 1923 to 1924.
217. WPC to AWD, July 2, 1941 (ms., SHSW).
218. WPC to DAW, July 11, 1941 (ms., MHS).
219. Auction catalog for Sale II of 19th & 20th Century Science Fiction, Fantasy and Horror Literature from the Inventory of Fantasy Archives, Swann Galleries, Sale 1650, February 17, 1994.
220. Cook to Wandrei, July 11, 1941
221. WPC to AWD, July 25, 1941 (ms., SHSW).
222. WPC to EHC, July 29, 1941 (ms., JHL).
223. WPC to EHC, August 2, 1941 (ms., JHL).
224. WPC to EHC, September 30, 1941 (ms., JHL).
225. *Driftwind* (July-August 1941): [broadside supplement].
226. WPC to AWD, August 15, 1941 (ms., SHSW).
227. WPC to EHC, July 15, 1942 (ms., JHL).
228. WPC to EHC, July or August 1941 (ms., JHL).
229. WPC to AWD, October 4, 1941 (ms., SHSW).
230. WPC to AWD, June 14, 1942 (ms., SHSW).
231. WPC to AWD, June 20, 1942 (ms., SHSW).
232. WPC to AWD, July 10, 1943 (ms., SHSW).
233. WPC to AWD, July 27, 1943 (ms., SHSW).
234. WPC to AWD, June 29, 1944 (ms., SHSW).
235. "The Mailer" (July, 1944).
236. *Opinions* (June 1944).

237. *National Amateur* (December 1944): 76.

238. Helen Crane Heins, "Boston National Convention Impressions", in *Eternal Feminine* (August 1944): 4.

239. "Amateur Dictionary" in *Lucky Dog* (1944): 19.

240. "A Guide to Charleston, South Carolina", in H. P. Lovecraft, *Marginalia* (Sauk City: Arkham House, 1944), pp. 199-237.

241. WPC to HCK, July 24, 1944, in Everts, p. iv.

242. WPC to AWD, August 5, 1944 (ms., SHSW).

243. WPC to AWD, August 12, 1944 (ms., SHSW).

244. Everts, p. 32.

245. HCK to AWD, May 24, 1945 (ms., Eugene Biancheri, Koenig's son-in-law).

246. HCK to WPC, July 20, 1945 (ms., Eugene Biancheri).

247. WPC to HCK, July 20, 1945.

248. HCK to WPC, July 20, 1945 (ms., Eugene Biancheri).

249. HCK to WPC, November 7, 1945 (ms., Eugene Biancheri).

250. WPC to AWD, August 30, 1945 (ms., SHSW).

251. Helen Wesson.

252. WPC to Helen V. Wesson, May 29, 1946 (ms., editor's collection).

253. EHC, "New England in Autumn", in *Interlude* (November 1947): 4.

254. WPC to DAW, September 9, 1946 (ms., MHS).

255. Quoted in Everts, pp. 29–30.

256. Edna Hyde McDonald, obituary, in *National Amateur* (March 1948): 53, 56.

257. *Churinga* (July 1949): 20.

258. EHC, "Footprints on the Sands of Time", in *Interlude* (February 1948): 2.

Recollections of W. Paul Cook

BY ARTHUR HENRY GOODENOUGH

I have sometimes wondered how I should begin this last chapter of my remembrances, which I have determined to devote to W. Paul Cook; but I can arrive at no beginning more fit than these words penned by him in 1916. In concluding an editorial article in his *Vagrant*, he says:

> Cook's name will never go into A.J. history, because he has never been a great politician, he has never been a great writer, he has never been a great publisher,—in fact, he never was, and never will be, great. But Cook may be set down as a lover of Amateur Journalism, in whatever form it may flourish, and by whatever name it may call itself. Therefore he says to all other amateur journalists—'Greetings!'

Thus writes Cook, W. Paul Cook, immortal Paul Cook, if you will assimilate the expression, in 1916. And if I remember correctly this is the same Cook who in 1913 issued a 76-page and cover, *Century*-size *Monadnock*, the finest amateur magazine I ever beheld in thirty years' experience; who in 1918 got out that marvelous *Vagrant* on one hundred and forty-eight pages (148); who has been Publisher of the United A.P.A. and gotten out the finest *United Amateur* that has ever appeared and gotten it out regularly; who has been elected Official Editor of the National A.P.A. and gotten out the largest and handsomest volume of the National Amateur ever issued, bar none; who has been elected to the Presidency of the National Amateur Press Association, and what is even more remarkable, sustaining his previous record of activity after election!

Have you, dear reader, any idea that in the world of unprofessional letters this record will ever be beaten? Frankly, I have not.

Besides, he has undoubtedly enriched our literature with a collection of examples of strong fiction which alone would serve to forever redeem him from the "faint praise" with which some lesser lights are habitually damned, and inscribe his name, in shining characters, high upon the entablature of our authorship. The fact that he has for years contributed tales to the amateur press over a *nom de plume*—that of "Willis Tete Crossman"—in no wise detracts from this merit, but rather gives his literary work the attraction of modesty. Some of the stories that have most impressed me I will list here: "The Square-Jawed Man Wins," "Informally Announced," "The Penalty of the Law," "The Clock of Paris," The Proof of the Theory," "The Regions of the Damned," etc. I give only a few that I can place at this time, but they are all striking stories, and tales inferior to any of them are appearing in the professional press every day.

If Paul Cook can escape going down in amateur history he is more clever than even I have given him credit for!

I got my first knowledge of Cook back in 1905–1906, when he first sent me copies of his superb *Monadnock Monthly*, and later we exchanged letters; afterwards I became a contributor to his publications, and this state of things has continued even to the present writing.

In the meantime Cook has been prodigiously busy. In addition to his regular arduous duties in the office of the Athol, (Mass.) *Transcript*, where he holds the responsible position of foreman, he has printed the *Monadnock Monthly* regularly, he has issued his monthly *Vagrant*, pretty regularly, he for a whole year published both the official organs of the United and National Amateur Press Associations; has well in hand a book by Will H. Greenfield entitled *Ring and Diamond*, has published in book form, William C. Ahlhauser's *Our Ex-Presidents*, besides a vast volume of miscellaneous work that I have neither space nor time to chronicle here. In fine, to state the truth strictly and without reservation, W. Paul Cook has displayed more enthusiasm for Amateur Journalism, and made more sacrifices in behalf of it, than any other individual I ever knew. If there are those who are inclined to disagree, I shall refer them to his record as a writer and publisher.

Cook and Parker have both at times threatened me with an invasion, (and Charles A. A. is still threatening, though he hasn't materialized yet), and it was not until a crisp, bright morning in October, 1918, that Cook actually made his appearance in the flesh.

We are supposed to be farmers,—at least we live on a farm and do our best to make a living at it,—hence rise earlier than city dwellers are supposed to; but the indefatigable Cook walked in on us on the day in question before we had completed the matutinal meal, and with that magnetic smile which is his own peculiar personal attribute, inquired, 'How are you, Arthur Henry?' and we struck hands.

Needless to say, I was clothed not as the lilies of the field, by any means, nor even as becomes a man of letters of sedate years, having only recently completed my barn chores; whereas W. Paul appeared in purple and fine linen, his countenance partaking somewhat of the splendor of the newly risen sun, but as the late Bill Nye would have it, Cook made me feel at home right off, and extraneous and ulterior details were soon lost to sight in the animated discussion of amateur affairs in which we soon engaged.

Now, it is rather 'bad form' for a city man to walk in on a farmer before he has had proper time to eat his breakfast, but I realized that Paul did not know the enormity of his offense, so I forgave him for it, and we got along very well.

Prior to his advent I had been notified thereof, but the description which accompanied the same was grossly misleading, and I confess that I was disappointed in my visitor. I had been warned to be on the lookout for a chap about five feet, weighing upwards of two hundred pounds, dressed in 'hand-me-downs' and a plaid cap, from beneath which flashed an abundant crop of hair of reddish cast.—Nay, I will say it was honestly and undeniably red. In fact so different was he, that at first blush I did not recognize him from his description. A slender, alert man of medium size, with dark hair and eyes—a countenance with good features, re-enforced by a magnetic smile, clothed in the conscious habiliments of the well-bred, and wearing eye-glasses,— such I found the Real Paul Cook!

It did not take him a great while to ingratiate himself with my good wife, and he and my son Rupert, then about fifteen, became friendly on the spot, and Rupert proposed and dealt out butter-nuts and sweet-cider with unstinted cordiality and the open hand of youth. Neither of which did the visitor appear to regard with disdain.

Willis [sic] Paul Cook possesses a wide circle of amateur acquaintances, and he has also a fund of anecdote, the wealth of which is not lightly to be computed. So the winged moments sped all too merrily, and his hour for departure drew near; we had hoped to keep him with us one night at least but he drew such a pathetic picture of his family and business associates waiting for him to return, (he was a truant, and no one knew his whereabouts), that we were forced to let him go his way.

So after partaking of a specimen of our modest county fare (in the midst of sugar shortage and 'substitutes,' mind you) consisting in part,

I recollect, of warm barley cake and cottage cheese—our guest girded up his loins, and I girded up mine, and we struck out valiantly for the trolley car, two and half miles walk from our door.

(In my hurry I was careless enough, I may add, to leave what little worldly wealth I had in my 'other pants' pocket.)

Arrived at the trolley line, and I was pretty well 'fagged,' as I am by no means a prize sprinter; but Cook stood it very well, and as it would be thirty or forty minutes before the next car, he proposed that we keep on and do the remaining two and half miles or so to the Brattleboro railway station a–foot. I consented; I either had to, (since I hadn't a cent) or else part company with Paul, and this latter I was loath to do. So on we sped, Cook trying to keep up his standard and I trying to keep up with Cook—and not quite doing it. The uninformed doubtless mistook us for escaping criminals or harmless lunatics indulging in over–exertion, but that is neither here nor there.

On reaching the station we were dismayed to find Cook's train gone, and a long wait staring us in the face. I drew a long, weary breath and thought deeply; the other victim of circumstances lit a cigarette and buried himself in meditation.

It was now late in the afternoon of an Autumn day, and night only too close at hand. My aching legs, my weary feet, my scant breath—all clamored to me to save my strength by riding just as far toward home as an electric car would take me—about half way; but alas, I had not a cent in my pocket, and it embarrassed me not a little to think of 'striking' Paul Cook, Willis Tete Crossman, and all the rest of it, for the loan of six cents on the occasion of our first meeting. Can you, gentle reader, share my sensations?

No, it was impossible; I couldn't do it; in spite of cringing flesh pride should be my staff!

The shadows were getting very long indeed by this time, and the air had the warning chill so common to late Fall afternoons.

Reluctantly, I bade Cook good-bye.

Reluctantly, I set out alone and a-foot on my hilly homeward hike of five miles!"

First published as "Further Recollections of Amateur Journalism" in the *Vagrant* (Spring 1927): 126–34.

The Birth of *Driftwind*

BY WALTER JOHN COATES

Ye Editor has long been partial to the adjoining picture. It is vitally related, by association, to the original conception, and later establishment of *Driftwind*.

Thru *Mood Songs*[1] (the Editor's first slim book of verse) came his earliest acquaintance with W. Paul Cook and Vrest Orton.[2] Cook had achieved a long and noteworthy career as an expert compositor and pressman, as editor and publisher of *Monadnock*—one of the finest amateur journals ever published in America; as President of the National Amateur Press Association, and as a writer of essays, short stories and criticisms under the *nom de plume* of Willis Tete Crossman. Orton was then just out of college, back from a roving trip to Mexico and the Pacific Coast. . .a youngling imbued with vision and enthusiasm, ambitious to become free lance author and publisher.

Having read *Mood Songs*, these men—both Vermonters by birth but residents of the Bay State—were curious as to what this emergent Vermont poet might be. So they wrote him, and he replied; and in the late summer of 1925 personal acquaintance was effected by a foregathering of the three at North Montpelier. Orton, as a boy, had once lived a few miles distant, at North Calais; and, preliminaries over, it was agreed the trio should spend an afternoon there.

Entering the village, an old three-story brick dwelling, once used in pioneer days as a post-tavern, loomed before us. It was uninhabited, and we soon secured permission to headquarter in it. Eastward and westward rose ranges of picturesque hills; southward the road wound, like a distorted ribbon, valleyward toward North Montpelier; northward, a few rods distant only, spread the silvery-green waters of Mirror Lake, one of Vermont's most bewitchingly scenic ponds.

Dreamy laziness was the method; literature was the menu; utopian visions were the dessert. We smoked, of course. We built castles. We talked. Individuality ran rampant—for each had literary loves, literary aversions. But on one subject all were agreed: something must be done to stimulate more widespread and unified literary activity in Vermont—to encourage nascent writers and promote keener appreciation for their work. Both they and their local reading public were suffering from a self-imposed inferiority complex.

There had been one epoch, we recalled, when the State could boast a distinct literary atmosphere, with a nationally recognized group of artists and writers. Once, in Royall Tyler's time (1792–1805) a North Hills weekly, published in Walpole but largely inspired from Vermont, had been foremost among journals devoted to *belles lettres* west of England. At that period of early American letters, the so-called *Guilford School* of poets, essayists, dramatists, in *Vermont*—Tyler, Fessenden, Dennie, Denison, Chamberlain—were a power to be reckoned with. Why not again?—or, at least, partially again? A distinct spirit, it was conceded, haunts this Green Mountain region—a distinct egoism is peculiar to this terrain.

Afternoon waned. The dreamers departed. But the visions, somehow—or part of them—remained. Winter came, bringing sorrow and anxiety to one of the trio: his only son[3] was ill—desperately so—with tuberculosis. And Spring brought no relief. But in April, partly as surcease from morbidity, partly because of the North Calais conference . . . *Driftwind* was born. An antique Golding press, 8 by 12, foot power and of forgotten lineage (it was in operation back in the [eighteen] eighties) stood unused, disreputable, in a back room off the country store.[4] Out in the woodshed was a pile of newly-cut birch wood, bark smooth and satiny still adhering to it. From the air itself, lazily, came a title. Since the wind "bloweth where it listeth" and as the publication, so far, was purely tentative and natural—why, *The Drift-Wind*, or course! *"A Tramp Magazine Issued for the Love of Literature."* This was the first title. It was later on, and after it had become better known, that Percy MacKaye suggested *From the North Hills* as a proper sub-title. And on the cover of these original issues, over the display motto, appeared the legend *"Fari quae sentiat."*[5] A stanza by Saxe (our own poet) against *war* was the first cover slogan, and the initial issue, of fourteen pages, was dated *April, 1926.*

A very few copies were sewed up in original birch-bark covers, and this practice continued during the whole year, twelve issues being sent out in all.

Beginning with fifty copies in April, the editions run to a maximum of eighty during the year. . .and all were given away. So rare, in after days, became complete files of this year's harvest, that the birch-bark files brought as high as $25.00 per volume, bound, and the ordinary sets, loose, about $12.50. They are almost unobtainable.

The stricken youth bade farewell to us in November.

In March we thought—for finance and labor reasons—to discontinue the enterprise. We published an *Editor's Valedictory*, stating this as a possibility. Much to our surprise the mail was at once flooded with protests, from Vermonters, inland and outland, and from many outsiders. So urgent were these protests that, after some hesitation, the Editor promised, if given sufficient support, he would continue the venture another year.

He did so, making it a bi-monthly—increasing the pagination, broadening the scope. Response was instant; but growth, though sure, was slow. Not till 1929 did circulation reach to 300 copies. It is now over 400 . . . and no padding. Libraries, educators, artists and writers, the intelligentsia, are its subscribers and readers. It has fought its way by its own intrinsic merits—and the loyalty of its clientele—fearless of pro- or anti-propaganda, resolutely hewing to its tolerant course. And its influence has been all out of proportion to its paid circulation. Prof. Merriam (University of Montana), himself Editor of *The Frontier*, has classed it among the three or four most significant regional magazines of the country. Though it pays for no contributions—save in prize awards, many well-known writers voluntarily offer their verse and prose to its pages. And it gets ten times as much matter as it can print. A larger and better press, a better assortment of type and fixtures, more paid subscribers—yes, and a few liberal patrons who will offer awards of merit for verse—these are its needs.

"Little I ask, my wants are few" etc.

In one corner of a country store, in a crossroads village, alone save for the encouragement of a few local friends, this magazine has struggled into existence—and latterly into some degree of distinction. Hand-set, assembled and sewed by hand; edited, published, addressed, mailed by one man (wife and daughter assisting)—it is a work of individuality from beginning to end. A real demand exists, as *Driftwind* has proven, for this sort of free lance magazine.

Reflecting the sentiments of *writers* (many others having written to like effect), Harry Elmore Hurd says, in a letter dated Feb. 15, 1932:

"I am proud to be included among your poets. *Driftwind* is delightful in format, challenging in content, and fearless in its outlook. Long may it stand among the first magazines in the country!"

1. *Mood Songs: Voices within Myself* (Hartland, Vt.: Solitarian Press, 1921). 250 copies printed.
2. Vrest Orton (1897-1986): founder of the Vermont Country Store.
3. Coates's son, John Webster Coates.
4. Coates operated a country store in North Montpelier, Vt. It also served as the office of *Driftwind* magazine and The Driftwind Press.
5. *Fari quae sentiat*: a line from Horace meaning "to say what one feels."

First published as "Pictorial Reminiscences by the Editor" in *Driftwind* 7, 1 (July 1932): 5–8.

The Colossus of the North

BY EDWARD H. COLE

W. Paul Cook might well go down in the record of amateur journalism as the Colossus of the North. He does things on a big scale. Forty years ago his *Monadnock Monthly* was the most pretentious amateur journal published. Today his *Ghost* makes persons gasp and splutter, "An amateur paper? Impossible!" In between there have been his *Vagrant*, one number of which attained 312 pages, 5 x 7; his volume of the *National Amateur*, in which he wrote "Finis" on page 331, the final number comprising 124 pages., 9 x 13; and *The Recluse*, 1927, similar in format to *The Ghost*. Moreover, there have been occasional volumes of his writings under the pseudonym of Willis T. Crossman: "Protest Stuff," 1934, "Told in Vermont," 1938, and "Vermontiana Esoterica," 1938. Whenever he has a job lot of odd-sized stock left over from some printing job, he's likely to run off a few copies of one of his pungent Vermont tales and send them out to friends whose fancy he's sure they'll tickle. Besides what he has completed and sent to his circle of friends, there have been several gargantuan-sized projects that Fate destined to destruction before ever they left Cook's hands. There was one *Monadnock*, for instance, done on coated paper; rain spattered on the sheets and ruined the edition.

In respect to procrastination, to accomplishing his projects when, as, and if the urge impels, Cook is the amateur journalist *par excellence*. There's one characteristic of all amateur publishers: they can't be compelled. From earliest time, date lines have meant nothing to them. Cook has rarely issued a paper within six months of the date of publication, and sometimes the lapse has been years. There's no knowing how much that he has put into type he has never got around to printing, and the metal has been dumped as he went his way to other fields. No one grins more at this trait than Paul himself. If you haven't received a copy of *Revenant*, his latest paper, for example, the reason probably lies in this comment in a letter I've just received from him: "May even get up energy to mail it—someday." The reader's compensation for procrastination in Cook's case is that the reward is always worth the delay.

In two more years Paul will be rounding out half a century in amateur journalism. It is ironical that the first paper with which he was associated was called *Tom Thumb*. While living in Marlboro, New Hampshire, in 1897, he became acquainted with a Harry Morse who was a telegraph operator at early Elmwood. They both grew active in the Golden Hours clubs, and Cook became co-editor on the paper Morse was already publishing. Four years later Anderson G. Ulmer of Savannah, Georgia, proposed Cook for membership in the United Amateur Press Association. In the same year the first number of *The Monadnock* appeared. It remained a monthly for two issues! Then Cook began a series of wanderings in pursuit of his profession at a printer and did not come to rest again until 1905. For two years he was in Hanover, New Hampshire, working at the Dartmouth Press by day and studying English three nights a week with professor Charles Francis Richardson of Dartmouth, one of the country's greatest students of English Literature. In "spare hours" he issued several numbers of *The Monadnock*. 1906 saw him begin his wanderings again—to a majority of the states of this country, to Europe, and to Jamaica, where he came unscathed through the earthquake and fire. Then in January, 1913, he settled in Athol, Massachusetts, where he remained until August, 1930.

This period in Athol, where he had the facilities of a first-rate professional shop at command, was the most settled of Cook's highly unstable life. He promptly issued the May, 1913, *Monadnock*, the copy for which he had been accumulating for the preceding several years. He had plans for a later 200-page number, but they never matured. Instead, he turned to *The Vagrant*, which ranged in size from a 12-page number to a 148-page issue and finally to the "clean-up" issue of over 300 pages spoken of earlier. During these years, too, he gave the National its grandest official organ. To do it he labored fourteen to eighteen hours a day. Be it noted, too, that he paid full price for the work, though it was done in the shop in which he was employed; the amount that he contributed from his own pocket is his secret, but it rocks the imagination. He served the association as president in 1919–20. Meanwhile he became official publisher for the United Amateur Press Association and gave generously toward making *The United Amateur* the largest and best numbers in the entire career of that organization. His activities in the United endured until the faction to which Howard Lovecraft devoted his energies underwent a lingering demise, 1924–26.

The death of his wife precipitated his removal from Athol; furthermore it caused along period of physical debility and mental unrest that made his earlier activities distasteful. His chief contact with amateur journalism was his friendship with Howard Lovecraft. Occasionally they would come to Boston and I would join them in reunions that stimulated us all. Then Paul went with Paul J. Campbell in East St. Louis in an ill-starred enterprise which left Cook even more unsettled. Returning East, he spent much time with his sister in Sunapee, New Hampshire, and worked somewhat with Walter J. Coates at the Driftwind Press in North Montpelier. The death of Lovecraft [1937] had a most depressing effect on him; but, in turn, my insistence that he write some recollections of Howard for publication in the Lovecraft memorial *Olympian* in 1940 served as a tonic, for not long afterward he undertook his first organized effort in several years and produced the moving 74-page memoir "*In Memoriam* Howard Phillips Lovecraft: Recollections, Appreciations, Estimates."

A year or two thereafter [1941] Walter J. Coates suddenly died. His widow turned to Cook to take over the Driftwind Press, where he had often assisted; and since that time Paul again has been settled, this time in his native Vermont. The Driftwind Press publishes not only the monthly *Driftwind*, a magazine devoted chiefly to poetry, but also a surprising number of privately issued books. It occupies a small building in the center of North Montpelier, high in the hills of the Green Mountain State. Paul edits *Driftwind* and handles the business and mechanical details of the Press. There, too, in odd moments he linotypes page after page of his monumental *Ghost* and other occasional publications, and when the mood urges or the need for using the metal for other work arises, he puts the paper to press. Ultimately, often after undue time, he commits the product to the mails.

Because of the extraordinary amount of roving that has constituted his life and the fact that most of his settled years have been in remote localities, most of Paul's contacts with amateur journalism have been through correspondence. Consequently, he has a distinctly objective attitude. The native Vermonter has a thoroughly independent point of view, and Paul is quite the Vermonter. Of late his publications have conspicuously lacked editorial comment, but in the days when he spoke his mind his forthright utterances revealed sturdiness of judgment and perceptiveness sometimes startling. In the 1913 *Monadnock* he pronounced the opinion that time has confirmed on the relations of the United and the National, that each has its sphere and its right to separate existence. Moreover, his tracing of the simultaneous modification of Warren J. Brodie's campaign in the *Random Amateur* against the United and the appearance of *The Shillalah* with its violent attacks reveals that he had a rather clear insight into the identity of the anonymous Irishman long before Tim Thrift let the cat out of the bag in *The Aonian*. His pronouncement [Note: "A Plea. . ." Ghost No. 3, May 1945] in the latest *Ghost* against the harm that Lovecraft fans seem likely to do the reputation of their idol, proves that his own friendship and love for Howard have in no wise affected his insight into the merit of Lovecraft's achievements.

Cook's participation in conventions and in amateur politics has been inconsiderable; he has usually shunned them. Yet on occasion he has played a part. He was the recipient rather than the seeker of the editorship and the presidency in 1918–1920. His part in the affairs of the United was somewhat confused. At first he viewed the 1912 split as an ill-advised attempt to wreck the association, and he gave his support to the Seattle faction, probably because of friendship for Vincent Haggerty and Ernest Morris. Later he joined with the Daas–Hoffman faction and, largely because of his friendship with Lovecraft, became the "angel" of that branch until politics beset it, and it passed out of existence. He has cultivated friendships with a few rather than contact with the many; yet even in that respect he seems to be undergoing change. He was among the most active participants in the 1944 convention of the National at Boston, and many of the most important decisions reflected his influence. Now he is keenly looking forward to attending further meetings of amateur journalists whenever they may be held where he can arrange to attend.

Though amateur journalists commonly know him chiefly as a publisher, Cook deserves as individual a reputation as a writer. He began authorship young. As a boy he was confined to bed for nearly two years, "condemned," he says, "by the doctors to an early demise through consumption." His main solace was a rubber stamp outfit.

With it he printed a book on notesize pages, which his mother stitched together; much of it was original. At the age of ten he was on the staff of *The Epoch*, the paper of the grammar school in Rutland, Vermont. Shortly afterward acquisition of his first press stirred him to write and publish a book consisting of a ghost story that, as Paul relates, was so much of a thriller that it frightened its author to the point where his flight from darkness grew to be a family legend. When he was eighteen he became one of the founders and the first editor-in-chief of *The Red and Black*, the students' paper at the Stevens High School in Claremont, New Hampshire.

Cook has written under several noms de plume; most frequently he has employed that of Willis T. Crossman. Some of his work has had professional publication. Considerable has been privately printed and distributed among his friends. In 1934 came "A Day With Crossman" and "Protest Stuff," both of sociological import, ironic, sardonic, and occasionally bitter. They depicted the miserable and frequently shocking fortune of the unemployed masses in the midst of the Great Depression, and were frequently derisive of the ineptitude of the government's unsatisfactory attempts to cope with the situation. Unquestionably much of the writing is autobiographical, and Cook pulled no punches in revealing life as he lived it or as he saw it. "Protest Stuff" is prefaced by an account of the death of Crossman. According to Cook's report the unfortunate fellow had been seized with convulsions in the Municipal Lodging House in Boston, whence he had been removed to the Relief Hospital and later to the City Hospital. "Here everything possible was done for him, but apparently the inexcusable delay and lackadaisical attitude of the police had made it too late. The patient died early in the morning without regaining consciousness, causes being given as exhaustion superinduced by exposure and malnutrition." The "flat verses" of which the bulk of the volume consists were supposedly the relics of the deceased, his bitter indictment of the misdeeds of capitalism and governmental error that had brought him to his tragic end. Excerpts from "Paternalism" and "Boomerang" sufficiently indicate the theme of the whole:

> But something to eat,—
> Work or no work,—
> Must be furnished the unemployed.

Where it comes from,
How it comes,
Matters not at all.
This is the only governmental problem,—
How all our people shall be fed.
This is the first duty of statesmanship,—
To feed our people. . . . .
Paternalism if you wish;
Call it what you like,
Twenty million people
Cannot be kept on the ragged edge
Of starvation.

అఎ

The plan has worked,—
"Help" can be gotten at a pittance,
Men are begging for work,
Factories can be filled in a moment
With a working crew
At incredibly small wages.
But the employers, the fools,
Failed to see
That these men will not be as they were.
Hardship has taken its toll
In dulling intellects, wrecking mentalities,
Ruining the cunning skill of the hands,
Sapping endurance.
The workers have paid and paid
For the criminal greed of the capitalists.
Now the capitalist must pay and pay
For deliberately destroying
The finest body of workmen
Ever existent
In the history of the world.
The fools.

Happier in vein and most likely to give him individuality in literature is his extensive collection of Vermont tales. These are written in a form neither *vers libre* nor prose, but somewhat a mixture of both, —"flat verse," Cook calls it. Each develops an aspect of Vermont character. Years of research have gone into the making. Every name is authentic; every episode is out of Vermont life. The dry humor of the native Vermonter permeates every narrative and brings to each a climax that catches the fancy and provokes laughter. Several have been published in *The Olympian*; others have been circulated in limited editions as Paul has used up tag ends of stock. Many of them are to be found in "Told In Vermont," a volume of approximately 100 pages, of which 150 copies were published in 1938. Even more are in "Heard In Vermont," a book of 136 pages, the folios of which have been printed for several years and which sometime Cook hopes to bind. On these, I am sure, Cook's reputation as a writer will most firmly rest.

I have known Paul for nearly forty years. In the early days he seemed elusive and aloof. As in the case with so many amateur journalists, we have had sharp disagreements; and I must confess that some of the most inept criticism of Paul's magnificent *Monadnock*s has been found in the pages of my own papers. He has always exhibited a generous forgiveness, and I have come to know and to admire the warm-heartedness of this Prince of amateur journalists. Howard Lovecraft brought us into understanding acquaintance; out of the affection which Cook and I felt for Howard has come to a deep mutual regard.

Few have ever had a loftier concept of amateur journalism or labored more magnificently in its behalf. The July, 1905, *Monadnock* carried the by-line "An Amateur Magazine. You cannot Buy It." That was put even more succinctly in the recent *Ghost*: "Priceless." In the 1905 issue he declared editorially:

> We have no more right to make money from amateur journalism than we have from our public schools. The true amateur journalist—the exponent of the highest and truest in amateur journalism—never makes a cent on his productions. He puts in money with no thought of spending it in cash. He spends more than he can afford; occasionally he sinks every cent he is earning outside of absolute essentials. And it pays.

There is no doubt of it.

How consistently he has exemplified this lofty ideal of his early days the record relates in glowing measure. Yet he always deprecates his achievements. His modesty is great in proportion to his achievement; the most monumental of his accomplishments is accompanied by his deepest apologies that the work has been so poorly done. Perhaps that is the secret of his continuing effort, for the amateur spirit at its best represents a ceaseless striving for the ever elusive perfection. Certain it is that if Paul Cook ever satisfies the relentless taskmaster desires to achieve for amateur journalism, the product will be stupendous. Like the ancient Egyptians he builds the noblest of monuments for the gods and for the dead.

First published in the *Aonian* (Winter 1945): 269–74. Reprinted in Mike Horvat's *Oregonian* (July 1994).

In Memoriam: W. Paul Cook

BY EDWARD H. COLE

Of Paul Cook I cannot write easily or without emotion. He was a close friend; I cherished him deeply. I have known him since I was a boy, a novice in amateur journalism. There were large gaps in our acquaintanceship, years when we lost sight of each other; but those lapses served only to strengthen friendship as it was renewed. I know, too, that the passing of friends who were dear to us both—Howard Lovecraft, Tim Thrift—has brought us closer together in recent years, as we have realized how precious friendship is. To me he confided the fact of his illness and impending operations; he directed that in case of untoward event, I should be notified; and he and I knew that the outcome might mostly likely be as it was—fatal.

He died on January 22 in Burlington, Vermont. He had rounded out fifty years of association with amateur journalism. Though his publishing was intermittent, his output was voluminous. His *Monadnock Monthly*, 1901-1913, culminated with an issue of 76 pages, 7 x 10, liberally illustrated with handsomely printed beautiful views of New Hampshire. He projected a 200–page number, but it never came about, though he did print one issue on coated paper, only to have it so damaged by rain that he could not send it out. Then he turned to publishing *The Vagrant*, 5 x 7, the fifteenth number of which, dated 1923, finally appeared in 1927—312 pages! For many years he lapsed into inactivity, but maintained correspondence and companionship with such friends as Howard Lovecraft and me. I recall with abiding pleasure occasions on which the three of us would meet in Boston and go on jaunts to nearby communities like Marblehead or Hingham to visit places of historic interest. The death of Lovecraft in 1937 was so poignant a blow to Paul that he suffered a nervous collapse. In 1941, however, he responded to my urging for a memorial article on Lovecraft for *The Olympian*. The brief writing of his recollections apparently freed his mind of the pall that had darkened it, and he wrote and published his 76-page *In Memoriam, Howard Phillips Lovecraft*. Then came his *Ghost*, five sizable numbers of which appeared, the latest in 1947. Some of the material for a sixth number was in type at the time of his death. He also issued one number of *Revenant*, devoted to articles from the pen of writers who had not appeared in the amateur press for many years. During the past half dozen years he also intermittently issued numerous booklets of what he called "flat verse," tales of Vermont. Two complete volumes of these verses he had printed at the Driftwind Press in the late thirties, *Told in Vermont* and *Heard in Vermont*; I believe that they remain in folio form, unbound, to the present day. Add to his private publishing the largest volume of *The National Amateur,* 331 pages, 9 x 13, and several volumes of *The United Amateur*, 1919–1924, representing largely his own generosity to the two associations, and you have a lavish production ranking with the labors of Truman J. Spencer, John T. Nixon, Warren J. Brodie, and Tim Thrift.

To me, a remarkable aspect of his career and his achievements is that during his long activity he was relatively aloof from his fellow amateur journalists. Rarely did he attend a convention; moreover, his personal contacts with his fellow amateur journalists were comparatively few. Unquestionably, his friendship with Howard Lovecraft was his closest with any amateur journalist. This is understandable, for he was responsible for bringing Lovecraft from seclusion and leading him into the world about him. I have known Paul personally ever since he attended a Hub Club conference in mid–winter, 1907 or 1908. A quality that struck me then remained characteristic of him through the years; he cared to participate in gatherings only to a point; when he had had enough, he left without farewell and went about pursuits that pleased him more. In just that way he faded out of the 1944 convention of the National, even though he had played a major part in the events behind the scenes determining the outcome of the meeting. I have known him to fail to keep an appointment even with Lovecraft and me when we had a dinner engagement at another amateur's home. It was a characteristic you had to recognize and overlook, for so long as he was with you, he was companionable and genial.

In recent years I came to know Paul rather closely, yet now that he is gone, I am astonished to realize what large gaps there are in my knowledge. But it is all a part of the pattern of acquaintance with him; he opened the door of his life only so far to a friend; he closed it on much.

Ever since he has been in North Montpelier, Vermont, we have visited each other once or twice annually, except when gas rationing prevented. For the past ten years his health has been precarious. The visit to the 1944 convention was virtually his last journey away from home. After a life of numerous ventures that had included traveling to many parts of the United States, to Jamaica, and across the Atlantic, and after eighteen years as foreman of the press room of the Athol (Massachusetts) *Transcript*, he had finally come to haven at North Montpelier, where he became the business manager of the Driftwind Press. Though he detested the winters there, he was admirably situated for his own good, a fact which he well appreciated. Nevertheless, two years ago he confided to me that he was certain that life held at least one more adventure for him. An opportunity to leave did come in 1947, he confessed what I last saw him in September, but he had not felt equal to the demand, or free to leave. Sensibly, he had decided to remain.

At the end of each of my visits for the past three years there has been an undercurrent of feeling that we might never meet again. His heart was bad; there were other complications. But still other ailments occasioned his death. He failed to throw off an epidemic that afflicted the community in the late fall, and finally yielded to persuasion to have medical care. An operation proved necessary. Failure of his condition materially to improve necessitated a second major surgery. He wrote me of the seriousness of what faced him and added that he had left instructions that I should be notified if the outcome proved fatal. That sad word came to me on the morning of January 23.

So passed one who gave generously and richly for amateur journalism, ever as he inscribed on the cover of the final *Monadnock*: "For Love Only."

First published in *Interlude* (February 1948): 2–4.

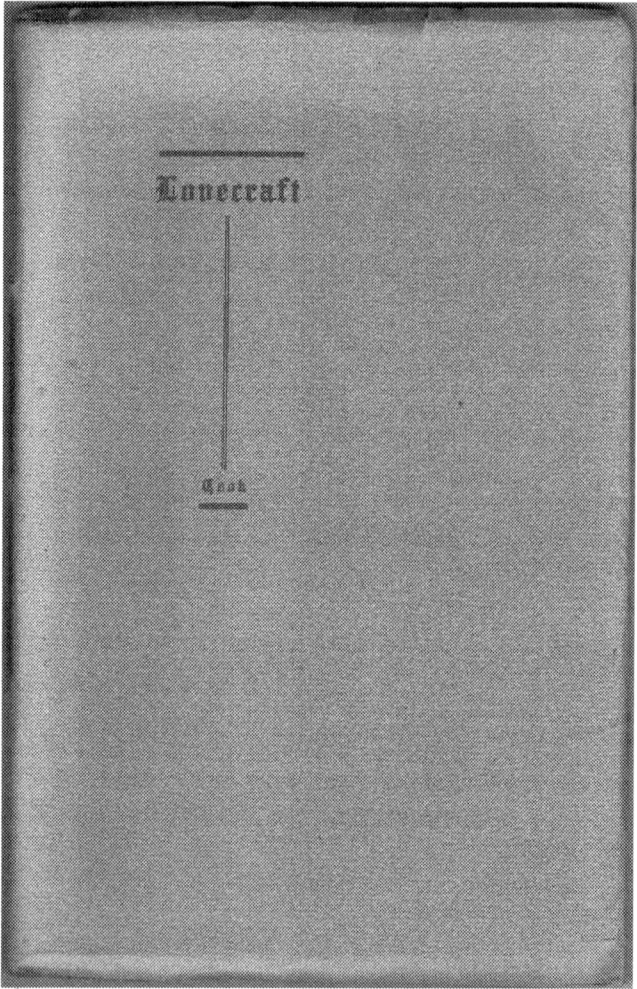

THE COVER OF COOK'S *In Memoriam: Howard Phillips Lovecraft* (1941)

A Bibliography of W. Paul Cook

BY SEAN DONNELLY

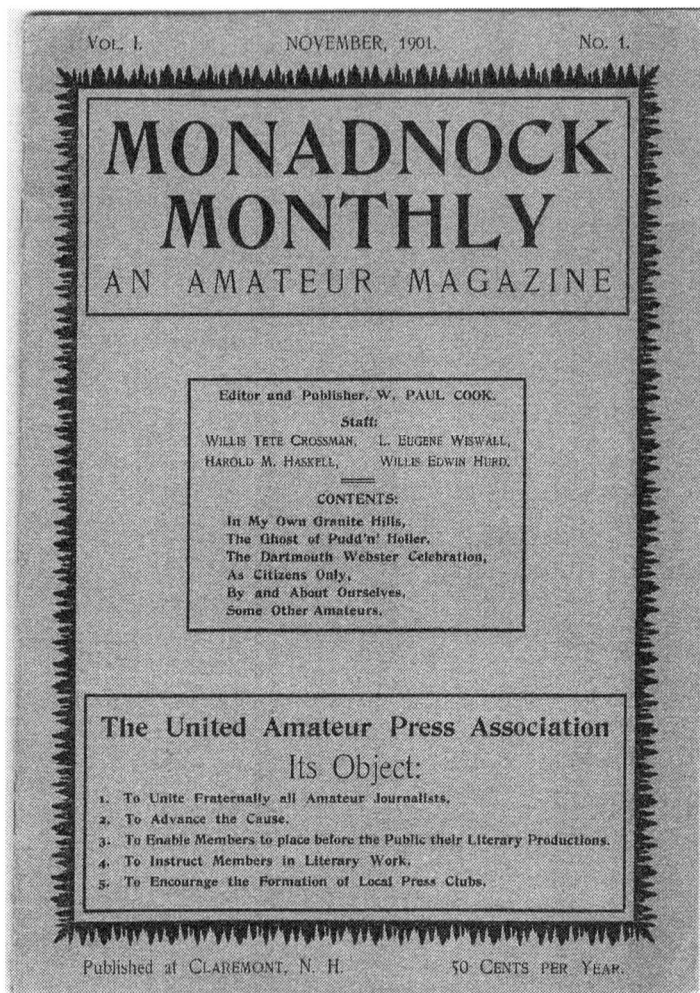

VOL. 1.   NOVEMBER, 1901.   NO. 1.

MONADNOCK MONTHLY

AN AMATEUR MAGAZINE

Editor and Publisher, W. PAUL COOK.

Staff:

WILLIS TETE CROSSMAN,   L. EUGENE WISWALL,
HAROLD M. HASKELL,   WILLIS EDWIN HURD,

CONTENTS:

In My Own Granite Hills,
The Ghost of Pudd'n' Holler,
The Dartmouth Webster Celebration,
As Citizens Only,
By and About Ourselves,
Some Other Amateurs.

The United Amateur Press Association

Its Object:

1. To Unite Fraternally all Amateur Journalists,
2. To Advance the Cause.
3. To Enable Members to place before the Public their Literary Productions.
4. To Instruct Members in Literary Work.
5. To Encourage the Formation of Local Press Clubs.

Published at CLAREMONT, N. H.   50 CENTS PER YEAR.

THE FIRST ISSUE OF COOK'S *Monadnock Monthly*.

I.

Arranged: A Legend of the Green Mountains
[North Montpelier: The Driftwind Press,] n.d.

Sewn brown printed wraps. 6 7/8 x 2 3/4 inches. Unpaginated [18 leaves].

Colophon: "50 copies of this crime committed just for the—er—fun of it by the so-called author. Set and printed one page at a time from a small job font of 18-point Cloister Oldstyle on a 3 x 5 press."

Contradictions
[North Montpelier]: The Driftwind Press, n.d.

Sewn printed wraps. 7 1/4 x 8 1/4 inches. 16 pages. A collection of seven poems first published in *Driftwind* magazine in the 1930s.

Colophon: "Vanityly printed at the Driftwind press. 51 copies."

Conversion: A Legend of Vermont
[North Montpelier: The Driftwind Press, n.d.]

Sewn printed wraps. 6 1/4 x 5 7/8 inches. 12 pages.

Colophon: "Fifty copies, minus done by the one responsible, when The Driftwind Press was off guard" [signed *W. Paul Cook*].

A Day in the Life of Willis T. Crossman. By Himself
Privately Printed. [North Montpelier: The Driftwind Press,] [1934].

Sewn yellow printed wraps. 5 x 7 3/4 inches. Unpaginated [14 leaves].

Colophon: Hand set and printed for the author by The Driftwind Press North Montpelier Vermont in an edition of fifty-four copies this being number [hand-numbered]."

Fiction: in which certain other fictions are exploded
[North Montpelier]: The Driftwind Press, n.d.

Sewn silver wraps printed in red. 6 5/8 x 5 1/8 inches. 14 pages.

Colophon: "done in the woodshed, by early candlelight (before breakfast), in the dead of a Vermont winter, on a contraption so ancient its makers have forgotten they ever committed the crime. I was very energetic, so I guess there'll be almost seventy of 'em."

Formula: A Fable for Children

[North Montpelier: The Driftwind Press, n.d.]

Sewn blue printed wraps. 8 1/2 x 4 1/2 inches. Unpaginated [8 leaves].

Colophon: "There is no special reason for this thing, except a complex of the pro to let no paper go out of the office unsoiled—(and there are those who will think this paper is considerably soiled.) This paper is waste and was headed for scrap channels. Now that the perpetrator of this atrocity has had his fun with it, he earnestly requests the recipients to drop it into the waste paper basket and hasten it on its interrupted journey. Fifty copies or a little less."

Heard in Vermont

North Montpelier: The Driftwind Press, 1939.

Cloth with paper label on spine. 6 3/4 x 9 1/2 inches. 129 pages. The second of two book-length Crossman collections; not bound and published until 1947.

It Happened in Dunbar

[North Montpelier]: The Driftwind Press, n.d.

Sewn printed wraps. 6 1/8 x 5 1/4 inches. 16 pages.

Colophon: "Forty-nine copies net for private distribution only. The Driftwind Press."

Lazy

[North Montpelier]: The Driftwind Press, n.d.

Sewn printed wraps. 6 1/8 x 3 3/8 inches. 16 pages. Illustrated with a linoleum cut by Frances Norton.

Colophon: "50 copies, minus, done by the author at the Driftwind Press with the proprietor wandering agitatedly around and murmuring something that sounds like "'corrigan'—probably a Sanskrit, Greek or Erse word expressing great admiration. Corrigan cut linoleumed by Frances Norton."

A poem; annotated after the latest manner, showing the how, the why, and the when, being an illustrated lesson on the mechanics of masterpieces, and a slight indication of the writings of the convolutions of a mighty brain in the throes of production

[North Montpelier: The Driftwind Press, n.d.]

Wraps. 6 x 9 1/2 inches. 24 copies.

Protest Stuff. Issued Posthumously With A Note About The Author.

[North Montpelier: The Driftwind Press, 1934.]

Stapled printed wraps. 5 1/2 x 7 5/16 inches. Unpaginated [26 leaves]. A collection of nineteen poems, some of which first appeared in *Driftwind* magazine. Includes an Introduction signed W. P. C. [W. Paul Cook] and dated April 3, 1934.

Colophon: "Sixty Copies of This Booklet Done by The Driftwind Press [hand-numbered]."

Note: According to a holograph correction in Cook's file copy, marked "No. One," 65 copies were published on April 2, 1934.

Secretive: a Vermont Idyl

[North Montpelier: The Driftwind Press, n.d.]

Sewn printed wraps. 5 3/4 x 6 inches. 17 pages.

Colophon: "49 impressions taken with the connivance of The Driftwind Press" [signed *W. Paul Cook*].

Surprise: A Tale Told in Vermont

[North Montpelier: The Driftwind Press, 1944]

Stapled brown printed wraps. 5 1/8 x 6 1/2 inches. Unpaginated [8 leaves].

Sympathetic: as told in Vermont

[North Montpelier: The Driftwind Press, n.d.]

Wraps. 5 3/4 x 6 1/8 inches. 52 copies.

Teeth (Being an extract from the notes of Willis T. Crossman, a down-and-outer, now deceased)

[North Montpelier: The Driftwind Press, n.d.]

Sewn printed wraps. 7 1/4 x 4 5/8 inches. Unpaginated [6 leaves].

Colophon: "Fifty-six copies of this thing printed by the author—the lord only knows why."

Told in Vermont

North Montpelier: The Driftwind Press, 1938.

Stiff brown printed wraps. 5 3/16 x 7 7/8 inches. Unpaginated [55 leaves]. Introduction by Walter John Coates. The first of two book-length collections by Crossman. Price: $1.00.

Colophon: "Hand Set and Hand Printed in an Edition of 150 copies at Rich's Hollow in the State of Vermont."

Vermontiana Esoterica: stories for initiates only

[North Montpelier]: The Silenus Press, [1938 or 1939].

Wraps. 4 3/4 x 7 1/2 inches. Unpaginated [11 leaves]. "Embellished by an interpretive, descriptive, realistically pictorial and inspirational wood cut by 'Janus' done directly on the block without crosshatching."

Colophon: "Twenty-six copies impressed on the Silenus Press by the Edonian Band. Done in the New Deal, anno VI."

Willis T. Crossman's Vermont: Stories by W. Paul Cook

Tampa: University of Tampa Press, 2005.

Edited by Sean Donnelly and Leland M. Hawes, Jr. With an Afterword by Welford D. Taylor. Published simultaneously in paperback and clothbound editions.

Note: Housed in the H. P. Lovecraft Collection at the John Hay Library of Brown University are manuscripts of thirty Crossman "poems" by W. Paul Cook. Some are unpublished. The manuscripts were probably acquired through Edward H. Cole, who was given some of Cook's papers by the widow of Walter J. Coates.

II.

Alhauser, William C. *Our Ex-Presidents.* Athol, Mass.: W. Paul Cook, 1919.

Blue cloth. Illustrated with frontisportrait of the author and photographs of the N.A.P.A.'s presidents. First published serially in *The National Amateur.* Price: $1.00.

Bullen, John Ravenor. *White Fire.* Athol, Mass.: The Recluse Press, 1927.

Gray cloth with paper labels to upper cover and spine. Illustrated with tipped-in portrait of the author facing the title page. A posthumous collection of poems anonymously edited and with a signed introduction by H. P. Lovecraft, and dedicated to Lovecraft, who was asked to undertake the project by Bullen's mother. The book's production was financed by Archibald Freer of Chicago, a wealthy friend of the late Bullen. Published Christmas day, 1927. Limited to 304 copies: 280 in gray cloth (sold at $2.00); 24 bound in dark green leather gilt for presentation (not for sale).

Coates, Walter John. *Land of Allen and Other Verse.* Athol, Mass.: W. Paul Cook | The Recluse Press, 1928.

Red cloth with paper labels to upper cover and spine. Frontisportrait signed by author. A collection of poems by the editor of *Driftwind.* Published December 8, 1928. 500 copies. Price: $2.00.

Cook, W. Paul. *In Memoriam: Howard Phillips Lovecraft. Recollections, Appreciations, Estimates.* Written in December, 1940. [North Montpelier: Driftwind Press, 1941.]

Sewn blue printed wraps. "Printed one page at an impression, by the author, April to June, 1941 by the courtesy and with the cooperation of the Driftwind Press. An edition of 94 net." Not for sale.

Fowle, Charles H. *Out of the Past. The Life and Career of Charles H. Fowle: Together with a Selection from His Contributions to the Amateur Press.* [Athol, Mass.]: Published for the Author | The Recluse Press, 1926.

Red cloth with paper labels to upper cover and spine. Published in April 1927. 400 copies. Price: $2.00

Goodenough, Arthur H. *Songs of Four Decades*. Athol, Mass.: W. Paul Cook, 1927.

Red cloth with paper labels to upper cover and spine. Published in February 1927. 315 copies. Price: $2.00.

Goodenough, Arthur H. *Twenty Years' Recollections of Amateur Journalism*. Published by W. Paul Cook, 1920.

Unbound signatures of 148 pages. The sections of the book were printed sporadically by Cook between 1919 and 1924. He evidently intended to bind up the sections but never did so, as he was becoming less active in amateur journalism by the early 1920s.

Greenfield, Will H. *Ring and Diamond*. Athol, Mass.: Cook Publishing Co., 1921.

In Memoriam: Jennie E. T. Dowe [Athol, Mass.: W. Paul Cook, 1921.] September 1921.

Includes an article by Cook called "Two Viewpoints" and "My Mother—As She Seemed to Me" by Edith Miniter.

Kleiner, Rheinhart. *Pegasus in Pasture, Latter-day Limpings of a Light Versifier, With some Callow Cavortings from More Coltish Days*. 100 copies Reprinted from *The Ghost* for "Spring of 1943" by W. Paul Cook at The Driftwind Press, North Montpelier, Vermont.

Brown sewn wraps printed in black. Unpaginated [8 leaves]. A collection of 14 poems. Not for sale.

Long, Frank Belknap, Jr. *A Man from Genoa and Other Poems*. Athol, Mass.: W. Paul Cook | The Recluse Press, 1926.

Blue cloth with paper label to upper cover. The first book issued by the press. Published in January 1926. 315 copies. Price: $2.00

Lovecraft, H. P. *The Shunned House*. Athol, Mass.: W. Paul Cook | The Recluse Press, 1928. Preface by Frank B. Long, Jr.

The sheets were never bound by Cook. Several sets were bound by Robert Barlow. A hundred were bound by Arkham House in 1961.

Loveman, Samuel. *The Hermaphrodite: A Poem*. Athol, Mass.: W. Paul Cook | The Recluse Press, 1926. Preface by Benjamin De Casseres.

> Black cloth with paper label to upper cover. Published in July 1926. 350 copies. Price: $2.00

Loveman, Samuel. *The Sphinx: A Conversation*. [North Montpelier, VT]: Published by W. Paul Cook, 1944.

> Sewn wraps. Reprinted from the *Ghost* (July 1944). Not for sale.

Symmes, Mrs. William B. [Cassie Doty] *Old World Footprints*. Athol, Mass.: W. Paul Cook, 1928. Preface by Frank B. Long, Jr.

> A book of travel impressions by Long's aunt who probably financed the book. The preface was ghost-written by H. P. Lovecraft. 308 copies. Not for sale.

Walter, Dorothy C. *Lovecraft and Benefit Street*. [North Montpelier: The Driftwind Press, 1943.]

> Brown sewn wraps. Unpaginated [8 leaves]. Reprinted from *The Ghost* for Spring of 1943. 150 copies. Not for sale.

Wandrei, Donald. *Ecstasy and Other Poems*. Athol, Mass.: W. Paul Cook | The Recluse Press, 1928.

> Purple cloth with paper labels to upper cover and spine, in glassine jacket. A prospectus for the book was issued. Published in April 1928. 322 copies. The book was suppressed by the author within a few years of publication, according to Cook. Price: $1.50.

III.

Epgephi. (September, 1920) Some Impressions of the First Orgy. July 3 to 10, 1920. Issued by George Julian Houtain and W. Paul Cook.

> Brown stapled wraps. 7 x 10 inches. 24 pages.

> First and only number, issued to commemorate a meeting of the Hub Club of Massachusetts. Contributors include Cook, Houtain,

Edith Miniter, Michael White, Winifred Virginia Jordan, Rheinhart Kleiner, Charles A. A. Parker, and H. P. Lovecraft, all of whose names are playfully obscured and given Mason–like designations as members of the Epgephians. According to Lovecraft's account of events, what occasioned the formation of the group was "the capture of [the Hub Club] by the United Amateur Press Association."

The Ghost. This being the First Number. Spring of 1943. Issued for his own amusement and that of his friends by W. Paul Cook

Orange and black printed wraps. 8 7/8 x 11 1/2 inches. 48 pages.

[1] "Terra Incognita" by E. A. Edkins, [1]–8 "Whom We Call Dead" by Edith Miniter, 8 "A Mother's Wish" by Nelson Glazier Morton, 8–9 "Gleeson White" by Edwin B Hill, 10 "In Remembrance" by Bertha Grant Avery, 10–14 "Like a Voice From the Tomb" by Ethel May Stuart Johnston Myers, 15 "At the Portal" by Frank Roe Batchelder, 15–20 "The Romantic Story of Delia Bacon" by Truman J. Spencer, 20 "Butterfly Path" by Jennie Kendall Plaisier, 21–26 "Pegasus in Pasture; Latter-Day Limpings of a Light Versifier; [With some Callow Cavortings from More Coltish Days] by Rheinhart Kleiner, 27–29 "Lovecraft and Benefit Street" by Dorothy C. Walter, 30 "Waters of Lethe" by Willis T. Crossman [W. Paul Cook], 30–32 "On Liking Poetry" by Pearl K. Morton, 32 "An Old Sailor Muses" by Betty-Jane Kendall, 33 "This Ain't Love" by Paul J. Campbell, 34–36 "Yarbs" by Jennir E. T. Dowe, 36-39 "The Trend of History" by Edward H. Cole, 39–42 "The Greatest of These" by Nelson Glazier Morton, 43–44 "Book-borrowers" by Rheinhart Kleiner, 44–45 "The Sage of Brooklyn" by Edwin B. Hill, 46-48 "Books that Debauched Me" by Ernest A. Edkins.

The Ghost. The second number. July 1944. Issued for his own amusement and that of his friends by W. Paul Cook.

Stapled pink printed wraps. 8 7/8 x 11 1/2 inches. 42 pages.

1–4 "The Wehr Wolf" by John Edward Colburn, 5–17 "The Book of the Dead, Chapter 1: Farnsworth Wright" by E. Hoffmann Price, 18 "Winter Night" by Vrest Orton, 19–41 "The Sphinx: A One–Act Play" by Samuel Loveman, [42] colophon: "THE GHOST is an amateur publication issued for love of the hobby known as Amateur Journalism. It cannot be bought from the publisher; and it is his wish that it never, at any time, under any circumstance, be sold."

The Ghost. The third number. May 1945. Issued for his own amusement and that of his friends by W. Paul Cook. priceless.

Stapled black printed wraps. 8 7/8 x 11 1/2 inches. 56 pages.

1 "Cosmic Horror" by Dorothy Tilden Spoerl, 2–4 "Rathnaka" by Burton Crane, 5–32 "The Weird Tale in English Since 1890" by August Derleth, 33–34 "A Covering Letter from August Derleth, In regard to the preceding thesis" by August Derleth, 34 "Musings" by Jennie K. Plaisier, 35–36 "Creativity a Democratic Process" by Howard Davis Spoerl (first printed in *Driftwind*, September 1944), 37 "Amateur Writing" by John Wilstach (first printed in *Driftwind*, February 1945), 38–54 "The Book of the Dead, Chapter 2: Robert Ervin Howard" by E. Hoffman Price, 55–56 "A Plea for Lovecraft" by W. Paul Cook, 56 "Night Madness" by Martin Chesley Hutchings.

The Ghost. The fourth number. July 1946. This issue being entirely Burrowings of An Old Bookworm by Rheinhart Kleiner.

Stapled gray printed wraps. 8 7/8 x 11 1/2 inches. 32 pp.

Page [32] colophon: "why a colophon, anyway? | if I put one here | I'd have to print on this page."

The Ghost. The fifth number. July 1947. An Amateur publication issued for his own amusement and that of his friends by W. Paul Cook.

Stapled purple printed wraps. 8 7/8 x 11 1/2 inches. 50 pages.

1–6 "The Book of the Dead, Chapter 3: Mortonius" by E. Hoffmann Price, 6–9 "Comments on Mr. Price's Article" by Pearl K. Morton, 9–11 "Jim Morton" by W. Paul Cook, 11–15 "James Ferdinand Morton Jr." [two articles] by Edward H. Cole, 15–20 "James Morton" by Rheinhart Kleiner, 21–27 "The Isle of Tanet" [a poem originally published in *Driftwind*] by Jude Palmer, 28–30 "The Saw-man" by Eleanor Barnhart Campbell, 31 "Bongo" [a poem] by Chesley Partin Hutchings, 32–33 "All About Love" by John Wilstach, 33 "Parted" by Jennie Kendall Plaisier, 34 "The Old Brothel Keeper" by Larry Kebec, 35 "Beyond Doom" by Chesley Martin Hutchings, 36–44 "Ramblings of a Reader and Collector of the Weird and Fantastic" by H. C. Koenig, 44 "Untimely Sabbath" by Howard Davis Spoerl, 45–48 "Horror Transcendent" by Leland Lovelace, [50] colophon: "MAY MY CURSE | FOLLOW HIM | WHO EVER OFFERS | A Ghost | FOR SALE."

The Monadnock Monthly. An Amateur Magazine, Published for the United Amateur Press Association. Editor and Publisher, W. Paul Cook. Vol. 1, No. 1 (November 1901).

Stapled gray wraps printed in black. 9 1/4 x 6 3/4 inches. 16 pages.

1 In My Own Granite Hills by Willis Edwin Hurd, 2-7 The Ghost of Pudd'n' Holler by Leon E. Wiswall, 7-11 The Dartmouth Webster Celebration by Harold M. Haskell, 11-16 As Citizens Only by Willis Tete Crossman, 16 By and About Ourselves [by W. Paul Cook]

The Monadnock Monthly. An Amateur Magazine. W. Paul Cook, Editor and Publisher. Published at Hanover, N.H. Vol. 2, No. 3 (February 1905).

Cream stapled wraps printed in blue and gold. 6 1/2 by 9 3/4 inches. 36 pages. 400 copies.

[i] blank, [ii] frontisportrait of Elijah Kellogg, [1] Snowflakes by George Bancroft Griffith, [1]-4 Rev. Elijah Kellogg by W. Paul Cook, 5 The Barefoot Girl by Horace Eaton Walker, 5-7 A Few Amateur Reminiscences: New Hampshire Amateurs of the Seventies by George I. Putnam, 8 Addenda to Mr. Putnam's Paper, 8 [untitled verse] by Willis Edwin Hurd, 9 Eve O'er the Vale of the Ike-Be!-Su by Willis Edwin Hurd, 10-13 One of the Least by Ira Eugene Seymour, 13 Imagination by Mary M. Currier, 13-29 The Square-Jawed Man Wins by Willis Tete Crossman [W. Paul Cook], 29-34 By and About Ourselves [by W. Paul Cook], 34-35 Some Other Amateurs [by W. Paul Cook], 36 Why Pass It By? by Charles Elliott Fish

The Monadnock Monthly. An Amateur Magazine. W. Paul Cook, Editor and Publisher. Published at Hanover, N.H. Vol. 2, No. 4 (April 1905).

Blue stapled wraps printed in blue and red. 6 1/2 by 9 3/4 inches. 24 pages.

[i] blank, [ii] frontisportrait of John De Morgan, [1]-5 John De Morgan by W. Paul Cook, 5 To the Sphinx by Foster Gilroy, 6-9 The Penalty of the Law by Willis Tete Crossman [W. Paul Cook], 9 The Night Storm by George Bancroft Griffith, 10-18 The Kettle on the Wall by Flora Stewart Emory, [facing page 19, plate with view of "Asquam ('Squam') Lake, Holderness, N.H."], 19-24 By and About Ourselves [by W. Paul Cook], 24 Some Other Amateurs [by W. Paul Cook].

The Monadnock Monthly. An Amateur Magazine. Printed by the Editor at The Dartmouth Press [Hanover, N.H.]. Vol. 2, No. 5 (July 1905).

Yellow stapled wraps printed in red, green, and blue. 6 1/2 by 9 3/4 inches. 32 pages. 700 copies.

[i] blank, [ii] frontisportrait of Harriet McEwen Kimball, [1] The Swallows are Flying by Russell D. Chase, [1]-5 Harriet McEwen Kimball: Poetess and Woman by W. Paul Cook, [facing page 6, plate with "Two Views on the Connecticut River"] 6 The Other Self by Arthur H. Goodenough, 7-11 A Dual Evolution by Paul J. Campbell, 12 The Appeal by S. A. White Kismet, 12-15 Some Letters From Old-Timers [with plates, facing pages 12 and 15, captioned "Profile Falls, Smith's River, Bristol, N.H." and "Pasquaney ("New Found") Lake from Sleeper Farm, Bristol"], 15-22 The Clocks of Paris by Willis Tete Crossman [W. Paul Cook], [facing page 22, plate with "View from the Fayall Peak, Holderness, N.H."] 22-27 By and About Ourselves [by W. Paul Cook], [facing page 28, plate with view of "Sugar Loaf Road, Pasquaney Lake"] 28-30 Some Other Amateurs [by W. Paul Cook], 30-31 Some Thoughts on Amateur Journalism by Pearl L. Noble, [facing page 31, plate with caption "Canoeing on Sunapee Lake"] 31-32 He Laughed by Willis Edwin Hurd

The Monadnock Monthly. An Amateur Magazine. W. Paul Cook, Editor and Publisher. Published from Hanover, N.H. Vol. 3, No. 6 (February 1906).

Black stapled wraps, with plate tipped on, printed in blue and gold. 6 1/2 by 9 3/4 inches. 32 pages. 350 copies.

[i] table of contents, [ii]-[iii] blank, [iv] frontisportrait of Robert Mackay, [1] Orange Blossoms by S. A. White Kismet, [1]-3 Robert Mackay by Hugh Winn, 4 Sunset by L. J. H. Frost, 4-8 Informally Announced by Willis Tete Crossman, 8 Love by Marha Shepard Lippincott, 9-11 The Granite Echo and Contemporaries by Herbert Durrell Smart, 12 Elegy Y: Ad Matrem by James T. Kirby, 12-14 Addenda to Mr. Smart's Paper, 14 At Home On the Farm by Willis Edwin Hurd, 15-17 "Time and Chance": A Review by Flora Stewart Emory, 18 The World's Way by Henry G. Wehking, 19-21 In the Mills of God by Harry Hoyt Travers, 21 A Little Sermon by Mae Boss Patton, 22-27 Some Other Amateurs [by W. Paul Cook], 27-28 No More! by S. A.

White Kismet, 28-32 By and About Ourselves [by W. Paul Cook], 32 The Devil's Mortgage by Arthur H. Goodenough.

The Monadnock Monthly. Only An Amateur Magazine. Vol. 7, No. 7 (May 1913).

Black stapled wraps printed in gold and white. 7 x 10 inches. 76 pages. [i] Contents, [ii] dedication, [iii] contents continued, [iv] List of Illustrations, [v] blank, [vi] frontisportrait of Sullivan Holman McCollester, [1] Morning by Lucy J. H. Frost, [1]-7 Sullivan Holman McCallister: Author, Educator, Preacher, Man by W. Paul Cook, [facing page 2, plate with view of "Mount Monadnock from Keene"], [facing page 6, plate with view of "Echo Lake and Mount Lafayette, Franconia Notch"], 7-9 To a Rose by Russell D. Chase, 10-12 The Proof of the Theory by Willis Tete Crossman [W. Paul Cook], 12 Grandpa's Pants by Ira Eugene Seymour, [facing page 13, plate with view of "Wildcat River, Jackson Falls"], 13-17 The Law of Souls by Flora Stewart Emory, [facing page 17, plate with portrait of George Bancroft Griffith], 17 The Cherry Tree by John A. R. Forbes, 18 Epigaea by George Bancroft Griffith, [facing page 19, plate with portrait of C. Fred. Crosby], 19-23 Random Recollections of Amateur Days by C. Fred. Crosby, [facing page 23, plate with view of "Hanover, N.H. and Connecticut Valley"], 23 Just a Little While by Harry Hoyt Travers, 24 The Queen Moon by Samuel A. White, [facing page 24, plate with view of "Presidential Range from Mt. Pleasant House, Bretton Woods"], 25-28 The Call of the Cataract by Clinton Pryor, [facing page 29, plate with view of "Mount Lafayette and Franconia Notch from Sugar Hill"], 29 Love Crowned by Mae Boss Patton, 30 Music Hath Charms by Charles A. A. Parker, [facing page 31, plate titled "View of Hampton Beach"], 31 To Winter by Samuel A. White, 32-38 Woven by Circumstance by Frank D. Murphy, [facing page 32, plate with view of "A Street Scene, Charlestown"], 38 The Wreck by Lucy J. H. Frost, [facing page 39, plate with view of "Purgatory Falls, Mount Vernon"], 39-40 Noes of Old Timers [by W. Paul Cook], 41-42 The Vision of Mirza: A Paraphrase by Gladys M. Adams, 42-43 An Imp and Smoke by Hicks Clark, 43-44 My Summer Dream by Sarah M. Wheeler, [facing page 45, plate with view of "Lake Winn, From Red Hill"] 45-46 The Wooing of Bruno by M. Almedia Thomas-Bretholl, 46 The Old Valley Home by George Bancroft Griffith, 47-48 Reparation by Olive M. Delahaye, 48 The

Singing Ones by Arthur H. Goodenough, [facing page 49, plate with view of "Merrimack Valley From Hookset Pinnacle"] 49-50 Home Sketches: 1 by James Thomas Kirby, 50 The Calm of Eventide by Samuel A White, 51-53 The Breaking-In of Philip by Litta Voelchert, 53-54 Massacre of Lachine by John A. R. Forbes, 54-56 Till Death by Samuel A. White, [facing page 56, plate with view of "Governor Wentworth Mansion, Portsmouth"] 56 Evening Reveries by Mabel I. Moore, 57-61 The Vintage of Time by Paul J. Campbell, 62 The World Is Asking Why by Arthur H. Goodenough, 62 A Spring Morning by Samuel A White, 63 Silence by Henry G. Wehking, 63 My Sweetheart by Samuel A. White, [facing page 64, plate with view of "Presidential Range from Bray Hill, Whitefield"] 64 Says Purdy McFane by Willis Edwin Hurd, 64 The Bluebell by John A. R. Forbes, [facing page 65, plate with view of "On the New Hampshire Connecticut River"] 65 Stub-Toe Land by Walter H. Van, 66-76 By and About Ourselves [by W. Paul Cook].

The National Amateur. Vol. XLI, Nos. 1-6 (September 1918 to July 1919).

The National Messenger. Vol. 1, No. 1 (July, 1919).

Stapled brown wraps printed in black. 3 7/8 x 6 1/4 inches. 8 pages. This paper was issued by Cook during his tenure as President of the National Amateur Press Association. Includes a long open letter from Cook urging more active participation by the members of the NAPA.

[1]-6 open letter from Cook as president of the NAPA, 7 Our Beliefs by John T. Nixon, 7-8 To Our Association by Florence E. Goodale.

The National Messenger. Vol. 1, No. 2 (August, 1919).

Stapled blue wraps printed in black. 3 7/8 x 6 1/4 inches. 8 pages.

[1]-7 open letter from Cook as president of the NAPA, 7 quote from amateur Walter S. Goff, 8 Our Creed by W.E. Mellinger.

The National Messenger. Vol. 1, No. 3 (September, 1919).

Stapled green wraps printed in black. 3 7/8 x 6 1/4 inches. 8 pages.

[1]-7 open letter from Cook as president of the NAPA, 7-8 letter regarding Lone Scouts from Charles Merlin.

The National Messenger. Vol. 1, No. 4 (October, 1919).

Stapled cream wraps printed in black. 3 7/8 x 6 1/4 inches. 8 pages.

[1]-6 open letter from Cook as president of the NAPA, 7-8 letters from John H. Haseman, Jr. and W. Paul Cook.

The National Post. Semi-Monthly. Vol. 1, No. 1 (August 15, 1913).

Self wraps. 6 x 9 inches. 12 pages. Edited by Charles A. A. Parker and W. Paul Cook. Billed as "Amateurdom's only newspaper," the paper published news articles submitted by members of the NAPA.

The National Post. Semi-Monthly. Vol. 1, No. 2 (October 1, 1913).

Self wraps. 6 x 9 inches. 8 pages.

The National Post. Semi-Monthly. Vol. 1, No. 3 (October 15, 1913).

Self wraps. 6 x 9 inches. 10 pages.

The National Post. Semi-Monthly. Vol. 1, No. 4 (November 1, 1913).

Self wraps. 6 x 9 inches. 4 pages.

The National Register.

The Pilgrim. (November 1906). Edited by W. Paul Cook and Vincent Haggerty.

Self-wraps. 9 x 6 inches. 4 pages. Apparently a one-shot publication, "devoted to the approaching election of the Atlantic Coast Amateur Press Association."

1-2 Cook's Remarks, 2-4 Haggerty's Say

The Pot Pourri. Vol. 1, No. 1 (April, 1920). Issued in the Interest of The United Amateur Press Association of America, by Edgar A. Rowell [and] W. Paul Cook.

Stapled brown printed wraps. 5 x 7 inches. 20 pages.

[1] Immortal Things by Arthur H. Goodenough, 2-6 United Convention Impressions by A Well-Known Amateur, 6-8 A Heart Content by Julia R. Smith Johnson, 9-15 Billy Smith, Slacker, by Pearl Stoughton, 15

The New Day by William J. Clemence, 16-18 The Ouija Board by Mae Uhlman, 19 Something New by Ella V. Harris, 20 Don't Be a "Quitter" by C. Westover

The Recluse. Issued by W. Paul Cook, for His Own Amusement at The Recluse Press, Box 215, Athol, Mass. This being the First Number—[Fall] 1927.

Stapled green pictorial wraps (with cover illustration by Vrest Orton). 8 x 11 inches. 78 pages.

[1]-2 "Study List: Vermont Poets and Poetry;" 3-14 "Early Vermont Minstrelsy" by Walter J. Coates; 15 "After Armageddon" by Clark Ashton Smith; 16-17 "A Check-List of the First Editions of George Sterling;" 18-21 "A Fragment of a Dream" by Donald Wandrei; 22 "The Runner" by Arthur H. Goodenough; 23-59 "Supernatural Horror in Literature" by H. P. Lovecraft; 60 "Brumes et Pluies (From the French of Charles P. Baudelaire)" by Clark Ashton Smith; 61-62 "Heart Symphony for Daré" by Vrest Orton; 63-69 "The Green Porcelain Dog" by H. Warner Munn; 70 "Ballad of St. Anthony" by Frank Belknap Long, Jr.; 71-75 "Hubert Crackanthorpe: A Realist of the Nineties" by Samuel Loveman; 76-77 "In the Grave" by Donald Wandrei; [78] "Intentions" by W. Paul Cook.

The Reflector Vol. 6, No. 5 (July 1906). Grand View, Tenn. Edited by W. Paul Cook, Lee S. Nelson, and Louis M. Starring.

Self-wraps. 6 x 9 inches. 4 pages. Published for the N.A.P.A. and the Southern Amateur Journalists Association.

The Reflector Vol. 6, No. 6 (August 1906). Grand View, Tenn. Edited by W. Paul Cook, Lee S. Nelson, and Louis M. Starring.

Self-wraps. 6 x 9 inches. 4 pages.

The Reflector Vol. 6, No. 7 (September 1906). Grand View, Tenn. Edited by W. Paul Cook, Lee S. Nelson, and Louis M. Starring.

Self-wraps. 6 x 9 inches. 4 pages.

Revenant. An Amateur Publication. Number One, 1945.

Stapled red printed wraps. 6 1/4 x 9 1/2 inches. 28 pages.

[1] title pages, [2] blank, 3 "Interlude [a poem] by Bertha Grant Avery, 4-9 "And This I Remember!" by Jennie Maloney Kendall Plaisier, 10-11 "Generosity and Selfishness" by Amanda E. Thrift, 12-21 "I Dined with a Sheik" by Ethel May Stuart Johnston Myers, 22 "Smiles" by Jennie K. Plaisier, 23-24 "Hi-Powered Convention" by Amanda E. Thrift, 25-27 "A Summer Episode: Boy Meets Girl" by J. Irene Maloney, [28] colophon: "Published by W. Paul Cook | simply because he had nothing else to do. | Printed by an ordinary printer | on an ordinary press | in ordinary ink | on ordinary paper | from slugs set | on an extraordinary linotype | —the brute!"

The United Amateur. 1918: July, September, November; 1919: January, May, July, September, November; 1920: March, May, July

The Vagrant. The First Number. December, 1915. Containing Something of Interest Only to a Few "Old Timers." From W. Paul Cook, Athol, Mass.

Stapled yellow printed wraps. Unpaginated [6 leaves].

[1] title page, [2] blank, [3]-[12] Echoes from the Past (Amateur journalistic extracts from "Oliver Optic's Magazine", OUR BOYS AND GIRLS for 1871.)

The Vagrant. The Second Number. March, 1916. Containing A Few Verses and Some Pages of Matter of No Consequence. From W. Paul Cook, Athol, Mass.

Stapled yellow printed wraps. 5 x 7 inches. 16 pages.

[1] title page, [2] Lonely by Harriet L. Trieloff, [3] Autumnus—and October by Arthur H. Goodenough, [5] My Two Little Kids by O. Byron Copper, [6] The Length'ning Day by Robert D. Roosmale-Cocq, [7] June by John Osman Baldwin, [8] A Calamity by James Larkin Pearson, [9] The Revenge by William J. Clemence, [10]-[16] Inconsequentialities [by W. Paul Cook]

The Vagrant. The Third Number. June, 1916. Containing Some Poetry, Some Verse, and A Considerable Quantity of The Producer's Stuff. From W. Paul Cook, 451 Main St., Athol, Mass.

Stapled yellow printed wraps. 5 x 7 inches. Unpaginated [12 leaves].

[1] title page, [2] Destiny by Arthur H. Goodenough, [3] The Heart of a Woman by Essilyn Dale Nichols (Mae Boss Patton), [4] Misunderstood by Harriet L. Trieloff, [5] The Valley of Delight by George W. Priest, [6] To the British Fleet by Robert D. Roosmale-Cocq, [7] An Eye For An Eye by Edna von der Heide, [8] Die Menschenseele by Harriet L. Trieloff, [9] Mary by John Osman Baldwin, [10] Freckles by William J. Clemence, [11] New York Harbor At Night by Olive G. Owen, [12] My Thought of You by James Larkin Pearson, [13] Second-Best by Henry G. Wehking, [14]-[24] Junk: Old and New Stuff by the Editor

The Vagrant. The Fourth Number. September, 1916. Containing A Poem by Harriet L. Trieloff, A Ballad by Arthur H. Goodenough, and A Sketch by Paul J. Campbell. From W. Paul Cook, 451 Main St., Athol, Mass.

Stapled yellow printed wraps. 5 x 7 inches. Unpaginated [14 leaves].

[1] title page, [2]-[3] Our All-in-All by Harriet L. Trieloff [facing page 3, photograph of Trieloff], [4]-[9] The Sachem's Gift by Arthur H. Goodenough [facing page 4, photograph of Goodenough], [10]-[16] Going to a Funeral by Paul J. Campbell [facing page 10, photograph of Campbell], [17]-[19] G. Wash. Darragh Sheds a Little Light by Geo W. Darragh, [20]-[22] Just to Fill These Three Pages [by W. Paul Cook]

The Vagrant. The Fifth Number. June, 1917. 451 Main Street, Athol, Mass.

Stapled red illustrated wraps. 5 x 7 inches. 40 pages

[1] title page, 2 The Evening Star at Christmas Time by Harriet L. Trieloff, 3-4 Articles of Faith by O. Byron Copper, 5 To Templeton and Mount Monadnock by Howard P. Lovecraft, 6 The Promise by Anita Roberta Kirksey, 7 Her Beauty by Arthur H. Goodenough, 8 The Vagabond by Robert D. Roosmale-Cocq, 9 O, Come Away by Harriet L. Trieloff, 10-12 Christmas in the Land of Heart's Delight by Jean Connell Hayes, 13 A Miracle by Essilyn Dale Nichols, 14 Christmas, 1916 by Edna von der Heide, 15 Christmas Day by Olive G. Owen, 16-19 The Star That Blazed O'er Balkan Hills by A. M. Adams, 20 You Jes' as Well Laugh as to Cry by James Larkin Pearson, 21-23 Kallima (An Indian Idyl) by Willis Edwin Hurd, 24-38 Thoughts Here and There by W. Paul Cook, 39-40 The First Fifty members of the UAPA [by W. Paul Cook]

The Vagrant. The Sixth Number. November, 1917. 451 Main Street, Athol, Mass.

Stapled brown illustrated wraps. 5 x 7 inches. 92 pages.

[inside front cover] The Flag by Franklin K. Lane, [1] title page, 2 Sonnet by Harriet L. Trieloff, 3-4 Old by Lucy J. H. Frost, 5 "Killed in Action" by Edna von der Heide, 6 J. C.—A Friend by Olive G. Owen, 7-13 Amateur Days—and After by Chas. S. Campbell, 14 Two Pearls by Anita Roberta Kirksey, 15-17 To Greece, 1917 by Howard P. Lovecraft, 18 Wondering by Mabel I. Moore, 19 Contemplations by James Larkin Pearson, 20 To My Library Companion by Chas. B. Spofford, 21-22 The House of Illusion by Arthur H. Goodenough, 23 Rest by L. Adelaide Sherman, 24 The Soldier by Ethelwyn Dithridge, [facing page 25, photograph of Flora Stewart Emory] 25-34 The Woman Who Grew Young by Flora Stewart Emory, 35 Failure by J. F. Roy Erford, 36 Surrender by William H. Greenfield, [facing page 37, photograph of William H. Greenfield] 37 Lucille by Rheinhart Kleiner, 38 Love's Magic by Winifred Virginia Jordan, 39 A Song of the West by Essillyn Dale Nichols, 40 Class Poem, Bethany College, 1913 by J. Clinton Pryor, 41-44 People As They Seem and Are by Pearl K. Merritt, 45-46 The Magic In the Man by Willis Edwin Hurd, 47-49 The Worshipper by Litta L. Voelchert, 50 The Death-Watch by Winifred Virginia Jordan, 51-55 The President's Diction by William R. Murphy, 56 The Hunger by Andrew Francis Lockhart, 57-58 The Land of War by Harriet L. Trieloff, 59-61 The Gingerbread Man by M. Almedia Bretholl, 62 Song by Elsie Alice Gidlow, 63-65 Peter's Progress by Ethel May Johnston-Myers, 66 A Promise by Margaret Trafford, 67-68 Advertising For An Army by Ben Winskill, 69-70 Susan Spreckles' Foxy Lover by O. Byron Copper, 71-74 Mice and Men by George W. Darragh [facing page 74, photograph of John Osman Baldwin], 75 Love's Heroes by John Osman Baldwin, 76-90 From Various Quills [by W. Paul Cook], 91-92 The Second Fifty Members U.A.P.A. [by W. Paul Cook], [inside rear cover] The Mother's Prayer, 1917 by Dwight S. Anderson

The Vagrant. The Seventh Number. June, 1918. W. Paul Cook. Athol, Mass.

5 x 7 inches. 148 pages.

1 title page, 2 Give Me the Love of a Child by Andrew Francis Lockhart, 3 Dawn in Winter by Harriet L. Trieloff, 5 Little Princess: Model by Flora Stewart Emory, 14 Profiles by Russell D. Chase, 15 Sonnets of a Bashful Man by J. Clinton Pryor, 17 The Church and the World by Maurice Winter Moe, 23 Where the Grape Vine is Twining Still by Andrew Francis Lockhart, 25 When Inspiration Fails by James Larkin Pearson, 26 To a Worthy Centenarian by J. E. Hoag, 27 I Have Tasted of the Waters by Winifred Virginia Jordan, 28 The Reason by Rheinhart Kleiner, 29 In the Regions of the Damned by Willis Tete Crossman, 40 The Mocking Bird by Anita Roberta Kirksey, 41 Nemesis by Howard P. Lovecraft, 44 The Elusive Muse by J. E. Hoag, 45 The Rise and Fall of an Amateur Newspaper by Geo I. Putnam, 50 A-Gypsying by Edna von der Heide, 51 In the Sweet Long Ago by Arthur H. Goodenough, 52 O Heart of Mine by Harriet L. Trieloff, 53 A War-Born Dream by Eugene B. Kuntz, 54 When der Frost Is On der Turnips by J. Morris Widdows, 55 "Losers Weepers, Finders Keepers" by Jennie M. Kendall, 65 Just Because of Her by Horace Eaton Walker, 66 If Love of Mine by Litta L. Voelchert, 66 A Gypsy Lullaby by Litta L. Voelchert, 67 Life's Story by L. Adelaide Sherman, 68 In Our Town by Will H. Greenfield, 69 The Vacant Chair by John Osman Baldwin, 71 Is Suicide Self-Murder? by Pearl K. Merritt, 77 Timely verse - 5 poems by Lawson Fields, 77 The Triple Alliance by Lawson Fields, 77 A Simple Request by Lawson Fields, 77 A Wager by Lawson Fields, 77 Uncle Sam's Toast by Lawson Fields, 77 The Kaiser by Lawson Fields, 79 Once by Roswell George Mills, 81 To Autumn by Anna Helen Crofts, 82 Two Fathers by Olive G. Owen, 83 Mrs Burke's Bridget by Charles A. A. Parker, 88 Adoration by Winifred Virginia Jordan, 89 The Master Musician by Eugene B. Kuntz, 90 A Song by Harriet L. Trieloff, 91 Our Inhuman Humanity by A. M. Adams, 94 The Chill of Remark by Bramleykite, 95 Two Lovers by Elsie Alice Gidlow, 97 These Two by Essillyn Dale Nichols, 98 A Spirit Christlike by Julia R. Johnson, 99 The King's Release by Will H. Greenfield, 102 Caught by O. Byron Copper, 103 At the Ol' Cider Mill by Willis Edwin Hurd, 105 Blunders and Democracy by Philip B. McDonald, 109 The Thing Has Often Been Done Before by Arthur E. [sic] Goodenough, 111 The Atlantic by John Milton Samples, 112 Life by Flora Stewart Emory, 113 The Beast in the Cave by Howard P. Lovecraft, 121 The Diary of a Fighting Man by Harry M. Konwiser, 126 On the Death of a Centenarian by Jonathan E. Hoag, 127 Lucy Jane Hutchins Frost [by

W. Paul Cook], 131 I Thought I Loved the Country by James Joseph Moloney, 133 Some Facts About the United's First Year by Ira Reely, 136 To Some One, Somewhere by Edna Hyde, 137 From an Empty Attic by W. Paul Cook.

The Vagrant. Eighth Number. July, 1918. Containing A Story by Arthur H. Goodenough and A Poem by Howard P. Lovecraft.

Stapled green printed wraps. 5 x 7 inches. Unpaginated [16 leaves].

[1] title page, [2] Success by Essilyn Dale Nichols, [3]-[12] "Remember Now Thy Creator..." by Arthur H. Goodenough, [13]-[23] The Poe-et's Nightmare: A Fable by Howard P. Lovecraft, [24] On Returning Home by Harriet L. Trieloff, [25]-[27] After the Curtain Falls by J. C. Pryor, [28] A Vagrant Mood by Litta L. Voelchert, [29]-[30] "Knights of the Broken Lance" by Verna McGeoch, [31]-[32] Continuing the United Membership List [by W. Paul Cook].

The Vagrant. The Ninth Number. September, 1919.

Stapled green printed wraps. 5 x 7 inches. 48 pages.

[1]-37 (the pagination jumps from 28 to 33) Twenty Years' Recollections of Amateur Journalism by Arthur Henry Goodenough [Written in 1913], 38-39 On the Road Down to Aurora by Winifred Virginia Jordan, 40-41 The Serious Year by Michael J. McNamara, 42-43 We Need More Ships by Abraham S. De Haan, 44 The Golden Gull by Dora Hepner Moitoret, 45-47 The First Scalp by Harriet L. Trieloff Schelin, 47 Visions by Martha Charlotte Macatee, 48 A Plea by "May Arthur."

The Vagrant. The Tenth Number. October, 1919.

5 x 7 inches, 48 pages.

Note: Goodenough's Recollections *are on pages numbered 37 to 44 but the pages revert to correct numbering thereafter.*

1 Toils of the Tropics by John J. Reid, 5 Memoralia by Samuel Loveman, 6 The City by Ward Phillips, 8 You Women by May Arthur, 9 The Poetry Fer Me by James Larkin Pearson, 10 Heaven Lies Around Us by Wilfrid Kemble, 11 The Mould Shade Speaks by Winifred Virginia Jordan, 12 The Winged Shepherds by Julia R. Johnson, 13 Psychopompos by Howard Phillips Lovecraft, 23 Tea flowers—A

Chinese Play by Roswell George Mills, 29 To Speak Is Not to Pray by Julia R. Johnson, 30 Brugmansia Suaveolens by Anita Roberta Kirksey, [31] Twenty Years' Recollections of Amateur Journalism (Part 2) by Arthur Henry Goodenough, 41 In June by John Osman Baldwin, 42 The Astral Guard by Julia R. Johnson, 43 (Some of our art school teachers) by Pauline Rubin, 45 The Cry of a Longing Heart by Julia R. Johnson, 47 For Youth Is Mine—Rondeau by S. Lilian McMullen, 48 Dans la Rue by S. Lilian McMullen

The Vagrant. The Eleventh Number. November, 1919.

5 x 7 inches, 48 pages.

Note: Goodenough's Recollections *are on pages numbered 44 to 56 but the pages revert to correct numbering thereafter.*

1 The river of the foxes by Agnes Richmond Arnold, 2 The Super Self by John Milton Samples, 3 To a Bluebird by Martha Charlotte Macatee, 4 God's Answer by Julia R. Johnson, 5 Mistress of Overflowing Woes by Eugene B. Kuntz, 6 The Mortal's View by Julia R. Johnson, 7 Thy Laughter-flowing Eyes by Eugene B. Kuntz, 8 Does the Rain Put Out the Stars by Julia R. Johnson, [9] Twenty Years' Recollections of Amateur Journalism (Part 3) by Arthur Henry Goodenough, 23 Dagon by Howard Phillips Lovecraft, 30 The Cloud That Is Silver Lined by Julia R. Johnson, 31 Official Criticism by W. Paul Cook, 36 Maurice W. Moe on Amateur Criticism by Maurice W. Moe, 38 Howard P. Lovecraft's Fiction by W. Paul Cook, 40 Prescience by S. Marion Wheeler, 41 Liking Poetry by Philip B. McDonald, 42 Life Without You by Flora Stewart McGraw, 43 More Painstakking in Amateur Poetry by Pearl K. Merritt, 45 It Is All Over by May Arthur, 46 A Hot Day at the Beach by Ethel M. Fincke, 48 My Man and I by Flora Stewart McGraw

The Vagrant. The Twelfth Issue. December, 1919.

String-tied stiff blue printed wraps. 5 x 7 inches. 16 pages.

1-2 The Voice by Charles L. H. Wagner, 3 Armageddon by Arthur Goodenough, 4-12 The Faun by Samuel Loveman, 13-14 The Nightmare Lake by H. P. Lovecraft, 15-16 My World by Arthur Goodenough

Note: Only 100 copies of this issue were saved, by H. P. Lovecraft, after some of the printed sheets were damaged by water.

The Vagrant. The Thirteenth Number. May, 1920.

5 x 7 inches, 48 pages.

Note: Goodenough's Recollections *are on pages numbered 56 to 73 but the pages revert to correct numbering thereafter.*
[1] Twenty Years' recollections of amateur journalism (Part 4) by Arthur Henry Goodenough, 20 A Letter from P. A. Spain by P. A. Spain, 23 A union of amateur forces by James F. Morton, Jr., 32 "A union of amateur forces" by W. Paul Cook , 36 Vagaries of a "Vagrant" editor by Henry Clapham McGavack, 41 The Statement of Randolph Carter by Howard Phillips Lovecraft

The Vagrant. Number Fourteen. March, 1922.

Stapled gray printed wraps. 5 x 7 inches. 90 pages.

Note: Goodenough's Recollections *are on pages numbered 74 to 91 but the pages revert to correct numbering thereafter.*
[74]-91 Twenty Years' Recollections of Amateur Journalism (Part 5) by Arthur Henry Goodenough, 20-40 A Vermont Pilgrimage by W. Paul Cook, 41-49 Bread o' Shame by Edith Miniter, 50-64 The Tomb by Howard Phillips Lovecraft, 66-68 Olive G. Owen, Idealist by Eben D. Pierce, 69-71 Extract from "Paths of Peace" by Olive G. Owen, 72 To you by Alma Myrtle Greenfield, 73 A Group of Poems by Andrew F. Lockhart, 74 This is My Day by Andrew F. Lockhart, 75 Sympathy by Andrew F. Lockhart, 76 A Memory by Andrew F. Lockhart, 77 Little Rose by Andrew F. Lockhart, 78 L'Envoi, 79 The Tryst by Andrew F. Lockhart, 80 To a Sobbing Child by Andrew F. Lockhart, 81 Foreword by Andrew F. Lockhart, 82 Little Blue Eyes by Andrew F. Lockhart, 83 Now I'm Old by Andrew F. Lockhart, 84 Maids of Broadway and Park Row by Rheinhart Kleiner, 85 Alma Myrtle Greenfield {by W. Paul Cook?], 86 Some Day When You Whisper Yes by Alma Myrtle Greenfield, 87 The Monarch by Alma Myrtle Greenfield, 87 A Valentine by Alma Myrtle Greenfield, [facing page 88, photograph of Alma Myrtle Greenfield] 88 Friendship by Alma Myrtle Greenfield

The Vagrant. "The End" Spring, 1927.

Sewn tan printed wraps. 5 x 7 inches. 312 pages.

Note: Goodenough's Recollections *are on pages numbered 94 to 135 but the pages revert to correct numbering thereafter.*

1 The Illusion by Flora Stewart McGraw, 2 A Young Worshiper by Beth Nichols, 3 White Star of Love by Winifred Virginia Jackson, 4 En Route to the Grave of William Henry Drummond o'er "The C.P.R." by Bramleykite, 5 Amateur Journalism Is Not Futile by Pearl K. Merritt, 9 The Lady of the Yule by Alma Myrtle Greenfield, 10 Ballad of :- the God of Tin by Lilian Middleton, 11 Dream Winds by Ella Z. Harris, 12 Sweetheart by Will H. Greenfield, 13 Memories of Boyhood by O. Byron Copper, 14 Roses by Roswell George Mills, 15 Soldier Boy by Will H. Greenfield, 16 Memory by James J. Moloney, [17] Further Recollections of Amateur Journalism (Includes "To Mr. Arthur Goodenough", poem by H. P. Lovecraft) by Arthur Henry Goodenough, 60 A Garden by H. P. Lovecraft, 61-64 Nathicana by Albert Frederick Willie, 65 United Amateur Press Association,: Philadelphia, 1897 by W. Paul Cook, 102 A Woman's Complaining by Clara L. Bell, 103-04 The Face in the Rock by Clara L. Bell, 105-07 A Kitchen Quarrel by Clara L. Bell, 108-10 A Thanksgiving Episode by Clara L. Bell, 111-13 Naming the Baby by Clara L. Bell, 114-25 My First Sunday in Church by Clara L. Bell, 126 The Evening Bell by Clara L. Bell, 127-34 Old Joe Piper by Clara L. Bell, 135-36 The Crossing Tender by Clara L. Bell, 137-39 At Seventeen by Ella Z. Harris, 140-41 To a Summer Cloud by Ira A. Cole, 142-50 The Divine Selfishness by Jennie Kendall Plaisier, 151-52 The Emerald Rainbow by Wilfrid Kemble, 153 The Nightingale by Willfrid Kemble, 154-55 The Passing of Tom, Dick and Harry by Michael J. McNamara, 156 A Newer World by Perrin Holmes Lowrey, 157-58 Dawn Patrol by James Hull Goss, 159 On the Heights by Esther T. Dalton, 160-64 The Casual Glance by J. C. Pryor, 165 Phoebus to Narcissus by Elsie A. Gidlow, 166 The Little Room by Anne Vyne Tillery, 167 Light the Old Pipe by Rheinhart Kleiner, 168 Three Balls of Gold by Joseph Thalheimer, Jr., 169-79 True Tales of a Penal Settlement by Eric W. McLean, 180 What You Can Do, Little Girl by Essillyn Dale Nichols, [181] A Few Pages of Loneliness by "May Arthur," 182 Being My Husband by May Arthur, 182 After Reading Some Old Love Letters by May Arthur, 183 A Tale by May Arthur, 183 Another "If" by May Arthur, 184 But One by May Arthur, 184 You, Dear! by May Arthur, 185 Longing by May Arthur, 186 O, Love! by May Arthur, 186 My Husband's Rival by May Arthur, 187 Dear by May Arthur, 188-95 The Green Meadow by Elizabeth Neville Berkeley & Lewis Theobald, Jr. [H. P. Lovecraft], 196 My Old Doll by Betty Jane Kendall, 197-98 The Foch Peace Parade by Jennie K. Plaisier, 198-200

Spring by Betty Jane Kendall, 201 Patriotic Verse or Prose by Pearl K. Merritt, 202-03 The Standard Christmas Story by Pearl K. Merritt, 204-05 My Treasures by Pearl K. Merritt, 206-07 A Mess in France by Pearl K. Merritt, 208-09 You Never Can Tell by Pearl K. Merritt, 210 Courage Also by Annie Pearce, 211 I Have Not Lost You by Ella Z. Harris, 212 "Unsuitable" by Ella Z. Harris, 213 Love's Influence by Ella Z. Harris, 214-16 "Human Stuff" by Pauline Rubin, 217 Fight on by Margaret Trafford, 217 A Kiss by Margaret Trafford, 218-34 Change by Vrest Teachout Orton, 235 The River and the Sea by James Larkin Pearson, 236 The Lives of Men by James Larkin Pearson, 237-38 The Grave-Tree by James Larkin Pearson, 239-53 At the Singing of the Sands by Willis Edwin Hurd, 254-55 M. O. H. by George Whitefield D'Vys, 256 Tomorrow by George Whitefield D'Vys, 257-58 Boyhood Memories by George Whitefield D'Vys, 259 The Poet's Crown by George Whitefield D'Vys, 260-69 In Behalf of Her neighbours by Essillyn Dale Nichols, 270 To One Left by Vrest Teachout Orton, 271-72 To One Gone by Vrest Teachout Orton, 273-74 To One at Delhi by Vrest Teachout Orton, 275-78 Copper Rivets by O. Byron Copper, 279 A Wind Waif by Winifred Virginia Jackson, 280 Smiles by Winifred Virginia Jackson, 281 O Heart of Me by Winifred Virginia Jackson, 281 The Rose of Friendship by Winifred Virginia Jackson, 281 But There is Love by Winifred Virginia Jackson, 282-83 When Deeper Moods Cry Out by Eugene B. Kuntz, 284 Morning in the Hills by Eugene B. Kuntz, 285 The Life I Want by Eugene B. Kuntz, 286 Freedom by Eugene B. Kuntz, 287-98 The Servant of the Gods by H. Warner Munn, 299-300 When the Moon and the West Wind Meet by S. Lilian McMullen, 301 Apple Blossom Time in Old New Hampshire by Herbert Durrell Smart, 302 In Dreamland by Herbert Durrell Smart, 303 Maybe Golden Gates Won't Open, 'Less We Find a Golden Key by Reba J. Bishop, 304 Story-tell Time by Reba J. Bishop, 305 The Unmothered Stitches by Reba J. Bishop, 306 God So Intends by Reba J. Bishop, 307 Lullaby by Mary Carver Williams, 308 Mother Sea by Ernest L. McKeag, 309 Moonlight on the Sea by Ernest L. McKeag, 310 The Slacker by William J. Clemence, 311 The End by W. Paul Cook. 312 "The End"

Year Book, 1906. United Amateur Press Association of America. Published for the Association by the Year Book Committee. W. Paul Cook, Chairman; Henry G. Wehking; Hal C. Bixby. Edited by W. Paul Cook.

String-tied purple printed wraps. 5 x 7 inches. 44 pages.

[1] title page, [2] Official Board, 1906-07, photograph of Wm. H. Greenfield, 3-9 Constitution and By-Laws, 9-14 Poem Laureate: The Angel of the Snow by Arthur H. Goodenough, 14-16 Honorable Mention: Poetry Laureate: Kansas by Ada Parkhurst, 16-[19] Story Laureate: "She Came Out of Missouri" by M. Almedia Thomas-Bretholl, [20] Roster of Conventions, Presidents, Secretaries, and Official Editors, photograph of Samuel DeHaan, 21-[26] Honorable Mention: Story Laureate: A Lost Dollar by Earle A. Howell, 27-[32] Essay Laureate: "Time and Chance": A Review by Flora Stewart Emory, [33] Laureate Record, 34-[38] Honorable Mention: Essay Laureate: The Raven by Louis M. Starring, [39] List of Official Organs, 40 Editorial Laureate: From "The East" by Wm. H. Moscow, 41-[44] Honorable Mention: Editorial Laureate: In Reply to Mr. Burchmore by Flora Stewart Emory.

Year Book, 1913. United Amateur Press Association of America. Published for the Association by the Year Book Committee. W. Paul Cook, Chairman; Arthur H. Goodenough

Stapled gray printed wraps. 5 x 7 inches. 36 pages.

[1] title page, [2] Official Board 1913-1914, photo of Ernest H. Morris, 3-9 Constitution and By-Laws, [10] Laureate Record, photo of Dwight S. Anderson, 11 Laureate Judges, 1913, 12 Poetry Laureate: Fight On by Olive G. Owen, 13 Honorable Mention: A Warning by Leston M. Ayres, 14-15 Story Laureate: Mrs. Murphy's Christmas by Roy E. Hanson, 16-20 Honorable Mention: Parson Jim's Gal by Jesse L. Robertson (with photo of Geo. O. Billheimer, photo of Ira Reely, 21-24 Essay Laureate: Government By the Mob by James F. Morton, Jr., photos of Samuel DeHayn and Thomas M. McKee, 25 Honorable Mention: Twilight by Edith Crawford Haight, 26-27 Editorial Laureate: From "Hoisington's" by Chester O. Hoisington, 28-31 Honorable Mention: From "The Chinook Wind" by George F. Wright, photo of William R. Murphy, 32-35 History of the 1912-'13, 36 A Note On the Year Book by W. Paul Cook

Year Book of The United Amateur Press Association of America, Issued by the Association Officially, and Containing the Laureate Winning Articles and Historian's Report for the Year Ending July, 1914, with Portraits and Other Historical Matter of Interest. Published for the Association by the

Committee. W. Paul Cook, Chairman; Florence Norcross; Sydney S. Whipple

Stapled red printed wraps. 5 x 7 inches. Unpaginated [42 leaves] [1] title page, [2] Official Board 1914-1915, [3]-[10]Constitution and By-Laws, [11] photo of Arthur H. Goodenough, [12] blank, [13] Laureate Judeges, 1914, [14] Laureate Record, [15] photo of O. Byron Copper, [16] blank, [17] Poetry Laureate: Autumn by William J. Clemence, [18] Honorable Mention: Let's Cut Him Open and See by James Larkin Pearson, [19]-[20] Story Laureate: A Son of the Soil (A Little Sketch in Black and White) by William Roy Christian, [21] photo from Eighteenth Convention, Norwich, Conn., 1914, [22] blank, [23]-[26] Honorable Mention: The Sky Actor by James Edward Morrow, [27]-[28] Additional Mention: Six Dollars Per (and a nice lunch) by Pearl K. Merritt, [29] photo of Flora Stewart Emory, [30] blank, [31]-[33] Essay Laureate: Principles of Democratic Government by Henry Cremer, [34]-[35] Honorable Mention: The Montessori System by Mary Junghany, [36]-[38] Additional Mention: School Government by Henry Cremer, [39] photo of Seventeenth Convention, Bellingham, Wash., 1913, [40] blank, [41]-[43] Editorial Laureate: From the "Baylor Literary" by W. Roy Christian, [44]-[45] Honorable Mention: Which Will You Be? by Edna G.Thorne, [46]-[47] Additional Mention: As the Hours Fly On by Ernest H. Morris, [48]-[52] Historian's Report (by Florence Norcross) with photos of Louis J. Cohen, Samuel DeHaan & Morris J. Cohen and a photo of Miss Florence Norcross, [53] photo of Sixteenth Convention, La Grande, Ore., 1912, [54] blank, [55] Poet Laureate Judges, [56] List of Laureate Poems, [57] photo of Dwight S. Anderson, [58] blank, [59] First Laureate Poem,U.A.P.A., 1899: The Bachelor's Shrine by Dwight S. Anderson, [60] Honorary Mention, First Laureate Competition, 1899: Immortality by William H. Greenfield, [61]-[63] Poetry Laureate, 1900: The Poem of the Day by O. Byron Copper, [64]-[65] Honorary Mention, Poetry Laureate, 1900: Wait and Hope by Wm. H. Greenfield, [66] Poetry Laureate, 1901: Summer and Winter by Wm. R. Murphy, [67]-[68] Honorary Mention, 1901: The Christmas Gift by John O. Baldwin, [69] photo of Fifteenth Convention, Bridgeport, Conn., 1911, [70] blank, [71] List of Official Organs, [72] Roster of Conventions, Presidents, Secretaries, and Official Editors, [73]-[84] Roster of Officers of the United Amateur Press Association of America, 1895-1914

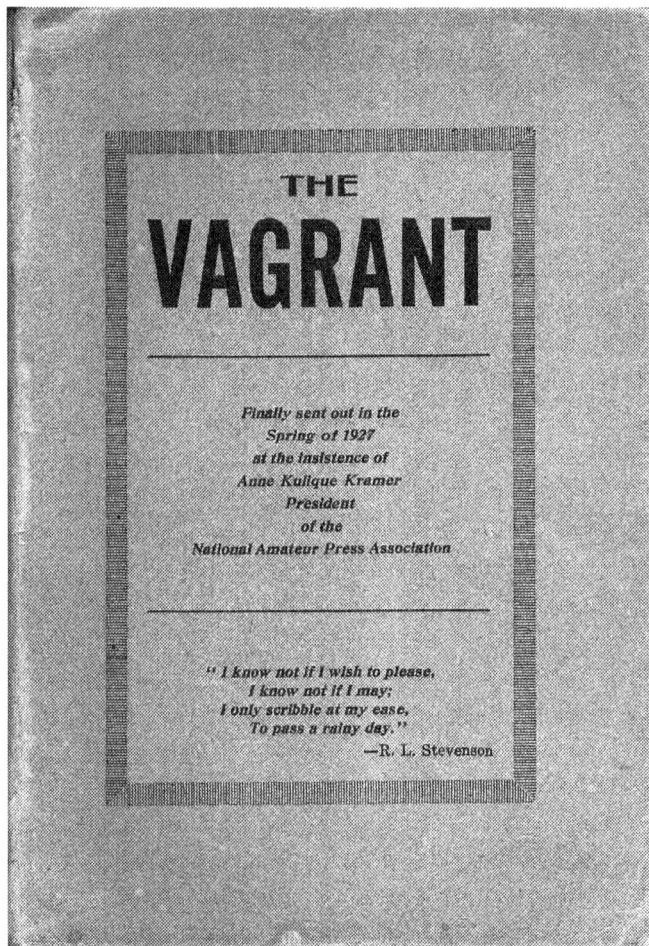

THE FINAL ISSUE OF *The Vagrant*.

BY W. PAUL COOK

John DeMorgan

AUTHOR AND REFORMER

It may safely be termed a most unusual, if not a unique thing, for a man to become famous in two countries in almost different lines. Yet such is the case with John DeMorgan, who is known by name and reputation to every amateur journalist in the country, from his having retained a membership in the United and National Amateur Press Associations for a number of years, and from his carrying on a large and kindly correspondence with amateurs. He is one of that number, and the active of that number, of men who have made a professional success, but who see in amateur journalism a true training school for professional work, and who are doing their best to aid and encourage us. But very few, even his friends by correspondence and his friends through books, appreciate what a privilege it is for us to receive his encouragement.

Mr. DeMorgan has been identified with amateur and professional journalism since he was eight years old. Although born in Ireland in 1848, he spend most of his early life in England, in which country he received his education in private schools and a junior college at Cambridge. For many years he was engaged in active public life, his work dealing mostly with social and political reform. He has always been an earnest advocate of Home Rule for Ireland and was one of the pioneers of the Irish Land Movement. This work led him to a close study, not only of the history of England but also of other countries, and we find in this where he gained that intimate knowledge of history, especially political or governmental history, which he works with such skill into his books for boys.

He lectured extensively on reform work, and one of his lectures, "How England Obtained India," was printed in pamphlet form, passed through twelve large editions in a few months, and is still in demand. He gained a wide knowledge of human life and nature in its varied phases through his experience in early life as a police court reporter, and he has published many amusing reminiscences in *The Green Bag*, a high class legal magazine published in Boston. He studied law but never applied for admission to the Bar.

Mr. DeMorgan also engaged in professional editorial work, editing a weekly paper and a monthly magazine, and making these organs important ones in their special subjects. He published two books, *The Secret History of the Court of England*, and a series of short biographies of the "Men of the Cromwellian Commonwealth," which were highly praised by the critics, and have passed through several large editions.

In his career in England and Ireland he became intimately acquainted with men whose names loom large on the pages of nineteenth century history, such as W. E. Gladstone, Cardinal Manning, Hon. Auberan Herbert, Lord Roseberry, Cardinal Newman and his brother, Prof. Francis, and scores of others.

Mr. DeMorgan was an earnest advocate of a Republican form of government, and his firm belief in the principles of the Declaration of Independence made him leave Great Britain and become a citizen of the land whose government was based on the Rights of Man. He has found (to quote one of his recent utterances, as reported) that "the real does not come up to the ideal, and that there is a danger of the principles enunciated by the Fathers of the Republic being forgotten, and instead of equal rights for all, class distinctions of the worst and basest kind are gradually making headway. The greed of commercialism, the lust for power, the indifference of the better educated classes on political questions constitute a great danger to the permanency of the Republic." But he hopes the good sense and inherent love of justice of our people will yet rescue the country before it is too late, and "bring back a recognition of those principles which made the republic the greatest, grandest, and freest on earth."

Mr. DeMorgan came the United States in 1880, and has made a new and different name for himself here. In England he was most widely known as a political writer and reform agitator. In this country he is *most* famous as a writer of stories for boys. Today he is an American in spirit and purpose and patriotism.

Soon after his arrival, in 1881, he founded and edited *House and Home*, a family paper which quickly obtained large circulation. In this paper he advocated the limitation of inheritance and many other advanced principles.

After selling out his interest in *House and Home* he was asked by George Munro to write a series of labor stories for the *Fireside Companion*. The stories were written and proved highly successful.

In 1886 Norman L. Munro arranged with him for some stories for the *Family Story Paper*, and later when *Golden Hours* was started Mr. Munro telegraphed from Florida to Mr. DeMorgan asking him to write the opening story, "A Brave Young Soldier," which was declared to be the most successful of any boys' story written up to that time. For eleven years he wrote for *Golden Hours*, and was an active member of the Golden Hours Club in its years of popularity, which shows where his interest in the enlarged Golden Hours Club (amateur journalism) originated.

Using his extensive knowledge of history as a background, after the publication of "A Brave Young Soldier," Mr. DeMorgan produced a long series of books designed for young people, having the faculty and the art to use history merely as a background or an adjunct to his story, and never allowing the dry facts—they are "dry facts," when used in a story—to usurp for a moment his story or distract or break the interest of his readers. He wrote over sixty serial stories for *Golden Hours, the Family Story Paper, New York Weekly, Fireside Companion, Saturday Night, American Fireside, Chicago Ledger,* and other papers of the same class. Many of these serials were afterward published in book form and had large sales. Most of Mr. Munro's copyrights of these works have been bought by Street & Smith, who are drawing upon them largely for their various "libraries" of publications.

When Mr. DeMorgan was writing stories of the Civil War he went to Richmond, Va., and visited all the great battlefields in that vicinity, becoming acquainted with many of the heroes, both Union and Confederate, who took part in that momentous struggle. He was thus able to give a true local color to his work, as well as impartially judge the motives of those who fought on either side, and to gain intimate anecdotes and incidents. His war stories have as a consequence been praised by Confederates and Unionists alike.

Mr. DeMorgan has also been a leading and welcome contributor to the best magazines throughout the country, and his utterances always command attention, coming as they do from *one who knows* whereof he speaks before he breaks his silence.

Mr. DeMorgan was in the foremost of the Politico-Economic campaign a few years back in New York, in which Henry George and his Single Tax theory were most "in the public eye." In this campaign Mr. DeMorgan was associated with Henry George, Father McGlynn,

Rev. Dr. Huntington and others. He has also lectured throughout the New England states upon those subjects of which he is an authority—Political Reform, Irish Home Rule, and kindred topics. He has been an earnest advocate of Trade Unionism, and numbers among his friends very many of the labor leaders on both sides of the Atlantic, including John Burns and Samuel Gompers.

At the time when pirated editions of H. Rider Haggard's books were flooding the country, before a rigid international copyright regulation, and when even the English copyright had expired, Mr. Haggard was at the zenith of his popularity in the United States and the names of his most widely read books were on everybody's lips. At this juncture Mr. Norman L. Munro asked Mr. DeMorgan to write a series of books which should be sequels to those of the English author. The result was the publication of *He, It, Bess, King Solomon's Treasures*, and *King Solomon's Wives*. So great was the success of these stories, that a rival publisher used the titles and burlesqued the stories, publishing a series under the name "Hyder Ragged," a deliberate insult to Mr. Haggard and Mr. DeMorgan, which we are glad to say was a disastrous financial failure, but not until Haggard and DeMorgan and Mr. Penny-a-Liner were so mixed in the public mind that people think they have read Haggard when they haven't, and people think they have read DeMorgan when they have only read Penny-a-Liner, and have gained false impressions of the real men thereby.

⌇

Mr. DeMorgan wrote the official voluminous *History of the First Light Battery, Connecticut Volunteers, 1861–1900*, which was published in two volumes, quarto, of five hundred pages each, and was the first history of a famous regiment ever written from the standpoint of a private soldier. In recognition of this work Mr. DeMorgan was elected an honorary member of the First Light Battery Veteran Association.

Two important works are shortly to be published from his pen, *The Literary Lives of the Presidents from Washington to Roosevelt*, being the lives of the presidents from a literary viewpoint, and *Irish Genius in the Nineteenth Century*, an exhaustive biography of Irishmen who distinguished themselves in the Army and Navy, in Law, Religion, and Literature, and in Science and Art during the century just passed.

Altogether Mr. DeMorgan's work counts up. He has written over a hundred serials and at least one thousand articles for magazines, besides innumerable short stories and a voluminous quantity of other work.

In the last two years Mr. DeMorgan's literary work has been confined to his leisure time in the evenings, for he holds the responsible position of Receiver of Taxes for the Borough of Richmond, in New York City. He handles nearly a million dollars a year, so the responsibility of his office may be imagined. With a conscientiousness all too rare in a New York official, he abstains from doing any of his own work during office hours, so it may be seen how little time he has. He has suffered for two years from an ailment which makes it impossible for him to walk or stand for more than a few moments at a time, so that when his official duties are discharged, in spite of his love of his literary work, it is often impossible for him to do a stroke of the pen for a week at a time. All admirers of Mr. DeMorgan, as well as of some other literary workers, often wish literary men would not feel obliged to accept a governmental position, no matter how much the man himself may think he needs it. Writers do not build for themselves alone, but for many others.

How Mr. DeMorgan is regarded by those who come in intimate personal contact with him may be inferred from the fact that at Christmas his subordinates in the Tax Receiver's office presented him with a handsome library edition of Balzac's works in sixteen double volumes.

Mr. DeMorgan is married and has one daughter.

Following is a list of Mr. DeMorgan's books of which the copyright is now controlled by Messrs. Street & Smith, and which are now in print.

BY JOHN DEMORGAN

Yankee Grit
Lucky Thirteen
Winning His Way
Robert Brendon, the Bell Boy
Louis Stanhope, Hero
A Daring Fire Laddie
Figures and Faith
In Unknown Worlds
Lost in the Ice

Always on Duty
A Bee-Line to Fortune
Napoleon's Double
Into the Jaws of Death
The Cruise of the Lively Bee
Fooling the Enemy
Marion and His Men
On to Quebec
Fighting Hal
The Hero of Ticonderoga
The Young Guardsman
The First Shot for Liberty
The Young Ambassador
Paul Revere and the Boys of Liberty

BY "FRANK SHERIDAN"

Walter Blackshaw
Merle Merton
In the Woods
The Boy Balloonists
The Knowlhurst Mystery
Nuggets and Nerve
Life-Line Larry
Bert Fairfax
Lionel's Pluck
Through Flame to Fame
Vernon Craig
Jack, the Pride of the Nine
From Midshipman to Commodore
The Cruise of the "Essex"
Dashing Paul Jones

BY "COMMANDER POST"

The League of Five

We have found it impossible to get a complete list of even those books of Mr. DeMorgan's which are now in print, to say nothing of attempting to gather a complete list of all his works. We will, however, try, try again, and if our efforts are finally crowned with success the list will be published as soon as we get it.

The copyright for Mr. DeMorgan's Haggard books was sold by Munro to the American Book Co., which failed; the books were scattered everywhere, and are very scarce.

First published in *Monadnock Monthly* Vol. 2, No. 4 (April 1905): [1]-5.

It should be noted that DeMorgan's works featuring characters created by H. Rider Haggard were intended as "sequels" rather than parodies. They apparently were not written as parodies. However, they have come to be regarded as such, in error, as reflected in their treatment in reference works like Thomas D. Clareson's *Science Fiction in America, 1870s–1930s* (Greenwood, 1984). One of DeMorgan's works, *He*, was also reprinted in an anthology of parodies titled *They: Three Parodies of H. Rider Haggard's She* (Arno Press, 1978) edited by R. Reginald and Douglas Menville.

By and About Ourselves

A Meeting at the Dartmouth Press

One pleasant day in October, 1905, a young man appeared at the general delivery window of the Hanover [New Hampshire] postoffice and inquired of the clerk, "Isn't a paper called 'The Monadnock Monthly' mailed from here?" Now it may be said here that we are not greatly in the favor of the postoffice clerks. They consider *The Monadnock* a nuisance. We persist in sending over–large bundles of papers at closing time at night, instead of early in the morning as they would like. Also there are other things. So when the young man in question sprung his query, the clerk frowned.

"Yes," growled he, "a fellow named Cook. You can find him in the Dartmouth Press building, across the street."

Looking across the street, the young man saw a large and dingy sign: "The Dartmouth Press." Having just come from a lengthened stay in Chicago, the young man succeeded in getting across the street without becoming a victim to the cable-cars or heavy wagons. Shortly he appeared in the business office of the Dartmouth Press.

"Does a fellow named Cook work here?" he inquired of a stout man with a broad expanse of forehead where hair once was, who was seated at the first desk with a pen behind each ear and a pencil in his mouth, making out a "job-ticket" with still another pen. "Yes, sir," answered the stout individual cheerily, after he had removed the pencil from his mouth and the pens from his ears; "you will find him in the pressroom. Right through that door." The young man went "right through that door" and found himself in a very small room containing another desk and a young lady seated at it. "Can you tell me where I will find Cook?" inquired the young man, sweetly. "Yes, sir," answer the young lady in the same glucose tone, "you will find him in the pressroom. Right through that door." The young lady went on marking "wf." and "tr."[1] and all the rest of it on long galley proofs, and the young man continued "right through that door." He found himself in a large room containing eight or ten girls and three men. As he entered he caught the tail-end of a conversation which had been going on among the "girls." "How many dances did you give him, Sue?" came from one corner. "Eight," was the prompt reply from another. Then the visitor was seen and murmurs of admiration rippled over the room, succeeded only by the sound of the type being languidly dropped in the sticks in the intervals between anything but languid movement of jaws, denoting gum. The visitor addressed himself to a man who was making up a newspaper form. "Can you tell me where I will find Mr. Cook?" "Yes, sir, you'll find him in the pressroom. Right through that door." The visitor passed "right through that door" and found himself in another room all alone with a Simplex type-setting machine and two girls, one of whom was vainly trying to punch out type faster than the other could justify it. No gum or dances here. "Can you tell me where I will find Mr. Cook?" asked the young man. "Yes, sir," was the reply, "you'll find him in the pressroom. Right through that door." The young passed "right through that door" and found himself in what was evidently the finishing room. Here the six girls, attempting to diagnose a recent elopement case and fold six thousand magazines at the same time. "Can you tell me," asked the intruder, despairingly, "where I will find Mr. Cook?" Every nose went into the air. (It beats the Dutch how those finishing room girls do admire me.) "Oh, yes, Mr. *Cook*," was the haughty reply. "In the pressroom. Right through that door." With a sigh our hero went "right through that door" and found himself—in the pressroom. Two young men were more or less busily feeding two job presses, while two rusty cylinders were standing idle. Approaching the one whom he considered the most A. J. looking the visitor inquired, "Is this Mr. Cook?" "No, sir," was the reply, "Mr. Cook just went into the stockroom. Right through that door." Now it happened upon the day in question that the boy in charge of the devil department[2] was indisposed because of an injudicious quantity of an injudicious mixture of G. O. Blake and Anheuser–Busch which he had partaken of the night before. Therefore we were chief cook and bottle-washer for the time being. A belt had broken and we were getting another from the top shelf, standing on a shelf four or five feet from the floor to reach it. A door opened and shut, and we glanced down. There was a young man of exceeding good inches and exceeding pleasant smile (in spite of his troubles) who inquired, "Is this Mr. Cook?" "Yes, sir," said we promptly. "Well, then," said he, "come down here and shake hands with a fellow amateur. My name is Moffatt, from St. Joe." "What!" shrieked we, jumping down and reaching up and shaking hands, "Elbert Moffatt?" "The same," said he. Now his name had been familiar to us since 1901, when both *The Clarus* and *The Monadnock* were given birth, and he was the first real, live, do-or-die amateur journalist we had ever met personally. If he is a specimen, A. J. is a great institution. Moffatt is a good fellow. Luck to him.

Do you ever dream?

Amateur friends, do you ever dream? Do you ever dream of what to you would be the supremist bliss? Do you ever dream of "what might have been"? Have you one idea which continually recurs to you of what above all things you would like to do? I am sure you have; more, I know you have. They tell us that our dreams are those ideals that will never be realized. When friends ask you about your dreams—your day dreams—do you reply directly and frankly? We are afraid not. And you cannot be blamed. I remember (it seems ages ago) that I used to dream of being a world-renowned author. I used to dream of a splendid home to which came pilgrims from all over the world to see the master. But this dream faded in time. Then I dreamed of being the editor of a great magazine, such as the *Century*, but greater than the *Century*. But this dream faded. Then I left home and entered into the hustling, bustling, busy, aggressive world. Here I learned the joys of boarding-houses and hotels. Here I learned what it meant to actually "work for a living." Here I learned the value of time—time to write, time to think, time to study, time to enjoy your own work in your own way. It was when, after working fourteen hours for my employer, I sought my rooms physically exhausted, that I longed for some of my time for myself to ease my still active brain by writing its fancies. But I must sleep, to be ready for the grind at the labor machine on the morrow. It was at this time that my high ambitions vanished, crushed out by toil. It was at this time that my present dream came to me. It is not a high dream. But it is my dream. I dream now of going back home, going back to the old folks. I dream of a cozy little room for a den. I dream of my desk cleared and myself at it whenever the mood strikes me. I dream of gathering all my books around me where I can continually see them—my Dickens, my Scott, my Dumas, my Shakespeare, my Dante, my Milton, my Whitman, my Poe, my Cervantes, and all the rest of them from Homer to my beloved Kipling. I dream of another little room with a small but complete printing outfit. Here much of my time would be spent upon my own amateur work; and I dream of my mother, my father, and my sister coming in frequently and chatting with me. Then I dream of the result of my labors at my desk finding its way into a few magazines, and of a small reputation in a literary way. But this is all a dream, and someone has said dreams never come true! Where is the man who said such a thing? Show him to me!

What isn't an American?

Someone has asked, "What is an American?" meaning by the question the inhabitant of the United States. We would throw the question back at this "someone" and inquire "What isn't an American?" If you came down closely to the question of nationality other than "American" we would be indeed "a man without a country"—so that we are an "American." To show just what the typical American is, and also to aid those biographers and historians who will be writing the history of this age, we will give briefly what we know of our blood. Our mother is full-blooded French, born in France. Our father's father is full-blooded Scotch, born in Scotland—the family name is McCook. Our father's mother's mother was full-blooded English, born in England. Our father's mother's father's father was full-blooded German, born in Germany. Our father's mother's father's mother's father was full-blooded Dutch. Our father's mother's father's mother's mother was a full-blooded Iriquois. Our father's mother's father's mother's father's mother's father's mother's—oh, hang it all, where are we anyway! But never mind, we've gone far enough. There's an American for you.

1. wf. and tr. are proofreader's marks for "wrong font" and "transpose."
2. Printer's devils are the apprentices in a printing plant.

Excerpts from *Monadnock* No. 7 (May 1913): 66–76. Subheadings provided by the editor.

Inconsequentialities

Upon the issuance of each number of the *Monadnock* we have been in receipt of letters couched about as follows:—"We other amateurs envy you the leisure and the means to issue such a paper! How quickly would many more of us print such papers if we but had the money! You are a lucky boy!" When we receive such a letter as this it causes us to feel a mixture of amusement and irritation. Since the issuance of the last number, these comments have been coming so frequently that perhaps it is due to ourself to set down the facts in the matter. We are not rich. We haven't even a little money. We are an ordinary, every-day printer working for an ordinary printer's wages—which are not high. These wages are all the income we have. Amateur Journalism is the only relaxation we have from the daily, weekly, monthly, yearly grind. Neither, because of the fact that we are a printer, do we get our paper printed any cheaper than an outsider. In fact, we pay more—for we spend long hours of our own time on our work and then find we are charged as much as an outside customer would be. We remember how once upon a time an employer of his own free will offered us the use of his lights and material to do our work on our own time (and we didn't bankrupt him either), but, (alas!) "them halcyon days" are no more. This work is most often done on our own time because we wish it done in a certain manner, and to do it yourself, John, is the only way to assure such manner. There are dozens of amateurs financially better off than we. Most of them never consider, however, making some small personal sacrifices to issue a paper. They cannot understand the point of view of one who does. To issue the May, 1913, number of the *Monadnock*, one of the things we did was to wear one suit of clothes a whole year and go all winter without an overcoat—and in New England, too. We also find here a record that to issue the July, 1905, number, we refused a four weeks' vacation. And then to have these people envying us, and wishing they had our money, and blaming us for not publishing more! It makes us somewhat impatient with some amateurs, sometimes.

Excerpt from an editorial in the *Vagrant* No. 2 (March 1916): [10]–[11].

First Impressions

If all those who contribute to this Experience Meeting[1] tell the truth (and of course they will!), it should create a sensation. Aeons ago I was compelled to attend some experience meetings. Probably in no other place have I heard so much prevarication, verging from plain lying to self-deceit. In numerous cases self-hypnosis was evident; but in others—

It has been a great many years since I allowed myself to discuss religion, and I do not intend to discuss it here. For a number of years I abandoned my steady diet of avowed fiction, and read largely upon the different religious beliefs of the world. I finally returned to the kind of fiction which you are not supposed to believe, being weary of appeals to superstition and of having my intelligence insulted by being expected to believe things which reason rejected. All this, however, is beside the point. I shall try to set down only first impressions—and these were, after all, but the natural first stages of a continuous growth along the same lines.

I have always been profoundly grateful for the fact that my parents possessed a certain independence of thought which set them apart, in a way, and was a cause of whispers and even open condemnation from the rest of the family and community of decidely hard-shell beliefs and gloomy aspect. I was not taken, a squawking infant (I am sure I should have squawked), and "baptized in the Kingdom of Heaven." My parents fully believed all the tenets of their faith, but they also believed in self-determination, and allowed me the opportunity to choose for myself whether I should go through the ceremony when I came to an age of understanding. I suppose that if I had died during infancy the whole family and acquaintances knew exactly where I would go!

My first recollection is of constant church-going and incessant reading of the Bible. First there was prayers in the morning, for which I was dragged out of bed at unearthly hours. Then there were graces before you were able to enjoy a meal—and when we had company who were asked to say grace, you had no appetite left for food after the company had shown what they could do along those lines. Then every evening the family must be assembled before bed time and due thanks given that we poor worms had been permitted to live all day. If one member was sick, the whole family gathered in the sick-room.

As to church-going, it was a constant round of dissipation. After prayers Sunday morning we managed to grab a bite to eat before going to church at 9:45. After church came Sunday School. Then home in time for the poor wife and mother to scratch like the dickens to feed the crowd for there was always company. Once, I remember, a female guest offered aid in preparing "dinner." It was a great shock. In the afternoon, at 3:30 there was a meeting of one kind or another. Then at 7:30 was evening service, containing a little less sermon and a trifle more lively music than in the morning. With Old Hundred, A Charge To Keep I Have, All Is Dying, Hearts Are Breaking, A Fountain Filled With Blood (my favorite—a most intriguing title), How Shall Fallen Men, With Trembling I Confess (though what I was confessing and why trembling I couldn't understand), And Are We Yet Alive (a most pertinent question at this juncture), Must I Be To Judgement Brought, As Pants the Hart, Condescending Love (a combination of words which always made me shiver), Hark, From The Tombs A Doleful Sound, and a dozen or so other hymns, we used to go home in a frame of mind gloomy enough to suit the most ardent Calvinist. Strange to say, it was after this period that I became fond of several religious poems, Abide With Me, Lead Kindly Light, and others--a fondness I cherish to this day. Well, Tuesday evening came a Young People's Meeting, at some home. Wednesday evening was a Neighborhood Prayer Meeting, at some home; Thursday evening the regular Prayer Meeting at the church. Friday evening there was a meeting for Bible study, in which the minister frequently got himself in wrong and was out-argued when he attempted to lighten the gloomy interpretation of various passages. In those days a minister was given a hard row to hoe if he was at all liberal in dealing with other beliefs than ours.

It was a mystery to me why so great stress was laid on the Bible in preference to various other books in the house. There was, of course, *Pilgrim's Progress* and Fox's *Martyrs*. (If I had a child the latter would be the first book put into his hands.) Everybody ought to have those two books. But we had some books of which the neighbors did not approve. There was *Robinson Crusoe*; and there was Shakespeare in a most unwieldly volume containing all his works—even the sonnets;

there were several collections of poetry; and there was Wordsworth, Gray, Byron (incomplete!). In fact we had a fair library of the classics in English. My reading was unrestricted, but disappointment was painfully evident when I habitually chose something other than the Bible for light reading. I have since come to appreciate the Bible as a stupendous compilation; as a contribution to the literature of the world it has its place on my shelves with other great works.; but at that time I was given too steady a diet of it to appreciate its beauties. It is laughable now to recall how, as a matter of duty, we solemnly waded through long genealogies, chapters of unpronounceable names, for the salvation of our souls. Doing penance because Adam and Eve ate the apple!

Playing-cards were regarded as an invention of the Devil for the subjugation and capture of men's souls. It was going pretty far when "Authors" was introduced as an educational game. (I am constrainted to remark here, that I afterwards acquired more education in a few stiff games of American Draw than I ever absorbed from "Authors.") When we moved to a rather broader community and word went back to our former friends that I had been allowed to learn Whist, I fear a shiver went through them.

Dancing could be spoken of only in whispers, and the immoral waltz, participated in by abandoned men and loose women, was quite unmentionable. It was hugging set to music, and there were those who wanted to do their hugging, all right, but in dark corners without music. It would be a pleasure to walk some of those old-timers out on a dance floor and give them a view of the "Shimmy"!

It was impossible for me to understand the scheme of things as pictured to me. Here was a world densely populated with living beings, animal and vegetable. The mighty, omnipotent power which had created this world out of nothing had likewise created other worlds, greater worlds, worlds without end. All this was told me to impress upon my imagination the fearful power held by the Creator. Yet from all these worlds without number, this small atom of a sphere upon which we dwelt had been chosen for the special care of this omnipotent being. But of all the thousands of complicated forms of life upon this globe, a certain division, called the human race, had been chosen for yet more particular care. When, by natural processes, all other forms of life died, they were dead, and that was all there was to it. But for the disposition of a certain emanation from human bodies at death, two places had been provided. One was a place of continual peace and delight, called Heaven. The other was a place of endless torment, called Hell. Out of the entire human race, a small number of persons had miraculously been given certain directions how to get to Heaven. We were, of course, among his select number. We were told to pray for the heathen (who were all those who did not believe exactly as we did), but were given to understand that their case was quite hopeless.

Something told me that the situation as pictured to me was false. Certainly my sense of justice revolted. It was in this frame of mind that I came to my school days—a condition of wondering doubt.

1. Paul J. Campbell, editor and publisher of *The Liberal*, an amateur paper published under the aegis of the U.A.P.A., had invited his fellow amateurs to submit short essays on the subject of faith. The works, collectively, would constitute an "Experience Meeting" in print. Among the other contributions to the Meeting was H. P. Lovecraft's "A Confession of Unfaith."

First published in the *Liberal* Vol. 1, No. 2 (February 1922): 27–30.

A Thought

How arrogant is this insignificant creature, man! How pompous in his self-hugged delusion that he is the superior of all other living things! He sets himself up a god, places himself to his own satisfaction as the favorite of that god, and then delegates to himself the functions of god-hood. Resting complacently in the fallacy that he is a superior being, he rides without compunction over other living beings, and is continually guilty of a cruelty which, if he could lose his hallucinations as to his divinely ordained position, would make him wish that there was, indeed, *no* hereafter.

Here is a little dog, one of a race on a par with man in every respect and far superior to the majority of our race in those rare traits of love, devotion, constancy, and self-effacement for those loved. The race of this little dog is celebrated for devotion "even unto death." Brought up in a family as "one of the family," nothing could ever have separated that little dog from the objects of his devotion. Taken a hundred miles away, and it would have found its way through storm and flood and in hunger and thirst back to its "own people." But what happens? Separated by a whim of its owner from its "master" for one night, it shows its love by crying softly, by going without sleep and grieving for long hours for the objects of its devotion. Man, lordly man, is disturbed slightly. He does not, as does the little dog, go without sleep. No, his sleep is simply broken. A brutal beating does not drive the love from the heart of the dog, but only brings kisses and forgiveness. So the common butcher is called, and the little dog, with no fear of death, but in grief at being separated from its loved ones, is consigned to death.

Oh, man, if there is a hereafter—shudder!

First published in the *Liberal* Vol. 1, No. 2 (February 1922): 13–14.

Howard P. Lovecraft's Fiction

Howard P. Lovecraft is widely and favorably known throughout the Amateur Journalistic world as a poet, and in a lesser degree as an editorialist and essay writer. As a story-writer he is practically unknown, partly because of the scarcity of publications of a size large enough to accommodate much prose, and partly because he does not consider himself as a competent story-teller. His first story to appear in the amateur press was "The Alchemist",[1] published in the *United Amateur*. This story was enough to stamp him as a pupil of Poe in its unnatural, mystical, and actually morbid outlook, without a hint of the bright outdoors or of real life. His second story, "The Beast in the Cave",[2] published in the *Vagrant*, was far inferior to "The Alchemist" in every respect except for its modern setting, and even this feature may be counted as against it in Mr. Lovecraft's case. The outstanding feature of this really slight effort was the skill with which an atmosphere was created, and the undoubtedly premeditated art with which the climax was made to appear anticipated and inevitable.

With "Dagon", in this issue of the *Vagrant*, Mr. Lovecraft steps into his own as a writer of fiction. In reading this story, two or three names of short story writers are immediately called to mind. First of all, Poe; and Mr. Lovecraft, I believe, would be the first to acknowledge his allegiance to our American master. Second, Maupassant; and I am quite sure that Mr. Lovecraft would deny any kinship with the great Frenchman. Third, and last, Bierce; and many will question, why Bierce? It is true that in only a few of his stories did Ambrose Bierce show himself in the role of an abnormal mentality, but this wonderful man, in common with Poe and Maupassant, while not going to the madhouse for subjects, yet certainly carried the atmosphere of the asylum into his stories.

Mr. Lovecraft with "Dagon" is not through as a contributor of fiction to the amateur press. He will never be as voluminous a fiction writer as a poet, but we may confidently expect to see him advance even beyond the high mark he has set in "Dagon".

I cannot fully appreciate Mr. Lovecraft as a poet—which is saying nothing against him as a poet! In fact, he should perhaps feel flattered! To me most of his verse is too formal, too artificial, too stilted in phraseology and form. But I can and do appreciate him as a story-writer. He is at this day the only amateur story-writer worthy of more than a polite passing notice.

1. *United Amateur* Vol. 16, No. 4 (November 1916): 53–57.
2. *Vagrant* No. 7 (June 1918): 113–20.

From the *Vagrant* No. 11 (November 1919): 38–39.

H. P. Lovecraft

Belonging, as I did, to the downtrodden proletariat, I was obliged to go to menial labor in the morning; consequently, I had to cut the session short about midnight. I left Howard sitting at my desk in the study, with the kitten curled up happily in his lap. The kitten, a part-Angora, was an unusually independent, self–centered, selfish, and cold-blooded member of his tribe, but had yielded to Howard's blandishments in spite of the fact that he had been referred to as "a member of the Felidae." About half–past six in the morning, before going down to breakfast, I poked my head in the study door. There sat Howard, in the same place in which I had left him six hours before, eyes heavy, but head unbowed, with the kitten apparently unmoved. "Good Lord!" I exclaimed, "haven't you been to bed?" "No," said Howard, "I didn't want to disturb kitty."

When you have known a man and have had contact with him for twenty years or over, an incident of this kind will first pop into your head when he is mentioned. And, indeed, such a recollection is sure to give an inkling of character. This was much more than a demonstration of Lovecraft's fondness for cats, although that was genuine and deep-rooted. I have never known a cat to refuse to make friends with him except one, very cold and haughty, short-haired, in Newburyport—evidently a member of one of the old families which, like the city itself, has been finished and frozen into immobility forever, except for an overweening pride of ancestors. Incidentally, I may say that Howard's predilection for cats resulted in perhaps the only time he was worsted in debate. An extremely voluble bird lover of the "feminine persuasion" simply overwhelmed him.

But this incident of the kitten in my study is a truer picture of Lovecraft than any he would willingly have conveyed. He considered it a part of a gentleman to possess poise, to keep a poker face at all times, to show emotion at nothing, to treat all things calmly, to wear his heart anywhere but on his sleeve. In accordance with this idea he had created a shell for himself and crawled into it. He had covered himself with a hard veneer. But this shell, this veneer, was thin, and anyone who knew him well knew his deep capacity for friendship, the aspirations and emotions which he attempted to conceal, and the genuine warmth of the heart which he would have liked to deny that he possessed. I shall never forget his outburst as we walked past the old estate of his grandfather in Providence. He lived with but one ambition—to repatriate the property before he died and restore it as it was in his grandfather's day. The crust was torn away, and you saw the man inside, red-blooded, seething with emotion.

"Why, the man in genuine!" exclaimed Howard, after our first call on Arthur Goodenough. Many of Goodenough's qualities as shown in his verse had appeared to Lovecraft as quite impossible. An almost unbelievable naivete, simple and sincere faith—sheer innocence, in other words—seemed to him quite outside the realm of the possible. During an exchange of poetic compliments shortly after they had come into epistolary contact, Goodenough had perpetrated the lines

". . . I make no doubt
Laurels from thy very temples sprout."

If one test of a poem be that it presents a picture, those lines were not lacking in poetry! The grotesqueness of the image presented struck Howard forcibly. Always extremely sensitive to literary values, he could believe only that Arthur was deliberately spoofing. I really had a hard job to convince him that Goodenough was simply incapable of the degree of malice necessary to the purposeful creation of such a caricature. Finally, Howard took my solemn word for it, and withheld his hand from a devastating reply. To all questions over a period of years I had replied, "Wait and see." Finally I was able to take Lovecraft for a meeting with Goodenough, the result being the exclamation above.

At that time I said, "Howard, you are yourself genuine, although different from Arthur."

I doubt if there was ever a more widely loved man than Howard Phillips Lovecraft. The immense correspondence which he carried on was one reason. I frequently pointed out to him that this could be only a detriment to his literary work. He would acknowledge the fact and resolve to cut various correspondents off his list, or at least to shorten his letters to them. But a chance remark in a letter would start in motion a train of thought, and the result would be a sizable manuscript. All of his correspondents, like myself, enjoyed getting his letters, but some of us groaned to see how the man was using up his energy (and he had only so much) on these private letters which, after all, amounted to very little, when he should have been working on such creative writing as would give him the place he deserved in literature. We wanted to see him world famous, and in a way he was, but we also wanted to see him in a position where he could indulge all his fancies and have aspirations fulfilled.

Lovecraft was so lenient toward the foibles and toward the literary efforts of his friends that he was not only forgiven but loved for his own very strong opinions on many subjects. The most ignorant and flag-waving American forgave him his Anglomania and his cutting remarks concerning the Revolution. A severe critic of his own work, he would go out of his way to find something to praise in the work of a friend. In some cases it took an imagination such as he possessed to find anything worth praise. Even in some of my own stuff (all a little less than valueless) he claimed to discern something to praise. What can you do about a man like that?

One outstanding trait of Lovecraft's which would not necessarily be associated with him was his love of *home*. This meant, first, Providence; second, "Rhode Island and Providence Plantations"; third, New England. On his yearly jaunts about the country to visit historic places, it was his custom to swing up into Massachusetts to make his last call on me. I would take him on his last lap home. As we swung down the Blackstone Valley on our way to Providence, Howard would straighten in his seat and sniff the air eagerly. Could you not smell the difference in the air as you come into Rhode Island! How much more sweet! How much more bracing! How much more homelike! This was not all play-acting, although it had that appearance. It was a real showing of his delight at getting home. We had just come from the Mohawk Trail, where surely, if anywhere in New England, the air should be bracing, but it did not hold the tonic properties of the air of home.

Howard's prejudices were many, but so were his enthusiasms. If you knew him but little, the prejudices were first evident. When you knew him well, he did not hesitate to show his enthusiasms. His love for Georgian architecture was well known to every one who met him. This was more than an esthetic sense of beauty—it was of the spirit. The last day that we ever roamed around Cambridge, we were not as usual making the rounds of the museums, but were seeing the new developments of the college itself. Harvard had, after the depressing (or maddening) period of "General Grant" architecture, come to itself and was erecting only purely Georgian buildings in well-planned groups. Howard meant every shiver as he passed some of these to-be-nameless buildings with his hand covering his eyes, and his ecstasy was not forced as he stood before a group of buildings on the Charles. He was inspired, his features glowed, his eyes shone with a true inner light as he gloried in Harvard rising from the depths of babbitism to a point where the vision to imagine architecture like this was possible. On other occasions I had taken perhaps low-class delight in dampening his enthusiasms for Georgian houses by crude remarks meant to be humorous, but on this occasion I was silent.

Tied up with Lovecraft's epistolary activity, and indeed a part of it, was his picture post card habit. All of his friends who kept the cards received from him had a five-foot shelf of them. After one of his trips—I think it was the one he took to New Orleans—I accused him of having an expense account something like this: Bus fare, $45.00; Food, $5.00; Post cards, $125.00. And he had to admit that I was more than half right. I have squatted on park benches, I have sat in drug stores, I have even leaned up against buildings when tables were not handy, signing dozens of cards as Lovecraft wrote them. Occasionally he even insisted that I write a line myself to someone mutually known. What postal clerks from Portland to Portland thought about them was another matter, for an infinitesimal space was left on a card for the merely incidental matter of an address after the message was written. However, I never knew of but one complaint. That was from a clerk in Paterson who wanted to collect letter postage on Lovecraft's cards. Thereafter each card to Paterson had a word or two for that particular clerk, he being "Paul Pry."

I could go on and on. But I will close these appreciations of Howard Lovecraft as a man by repeating what his old friends now end their letters with when he has been mentioned:

"We shall not see his like again."

First published in the *Olympian* No. 35 (Autumn, 1940): 28-35.

Introducing Vermont Names
(Prologue to a Study in Nomenclature)

During the last few years, for use in a "literary" way, the writer has been collecting personal names which have been used in Vermont. He at present has over ten thousand, and has by no means exhausted the subject. This is not intended [. . .] to imply that any or all of the names he has gathered are not common, or have not been used in other New England states; but names have been taken only from Vermont, good names from other states being excluded until discovered in Vermont.

The study of personal nomenclature has proved unexpectedly fascinating and "intriguing" (a horrible modern use of the word, which of course conveys the idea with great accuracy). Real puzzles are continually presenting themselves as to the origin, derivation, and gradual corruption of names, to bring them to the form in which we find them. It is a subject for a large book, and probably books have been written on it; but we have seen none.

Washington Irving was once speaking of the towns in western New York when he said: "Shallow affectation of scholarship . . . the whole catalogue of ancient worthies is shaken out of the back of Lempriere's classical dictionary, and a while region of wild country is sprinkled over with the names of heroes, poets, sages of antiquity, jumbled into the most whimsical juxtaposition."

While we are inclined to underrate the genuine learning of many of the early settlers, especially the ministers, as the discovery of classical dictionaries in the most unexpected places would indicate, still there is some truth in Irving's charge of "shallow affectation of scholarship," applied to personal as well as to other names. It is simply inconceivable that a child should be named "Elagabalus" or "Heliogabalus" (both forms appearing in our list), if the parent or the nominator knew just *what* Elagabalus was.

It is true that the classical dictionary, history, literature, humor (frequently fantastic), or wishful thinking, idea of euphony or even malice, have all been drawn on for personal names; but the Bible has been the first and the greatest of sources. It is to be doubted if there is a name in the Bible that has not been used. This use of the Bible has been carried to the ultimate extreme, it would seem, in the name "Ai," which appears to be resolving a name into its atoms, to be condensing until the very root was found. "Ai" must be the biblical city, as it was used before cross-word puzzles were prevelant and made us acquainted with the "three-toed sloth" and the "Japanese salmon." This use of the Bible we are inclined to credit to our ministers who baptized and frequently named the children—but we must not forget that there were here a great many descendants of Puritans of England who used entire sentences from the Bible as personal names. There has not as yet been encountered in Vermont a name equal to that of the famous Captain "Trib" or "Tribby" Clap (or Crabb) of Massachusetts, who was named "Through-much-tribulation-we-enter-the Kingdom-of-Heaven," but a Vermonter has been found who named his five sons Matthew, Mark, Luke, John, and Acts-of-the-Apostles. Also we find Early Sacred, Overcome Tribulation, and Valiant-for-the-Truth (all some of that hopeful thinking), as additional samples.

But the idea is unduly prevelant today that our early settlers were of a deeply religious, if not actually a pious, character. As a matter of fact, besides the many who "sat in the seats of the scornful," there was more than a sprinkling of athesists, free thinkers, agnostics and unclassical deists. Hence we have our classical names, like the unfortunate "Baalhamon."

Very interesting results can be obtained by properly matching given names to surnames for literary purposes. Also—"accidentally or on purpose"—this has been done in real life. A few to be encountered are: Preserved Fish (a name no one believes genuine until it is seen in print), Preserved Wright (what a name for an undertaker!), Increase Graves (who should have been a doctor instead of a minister), Pickled Ham, Medwell Strong, Ida Claire, Solomon Law, June Bugg, Flower Barrell, and so on, and so on.

We also run across interesting puzzles not solvable. For instance, why did the Onion family, on coming to Vermont and settling on Onion (Winsooki) River, change its name to Deming?

First published in *Driftwind* Vol. 15, Nos. 6 (June 1941): 380-82

More About Names

It develops that I did a very rash thing in writing a few casual remarks on personal names for the June *Driftwind*. The names haphazardly used in that article have been variously characterized as "fantastic," "grotesque," "improbable" and "impossible." I have been suspected, in fact, of "inventing" names. Even for literary purposes it is not necessary to invent names—and I question if a name can be invented that has not been really used. On at least two occasions I have thought that I was pretty clever in concocting a name holding some ironic significance, only to discover later that certain parents had anticipated me and had named the brat accordingly. So I have given up inventing names. It isn't necessary.

There are names for all occasions. It is forbidden in fiction to use the names of any living person, and it is advisable to avoid even using the name of anyone dead. I usually surmount this difficulty by taking a real family name and a real given name, linking them up as seems desirable. For instance, my undertaker is called "Willingly Woodbury." But, even so, I expect any day to hear from someone bearing one of my synthetic appellations. The experience of Mark Twain and Charles Dudley Warner with their "Colonel Mulberry Sellers" will be recalled by everyone.

But the epithets applied to the few names given in the previous article are quite unjust. Hundreds of as choice ones can be given at random. He was not a Vermonter, but Philip Physick was the name of a prominent American physician of the early nineteenth century. And only recently another doctor, George F. Pilz, petitioned to have his name changed. Neither of those names could have been used in a work of fiction without a charge of inventing it.

Coming back to Vermont, if the names of Publius Vergilius Booge, of Americus Vespucius Spaulding, of Most Noble Festus, of Shearjashub Spooner, Peter Pickle, Prince Soper, or even of Bunker Gay, were used by a story writer, he would be accused of farcical fabrication. Yet all these names were carried by people of some importance in their day. And in Vermont may be found the tombstone of Sir Isaac Newton. That is the actual name of the man whose grave the stone marks.

"Finis" is not at all an uncommon name, being borne by both boys and girls—for girls the name being occasionally altered to "Finia"; indicating, of course, a determination on the part of the parents to stop right there. But one Vermont family, after having named "Addenda", followed by two boys, called as they appeared, "Appendix" and "Supplement." Which ends our record of that family. It would be interesting to know how much the ingenuity of the parents was strained by further accessions.

In pursuit of names we continually find ourselves up against a stone wall when attempting to carry a family name back out of Vermont. Many names appear first in this State, the previous name being something else. The New Hampshire Grants, in a constant turmoil, with its own laws, was fighting for life against enemies in the west, the north and the east. Its inhabitants were not only feared but actually proscribed in more than one place—a good refuge to seek when in difficulties with the authorities in one's homeland. And many did take advantage of this asylum. The first Vermont historian, learned and cultured, himself came here under a cloud, although he did not change his name.

All these things make the pursuit of names an interesting subject to us.

First published in *Driftwind* Vol. 16, Nos. 1 & 2 (July–August 1941): 34–36.

A Plea for Lovecraft

The best thing that can happen to the memory and the future reputation and real standing of Howard P. Lovecraft is to have his admirers, disciples, acolytes, devotees, get at least one foot on the ground. At present they are floating or suspended in some manner in the rarefied air of the empyrean with nothing substantial to get hold of, or have their noses so closely pressed to the ground in the attitude of worship that they are blinded to all real values. As one of the idolators writes me: "Lovecraft is almost a god to me."

Irreparable harm is being done to Lovecraft by indiscriminate and even unintelligent praise, by lack of unbiased and intelligent criticism, and by a warped sense of what is due him in the way of publication of his works. In fact, I am afraid that what is due him has been entirely lost sight of, and that the only thing seen is the market for everything he wrote. So wide a circulation of even his worst stuff, and his worst was pretty bad, coupled with the assurance that it is the work of a master, is certain to have a definite reaction, and a very unfavorable one, as he comes to the notice of those whose knowledge of literary values is not blinded or stultified by personal friendship and unquestioning worship.

This awakening of the world outside of Lovecraft's comparatively small circle of admirers has already begun. In a review of *Creeps by Night* in the New York *Herald Tribune*, the writer calls *The Rats in the Walls* "pure clap-trap." This is the plain truth. Of all Lovecraft's stories, that particular one is most open to the charge. Superb clap-trap, it may be, but clap-trap none the less. August Derleth, the editor of the volume, has a keen sense of literary values in classing, analyzing, and putting in their place his own writings and the work of most others, but when he comes to the work of Lovecraft he completely mislays his yardstick and is singularly obtuse, or pretends to be so. If he brought to the Lovecraft work the same critical acumen which he applies to his own work, it would be of more benefit to Lovecraft.

Arkham House can not be blamed for cashing in on the present Lovecraft furore. With great faith, courage, personal sacrifice and hard work they published the first omnibus volume, *The Outsider and Others*, and for several years held the bag before they got back their cash expenditure on it. Strange to say, it was the publication of the second omnibus[1] (which should never have been published) that put Lovecraft over with a bang, and made the publishing of other weird books a lucrative business. This was due largely to the book being called to the attention of columnists like Vincent Starrett and others who were obliging and easy going rather than critical in giving it notices. Arkham House deserves rewards when "The Ghosts Pay Off," as John Wilstach calls it in *Variety*. The game of course is to publish anything and everything of Lovecraft as long as Lovecraft fans are howling for more and more. So it will go on as long as there is a shred of paper remaining with a word scribbled by Lovecraft on it. This is all right for the Lovecraft fans. They should have what they want. But the fact remains that nothing worse could happen to the future standing of one of the masters in the weird field. Indeed, he may eventually come to be considered one of the supreme masters, but it will be in spite of all the present over-praise, and when his work is boiled down to one well-chosen volume of no great size.

I confess that I view with some misgivings the projected publication of a volume of Lovecraft's *Selected Letters*.[2] It can be the very best of all his books—and should be. But it will be edited by a group who are much too "high" on the matter.

Of course there has been a conscious build-up for Lovecraft, and a build-up which has been eminently successful, in spite of the fact that it started with the distribution of the unfortunate second omnibus. The present boom in his name and works is loud enough so that he has even been heard about in Providence. Providence was the last city of any size to know about its native son, but even so, it was a triumph to make Providence hear at all.

Peculiarly typical of the Lovecraft criticism (or deliberate lack of it) is August Derleth's remarks on "The Outsider" in this issue of the *Ghost*. In his very important thesis, "The Weird Story in English Since 1890," Derleth in most of the article shows that same critical faculty which I have said he exhibits when dealing with his own work. But when he comes to deal with Lovecraft, suddenly his faculties are seemingly dormant. It may be said that since the writing of the thesis he has come to prefer "The Colour Out of Space" to "The Outsider" as one of the very greatest of the Lovecraft stories; but at that time he thought the latter topped them all. In connection with "The Outsider" he says "....the revelation, which the author conceals to the very end." I am most certainly casting no reflection on Derleth's intellectual integrity, in which I thoroughly believe, when I say that he must know better than that.

When I first saw "The Outsider" it was in the typed manuscript, and at the bottom of a page were the words: "My fingers touched the rotting outstretched paw of the monster beneath the golden arch." There was the revelation; there was the story. I was struck with admiration at the artistic restraint of the work, and started a note of praise to Lovecraft when, lifting the sheet, I found there was more of it. Restraint disappeared and the author enjoyed himself throwing words around. All the rest was just verbiage, words, padding, anti-climax. I wrote him then that the story should have ended there. And I still think so.

1. *Beyond the Wall of Sleep* (Arkham House, 1943). An abridged version of Cook's memoir, *In Memoriam: Howard Phillips Lovecraft* (1941), was published at the end of the book.

2. Lovecraft's letters were eventually published in five volumes by Arkham House (1965 to 1976). Those have since been supplemented by *H. P. Lovecraft: Letters to Alfred Galpin* (Hippocampus, 2003), *H. P. Lovecraft: Letters from New York* (Night Shade Books, 2005), and other recent publications edited by S. T. Joshi and David E. Schultz.

First published in the *Ghost* (May 1945): 55-56.

The Great "What Is It?"

What is Amateur Journalism? The question is a bromide to ask; and it is a bore to the one who answers it and to those unfortunate enough to read or hear the answer. For there are as many answers as there are amateur journalists.

What is an amateur paper? Charlie Parker thinks anything is not an amateur paper unless it is filled with chit-chat "about amateurs and amateur papers." It was not a genuine amateur paper to Howard Lovecraft unless it showed a conscious striving for improvement in self-expression. He spent many years trying to mold organized Amateur Journalism to his model, but failed. Doc King publishes a very well-done account of his European travels and a cry goes up that the paper in which it appeared was not an amateur. Tony Moitoret publishes his political experiences, and a groan goes up that this isn't Amateur Journalism. Both were very good Amateur Journalism, though as far as reading them goes, they might have been approached with fear and trembling—if at all. Burton Crane has in a recent *Masaka* an example of versatile brilliance that has never been surpassed in Amateur Journalism or anywhere else, writing the essay, poetry, fiction, sketch and editorial all himself, and, incredible as it may seem, I have received at least one letter complaining that this isn't Amateur Journalism! ‡🍎ʃ•ἰ¿Ω∞. He should probably have applied to the Manuscript Bureau for his table of contents.

The *Ghost* isn't an amateur paper because I don't fill it with editorial drool. When I am forced to look at some of the editorial goo I perpetrated in the old days, I am convinced that the heading I sometimes used, "Idiotorials," is the correct one, and I have no ambition to repeat the performance in this day and generation. And an occasional glance at the contemporary efforts of some of those who were my contemporaries does nothing to convince me that I could do any better today that I did then. But the *Ghost* would be an amateur paper if I did not have in it a single contribution by a member of the National Amateur Press Association nor circulated a copy in the National Amateur Press Association.

There are thousands of genuine amateur journalists in the country who never heard of organized Amateur Journalism, and who might be totally uninterested in it if they did hear of it—especially after receiving the "National Bundle." But they are amateur journalists nevertheless.

The high water mark of Amateur Journalism was undoubtedly Truman Spencer's *Investigator,* which had everything. But, look it up and you will find that some of its contemporaries carped that it was too well printed and cost too much for an amateur paper. From the "thumb nail" sheet printed with a rubber stamp outfit to the *Investigator*, if issued without hope of reward in either cash or appreciation, they are all amateur papers, absolutely regardless of contents.

And it is Amateur Journalism to deny any other paper than your own the title of amateur, and it is Amateur Journalism for me to say that everybody is wrong, including me.

As for me, I have a big project on hand to round out my amateur "career." I may issue a number of issues of this or that, but none of them will mean anything. My first paper was a rubber-stamp printed paper, but it was printed a whole line at a time in the little "stick" furnished for the purpose. This was entirely too elaborate an apparatus for an amateur. My ambition is to print a rubber-stamp paper one letter at a time. When, and if, you get such a paper from me, it will mean "30."[1]

1. "30" is used in the traditional world of handset type and letterpress printing to indicate "the end."

First published in the *Aonian* (Winter 1945): 275–76.

Jim Morton

W ould that at least a dozen different people could give us as living a picture of Jim Morton in as many activities as Hoffman Price[1] has in his sketch of the mineralogist!

It would seem to be destined that James should be more of a legend in his life than after he had left it. Nearly fifty years ago when I first encountered amateur journalism, James Ferdinand Morton Jr. was a legendary character, though intensely active and personally known. Beginning with his brilliant but erratic studentship at Harvard, stories were current everywhere of his equally erratic if not equally brilliant career after he left college.

But after he "settled down" at last in Paterson [New Jersey] he really and truly settled down, and, while his interests were as varied as ever (as, with his mind, they *had* to be) the erraticism largely if not wholly disappeared, the radical effervescent spirit was calmed, and the tales began to be forgotten as those who had known him well dropped out. He was still the great liberal (so liberal that, as some one said, he "leaned over backward") but there came a solidity, a sense of responsibility to himself and to his "job", that had been wholly lacking. After sixty years of following will-o-the-wisps, and living as precariously as that indicates, he became a "substantial citizen." Instead of being the friend of Emma Goldman and the rest of the "Paterson Reds" when they were *red* and not a confused pink, and presiding at a meeting at which Emma spoke in New York which caused several riot squads to be called out, James disappeared from the more livid news items, and was mentioned only in the reports of meetings of literary and learned societies and in *Who's Who*. The balance wheel, the gyroscopic device which he had always possessed somewhere, had started turning. But who am I to talk of balance wheels!

One sentence at least in Hoffman Price's article[2] will cause a smile from those who knew James in his younger days: "He was moderate in all things, even in the expression of firm convictions." I can imagine a few whom I could name crying, "what a change, what a 'settling down' indeed!" (There is the story of the new straw hat: For year after year Jim appeared at conventions with the same straw hat, which was getting browner and browner with the years until another shade would make it black. One year, I fear not entirely from charitable motives, a number of the boys took up a collection, bought a new hat, and presented it to James with due ceremony. For once Jim was speechless. He took that new hat, slammed it on the floor, and jumped on it.)

There was a change, indeed, from the fiery red-headed radical of the Paterson Reds era to white-haired Curator of the Paterson Museum, but not such a change in that exploring mind as it would seem.

There is even a connection or something between the *Ghost* and Morton. Just as I was preparing to issue the first number, James told me that his collection of school readers, on which he had been working for years (I had seen him add to it in Eddy's in Providence and at Day's and Colesworthy's on Cornhill) was as complete as it ever could be made. I at once commissioned him to write an article on it, which he promised to do. But as far as I know the article had not been started when he died.

Three pictures of James remain, curiously, with me. The first, a slender young man with an ancient straw skimmer perched on top of a shock of red hair. Next a rather more portly (but never fat), genial and suave white-haired scientist demonstrating with delight the fluorescence of minerals. Then, during an evening spent at my room in Boston, (the last time I saw him, I think), saying "Paul, why don't you tell me to remove my coat? It's hot here." And my saying, "Migawd, James, I didn't know you were such a stickler for etiquette. Am I supposed to help you off with it?" At this same meeting he had a paroxysm of stifling and coughing, at which I was alarmed. "It is nothing," said James, "I have made a study of the condition, and while incurable, it will never kill me." And it didn't.

As to everything being "ship–shape" in Jim's bachelor kitchen, I can only say that Ed [Hoffmann] Price visited the place on a different day from that on which I saw it, although it was probably the same year, within a few weeks, and possibly within a few days or even hours.

While in the Paterson Museum I purposely called him "Dr. Morton," in which way he had been introduced on a radio broadcast, only to be rebuked for the formality, and assured that he had no Doctor's degree anyway—had never regarded the title worth going after.

The real caliber of the Morton mind had perhaps its best demonstration when he performed the feat that made him the curator and "settled him down."

Now this story came originally from Lovecraft, but was later verified by James when I asked him about it. "How in the world did you do it, Jim?" I asked. "Oh", said he, "anyone can do anything under the spur of necessity and if they become interested. It was not as difficult as it looked!"

There was a reorganization planned of the Paterson Municipal Museum and a Curator was needed. Friends told Morton about it and urged that he apply for the position. It was a competitive examination, it being necessary that the new Curator have a definite program and show ability to carry it out. Hitherto there had been only a loose organization of the Museum and no set plan by which it was run. James at the time was at loose ends and looked over the possibilities. He decided that the Museum should specialize in minerals. Paterson lies at the centre of a very interesting country, mineralogically, but the Museum's mineral collection was small and poorly displayed and arranged. Morton told the group they would not see him for three weeks. He shut himself up in his room with a library. At the end of the three weeks he appeared and announced that he was ready for the examination. He presented his plan to the museum board, underwent a stiff examination by experts, and was appointed Curator. In other words, in three weeks James had taken a several years' course in mineralogy. He at once became widely known in that science. I doubt if such a feat was ever duplicated.

It was in connection with his minerals that James told me a story that he said was such a series of coincidences it could ever be used in fiction. There was one mineral the museum did not have and it was to be found only in one place in the East, a quarry located in Providence, Rhode Island. James knew but one person in Providence, that being Howard Lovecraft. The owner of the quarry was a "foreigner," not of a benign disposition and suspicious of everyone. There was one mortgage, and one only, held on the quarry. That mortgage was part of the small estate owned by Lovecraft. The owner thawed and aided Morton in securing what he wanted.

As one result of this mineralizing expedition to Rhode Island there was piled in the corner of Lovecraft's room for over a year a ton or so of rocks left there by Morton. When I suggested that each chunk be carefully wrapped in tissue paper and the collection packed in boxes and shipped to Morton to get them out of the way, Lovecraft treated the suggestion with a snort. They were going to stay right there until Jim came for them. He eventually did.

1. E. Hoffman Price (1898–1988), prolific pulp writer who met many of his fellow authors, including Lovecraft, Robert E. Howard, and Clark Ashton Smith, during his travels. He wrote essays on Morton, Howard, and Farnsworth Wright, editor of *Weird Tales*, for Cook's *Ghost* under the series title "The Book of the Dead." A book of that title, collecting those essays and other memoirs, was published by Arkham House in 2001.
2. "The Book of the Dead, Chapter 3: Mortonius" in *The Ghost* No. 5 (July 1947): 1–6.

First published in the *Ghost* No. 5 (July 1947): 9–11.

A Day in the Life of
Willis T. Crossman

by Himself

꿎

A DAY

WITH

CROSSMAN

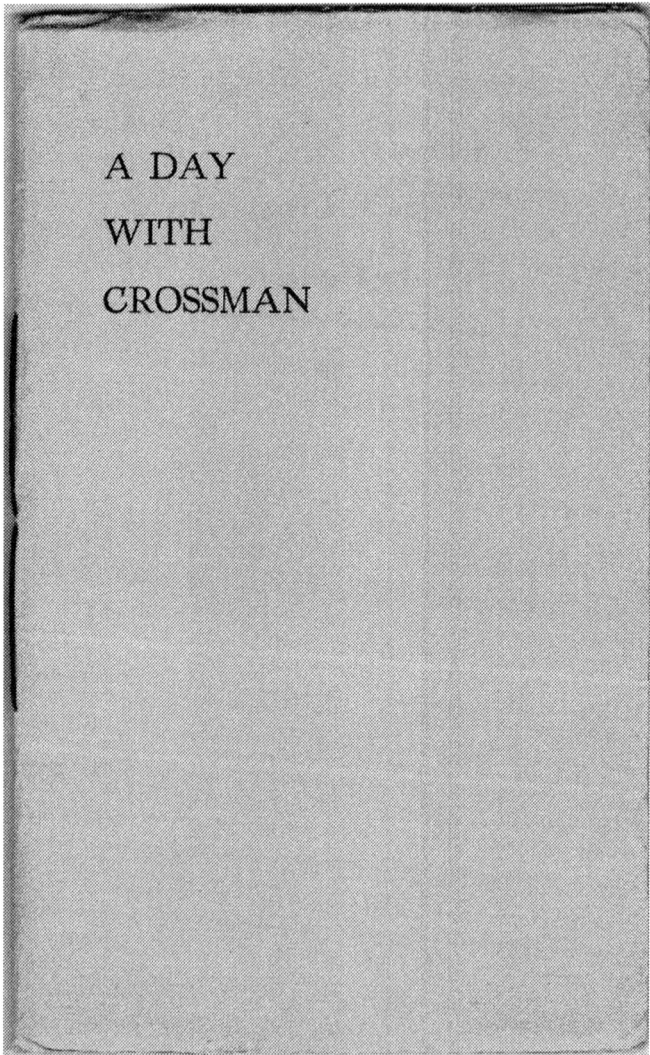

THE COVER OF *A Day in the Life of Willis T. Crossman.*

A Day

"Willis," said an acquaintance as we sat on a bench in the Public Garden, watched the swan–boats, and wondered how we were going to manage for coffee and sinkers the next morning, "You seem to have a plain and cogent, if not an elegant, style. Why don't you write a little something designed to give some of our good friends a glimpse into the life of the under–dog?"

"In heaven's name!" I exclaimed, (only that wasn't the place I mentioned), "You know my circumstances—how do you think I can get time to write an coherent article, to say nothing of getting the money to see it printed?"

"Well," answered the individual in question, "When you get a job and a room you can go without sleep some night and write whatever is necessary. As to financing, you can manage to save 25 or 30 cents a week, if you are careful, to pay toward expense of publication."

And that is how it happened. I have a job—more about which later; I am going without sleep tonight to write this drivel; and I have been putting aside 20 cents a week until enough has accumulated to either buy me a square meal or pay for this paper. It has been decided to issue the paper—I can go without eating but the habit of breaking into print can not be restrained.

What I am at times pleased to call my mind being absolutely barren of ideas as to what to write about, it has been suggested that I employ the perpendicular pronoun extensively and write about myself; not in any spirit of trying to emulate bad old Walt or the lady from Butte, but to give the history of a typical day in my life, thus explaining the difficulty in finding time, ideas or money to get an article in print.

Of course autobiography is the lowest form of fiction. I am not especially fond of autobiographical stuff, especially when it stresses the sordid side of one's existence—as anything I write necessarily must. But with such examples before me as Jack London and Harry Kemp, why should not I, being impelled to write and lacking any other subject, do it myself? Besides, Kemp's book has supported him (in a state of nudity on Cape Cod) ever since it was published—and who knows what might happen to this!

I shall not attempt to imitate these two muckrakers, nor on the other hand shall I ape that old rake Ben. His autobiography is merely a glorified maxim for the edification and uplift of the young. Ben did not tell any more than he thought wise for the purpose. As for Walt and Mary, I fear my knowledge of my own anatomy is not complete enough to enable me to profit from their examples.

On the other hand I do not want to be sentimental and try to work up any maudlin sympathy on the part of the public. If you do not want to be slobbered over, keep away from sentiment. John Brown kissed a negro baby and 'Gene Debs kissed a negro convict, and they have both been drooled over ever since. I will say in John's favor, however, that he did not have a photographer present when he pulled off his stunt.

But to our muttons—a day in my life. Yesterday will do as well as any, as there is little variation from day to day.

At about four o'clock ante mortem I am awakened by a raucous noise in the next room. I have no alarm clock and Uncle Mayer has my Ingersoll, so I have arranged with the man in the next room, who works nights, to allow his alarm to go off at this hour.

Reaching out of bed and groping around on the floor, I finally find a match which I had placed there the night before. Striking this on the wall at the head of the bed I get sufficient light to find a lamp on the stand in the corner. Removing the chimney carefully, for it is cracked and threatens to disintegrate at any moment, I finally secure a light, enough of which seeps through the soot on the chimney to enable me to see my surroundings.

On just what floor of the house this room of mine is situated I do not know. Once or twice I have counted up to eight as I climbed the stairs, but am always too tired by the time I get that far to care exactly how many flights it is—whether nine or ninety. Either ten or eleven, I should judge. The room is what is denominated a "hall bedroom," the dimensions being roughly six by nine feet. It has one advantage over a room in the Y.M.C.A. in the fact that I do not have to undress in the hall and back into bed. There is just a nice fit for stretching the arms to put on a coat. Furnishings are simple and homely, but practical. A low cot bed occupies one end of the room. The opposite end has a window, and the door is the centre of one side. A small stand behind the door contains the lamp, a package of smoking tobacco, [some tobacco manufacturer is throwing away a fortune by not making me an offer to name their product here], a pipe, matches, and a skull match-holder—a symbol of mortality I always like to have about me to bring me up short when I get cocky and think that I am somebody, that I amount to something in the cosmos, and that anything at all is worth while. In other days I owned a tobacco jar made from a genuine human skull, and tobacco kept in it for a month acquired a mellowness and a richness of aroma unsurpassed in my experience. That skull utterly vanished between darkness and dawn. I have wondered if he came after it.

Beneath the stand is a wash-bowl and pitcher, the pitcher being half-full of water, in other words, filled as far as the hole in one side approximately half-way up. Tradition in the house says that the hole was caused by the bullet with which a lady eliminated her boy-friend some fifteen or sixteen years ago. Said bullet passed through the boy-friend's cardiac region, hit the pitcher and dropped, spent, inside, where it was found. I wish to correct at this time an entirely erroneous account of subsequent developments in the affair which was bruited about at the time and is still current. It is not true, I am assured by those living in the house at the time of the tragedy, that the lady pushed the remains of her friend under the bed and forgot all about them until a week later, when she started to sweep the room. The story goes on to the effect that she then called up the police station and asked them to please come and get the body, as it was in the way. This version of the tale is purely apocryphal and is a vile canard or something smirching the memory of one who later went on the stage and still later adorned an evangelist's platform. As a matter of fact, the girl gave herself up the next morning. The evidence being purely circumstantial, admirers buying her some very becoming additions to her wardrobe, she being able to always smile when the tabloid photographers were snapping her, and her expertly displayed abysmal ignorance of which end of a firearm was which, united in causing a male jury to acquit. After a hunting trip to the Adirondacks, she went on the stage, as has been said. Having straightened this matter out, I can go back to where I was when I was interrupted.

The night before I have brought the pitcher of water up from the fourth floor, that being the highest bathroom in the house. On going down this morning I take it along and leave it there. The room also contains a small chifforobe or whatever you call them with four drawers, three of which can be opened, and a mirror in pretty fair shape, there being only a large horizontal crack and a smaller vertical one. It is somewhat perplexing, until one gets accustomed to the vagaries of said mirror, to decide which of the four faces reflected therein to shave, but it proves quite simple after some practice. Shave 'em all. A row of hooks on the wall are occupied by my other trousers, hat, coat and weskit, with an empty hook begging for the winter overcoat which I haven't any of yet.

On the floor underneath the cot is the book. I make it an invariable rule to have a book in my room. Not necessarily to read; but if one has company it sort of lends an air of tone to a place, as it were. The present book is a paper copy of Haeckel's "Riddle of the Universe." I am now reading it through for the fourth time and on each reading my mental fog gets denser on the subject, whatever it is. I got this particular copy from a sidewalk box on Cornhill for a thick nickel.

Having laved my face (I think that is the proper thing to do to a face), I empty the wash bowl out of the window. At this hour of the morning there are few about, and even if the landing of the water on the sidewalk and the passing of a pedestrian should coincide, it would be difficult to ascertain its exact source. I suppose it is all dissipated in fine mist before it gets down so far, anyway. But possibly I am malicious in thinking it might be my luck some severely cold morning the coming winter to have the water freeze in a solid lump and make connection with a policeman—preferably the one who tore all my newspaper coverlets off me on the Common last winter and told me I couldn't sleep there. As if I didn't know I couldn't! It was too cold.

Using some care to avoid stretching arms too far or kicking too violently, I get into my clothes and leave the room, first removing the wedge-shaped piece of shingle from the bottom of the door inside. When I go out I put the wedge on the outside and kick it in hard. Without knowing just what method is used in locking the door, anyone trying to enter would be perplexed. As a matter of fact there is a lock on the door, but a somewhat unreliable one, and after failing to unlock the door on two consecutive nights and being obliged to enter the next room and crawl from window-ledge to window-ledge like an almost-human fly, I finally broke the key off in the lock when the lock was closed and devised the present plan. You don't lose your key, anyway. "How," asked the landlord one day, "do I get into that room of yours? We were looking for a fire today and I couldn't unlock the door." "You don't get in," said I. I felt it unnecessary to explain that a little twist with a jack knife would be the open sesame. If there is a fire, the firemen will know how to get in—with an axe. Who ever heard of firemen unlocking a door, anyway, even when the key was in the lock.

So I climb down one flight after another (the banisters are too rickety and slivery for riding) and emerge on the sidewalk.

I am now approximately two miles from my work, and must be there at ten minutes before five to take the elevator down, so I have little time to waste. Down the street and around the corner is a restaurant conducted by the Salvation Army where I can get two doughnuts and a cup of coffee for four cents. It is run largely for the benefit of night workers, night prowlers, the homeless, and early workers. I dispose of four doughnuts and two cups of Java, and on leaving hasten my steps somewhat, arriving at my place of employment not far from the waterfront at 4:49. Two are already there and the elevator is ready with the night watchman operating it. The building is only a squat three stories in height, and no one would imagine that most of it is underground. But such is the case, for it sinks seven stories beneath the street. Therefore the elevator. One man has not shown up at 4:50, and it is forbidden that the elevator wait for him, as the operator has to punch a clock at 5:00 precisely, failure to do so being automatically cause for losing his job. As we start down and the gates are falling into place, the fourth man of the gang hurries up one-half minute late. But that half-minute means a half-day's pay to him, as this is his last chance to get down and go to work before noon.

The elevator goes only to the fourth sub-cellar, or in other words to the fifth story underground. There we get off and walk the last two stories down ramps, constructed with a gradual slope to allow the wheeling of large vegetable trucks from the lower regions to the elevator. I forget the reason assigned for not extending the scope of the elevator when the two lower floors were added, but it is beside the point—this is a plain narrative of fact and not a technical treatise.

Reaching the seventh and last story, we are now far below the level of the bottom of the harbor, though not actually under it. The air is not moist here, but is actually dry, the walls of cement glazed with a hard, smooth finish show no moisture, in striking contrast to the third and fourth stories above us, which are actually sweating and in places even covered with unhealthy-looking pale lichens. This entire structure is absolutely fire-proof against anything less than such a blaze as will melt the so-called everlasting rocks. In the entire structure, furnishing and all, there is not a quarter cord of wood or other inflammable matter. The builder warned the firm that he would not, for any consideration, take the contract for wrecking it. The ages working on it with the remorseless wear of time, just time, is thought to be the only force which will destroy it, and then only by disintegration. All this is a most consoling attitude to take when you are immured helplessly fairly deep underground—but it is to laugh! A little irritation on the earth's skin, a slight wrinkle of annoyance, and this structure with the entire ant-heap of which it is a part would be as if they had never been. Those of us who are still capable of certain degree of thought and are cursed with some imagination can feel, down here, the possibilities of the situation. Down here we get signals, messages, can see signs and portents never sensed by those on the surface, brought to us from afar over or through the marvelous system of nerves of the earth itself. I was once down in a coal mine in Missouri, (Lexington, I think) and there were, faintly, these earth noises. But there they were dulled or entirely obscured by the noises of the mine themselves. Here they come to us faintly but unmistakably in a perfect Morse. It cannot be said that this is over-easy on sensitive nerves. We had one man come to work with us who lasted just four hours. He was in a state of semi-starvation, having come to the city in early middle-age from the farm in order to make money enough to go back and live on the farm. After four hours down here, it took four of us to partially restrain him while emergency measures were being rushed to get him out of the place.

Our level consists of one huge room, partitioned off high enough (about four feet) to make eleven potato bins. In the center of the room is the "well," a hole twenty or more feet deep and five feet square, which collects all the water that may try to accumulate in the sub-cellars. It is covered with a wooden lid; through which goes the pipe for the pump which is pretty constantly in action pumping the water from the well to the ground level, where it discharges to a drain leading to the harbor. The air is slightly below moderate temperature, fans constantly renewing it from above and conditioning it before it reaches us, other fans removing the ill-conditioned air. No, this costly apparatus and excessive care as to conditions are not for the benefit of the employees. They are solely for the sake of the potatoes. Employees are plentiful and therefore cheap, but potatoes represent money. Luckily, conditions ideal for potatoes are exactly suited for the well-being of the human animal when he is exercising gently.

The four of us in this room are supposed to be more or less experts at the grading and sorting of potatoes, but really there is no expert work to it, consisting merely of labor in sorting potatoes of five kinds into four grades. There are four named varieties that are thus sorted, the fifth being a mixture of any and all varieties that come to hand. Any boy can sort as to size, and a very short period of practice is all that is necessary to learn to distinguish the grades by merely handling them.

How I became, of all things, a potato "expert," is another story, too long for this occasion. Suffice it to say that I was stranded high and dry up in Maine some years ago and spent a season on a large Waldo county potato farm, getting out of the state only by going to Boston with a carload of potatoes as a caretaker in the winter. I rode in the potato car and my duty was to keep a fire going in the stove to prevent the potatoes from freezing. The consignors were perfectly safe in thinking the caretaker would not let that fire go out. If he did it would have been just too bad for him. He would have been as stiff as a salted cod-fish the next morning. It occasionally happened that a car arrived in town full of frozen potatoes and a candidate for the North Grove street morgue and the Harvard medical school—but my carload got through all right. This method of transportation of potatoes has, I think, been done away with long ago in favor of more modern methods. On this occasion I ate potatoes and salt exclusively for ten days. Which brings me back to lunchtime in the cellar. We have in one corner of the room a sort of brazier (no, I did *not* say brassiere), a fire of very dry wood chips. When there are nearly burned out, we place potatoes in the hot ashes. At noontime the potatoes are splendidly cooked, baked with the jackets on (the only way to cook potatoes) and as mealy as though made of flour—as indeed they are, and may be, and are, cooked like flour in all ways and served in shapes varying from an adamantine or doughy lump to a delicious mealy morsel. We have a bag of salt on hand, occasionally when someone is flush and we want an hilarious (yes, I now what article I used there—I did it on purpose) time, he brings in a quarter–pound of butter, affording us a real banquet two or three times a week. The diet is nourishing and most certainly healthful, for we are all strong and never ill, but it is not fattening. I myself have dropped from 143 pounds to 121 in the six months I have been on this job, one of the other men is down to 109, which is all bony structure, and a third has built himself up to 115 from the 97 he weighed when he came to work here. But at that time he had fasted for so long that his first hearty meal of potatoes made him violently sick. He should have started on soup, but there was hardly any choice in the matter. He is feeling so well now that he is beginning to have ambitions to go out and get a better job. I am sure I don't know why.

While speaking of the varieties and grades of potatoes, I am tempted to say something about a kind of potato of which I have never seen a mention in print, and which as a matter of fact is little known even among those who make the growing and marketing of potatoes a business. The firm by which I am now employed handles practically all of this potato grown. In a very restricted area of New Brunswick, and in a still smaller one in Maine, a hill of potatoes will occasionally be found of so distinctive a character as to distinguish it unmistakably from its fellows. The tubers have actually grown out of the earth and lie on the ground exposed to the weather. This may occur to any variety of potato planted in these localities. The potatoes are a dark purple in color when raw, but when properly baked turn to an inconceivably pure white and are of an unsurpassable mealiness and flavor. The demand for these potatoes among the cognoscenti far exceeds any available supply. When found they are packed in cotton in small packages and shipped to us by express. We wrap each tuber in soft tissue paper (air must be admitted) and put in a cardboard box. These potatoes sell for from 25 cents to 75 cents apiece, and the firm has standing orders every year for more than can conceivably be received. These orders are filled in rotation, each customer being drastically limited as to quantity. The phenomenon is one that has not been explained. Analysis of the soils of these two localities reveals no difference from that in any potato-growing district. These freak potatoes if planted almost invariably return to common potatoes of their kind. Where this does not happen, the seed produces nothing. Never are freaks produced. Analysis of the potatoes themselves shows a slight, and possibly no, upset in the proportions of the element present. Therefore all attempts to propagate these freaks as a separate variety fail. The best of scientific attainment has been brought to bear on the subject without result. So there the matter rests—a natural phenomenon without parallel so far as I can ascertain; cause for sending naturalists to Matteawan, East Gardner or the Brattleboro Retreat, and for making the shades of Darwin, Asa Gray and Linnaeus tear their hair in anxiety.

The ordinary potatoes come to us in bags from the elevator floor two levels above, down a chute. The bags are opened and emptied by helpers and we grade and sort them into various bins. On orders they are rebagged and taken on small barrows up the ramps to the elevator. They are never washed and no water is allowed to touch them until they are sold, when some of the finest and most expensive grades are carefully wiped with a damp rag. But with all this we have nothing to do.

And this is all there is to it, handling potatoes until seven o'clock, when we "call it a day." I do not dare to tell how many bushels of potatoes I have handled on some days, because I do not want to be accused of bragging or suspected of telling an untruth. Back up the ramp to the elevator. Sometimes it is ready for us and sometimes not. They are not as fussy about getting us out as they are about getting us in. Frequently it is 7:30 before the elevator comes for us. If we get anxious to be out, it is possible to walk up the five stories by stairways, but there are as many doors to be unlocked and locked again, and little or no time is saved. Besides, while the others haven't as much climbing to do when they get home as I have (one of them lives in a cellar and another has appropriated a nook in an abandoned subway), still we are all too tired to willingly undergo unnecessary exertion. When I ask these two fellows how it seems to spend practically their entire time underground, they say they feel like troglodytes or whatever those old guys were, except that the troglodite (one of these spellings ought to be right) was on the way up and they were on the way down. When on the surface they are timorous, darting furtively around corners at the least alarm and continually getting themselves chased by the flatfeet. When we finally get out into the street we have the satisfaction of knowing we have $1.14 2/7 coming for the day's work.

On my way to the room I stop in the hospice of the Volunteers of America and get a beef-stew with vegetables for four cents, two slices of bread with butter for two cents, a cup of coffee for two cents and two pieces of pie for three cents a piece. At a waste paper receptacle on the corner of my street an afternoon paper may invariably be found at this hour, and frequently a dog-eared copy of the *Argosy*, *Snappy Stories* or *Hooey*, or a copy of some privately printed book of poetry—the latter doubtless deposited there by the author after he had actually read his stuff in cold print. So I am supplied with all the reading matter I have the time or inclination to indulge in. The daily paper is the only thing that I would really miss of this assorted literature. In the daily papers the humorous columns are scanned with most enjoyment. Here I find the latest dope on who won the war; the exact number of casualties in a group of female "Reds" who tried to see the office boy of the third assistant secretary to the lieutenant-governor; the statement that the employment situation is much relieved; that the average pay of the employed is twenty dollars for a week of forty-eight hours; the latest infantile utterance of the governor of Vermont; assurances from the mayor that not a man, woman or child in the city lacks the necessaries of life; a despatch from Washington to the effect that France may possibly pay part of the interest on the installment of war debts due next Wednesday; and the rest of the humorous items gathered by reporters or sent out from the various propaganda headquarters.

This is the story of a typical day in my life, which means seven days a week, except that very often we celebrate Sunday by working one or two hours longer, as large loads come Saturdays and must frequently go out Monday.

Upon reaching my room I shrug off my outer clothes, kick off my shoes, and throw myself on the bed for a time. If too exhausted, I frequently fall asleep, waking about twelve and taking off the rest of my duds. Usually, however, after resting for a half-hour or so, I get up and look over the paper. Then I kneel down and draw from underneath the bed two sheets of newspaper. The lifting of the top sheet reveals the pieces of a so-called jig-saw puzzle spread out on the lower one. Various small sections here and there are put together, but it is yet a mixed-up affair. I have been playing with the thing for five weeks, and have begun to suspect that when a former owner consigned it in disgust to the waste receptacle on the corner some of the three hundred or so pieces were missing. Well, it serves to distract us from our troubles, if any. There is exactly enough room on the floor for the puzzle and for me to lie prone, resting on my elbows, taking a chance in moving the lamp to the floor for better illumination of the intricacies of design and color. When the puzzle is completed as far as the pieces I have will go, I shall pass it on to the others in the crew.

I cannot complete this record of a day without a brief account of one of those pleasant little incidents that occur occasionally even in the most uneventful lives to break up the monotony of existence and relieve the daily grind. A few mornings ago on my way to work I found on the sidewalk a perfectly whole, unlighted cigarette, unnoticed when dropped by someone removing a cigarette from a package. Luckily having a match, I lit it up. I have to pass over a bridge spanning a roadway and a small stream of water. On this bridge, the cigarette being smoked to the point where it scorched my fingers, I tossed it overboard. A car was coming along the roadway a short distance off. I had taken but a few steps when there was a crash below and an eruption of language. Peering over the railing and under the bridge, I saw a car, (an open model), mixed up with one of the upright supports of the structure, while the driver was hurriedly crawling out, clutching frantically at his back, spouting language which seemed to consist mainly of extracts from Holy Writ, and finally making a dash for the stream and lying down in it. Evidently an escaped maniac and a person of violent tendencies. I hastened my pace a little as I continued on to work. I shall never know just what happened, it will remain forever an unsolved mystery, but the incident had broken the monotony of existence, and I worked all day with more heart in my labor.

There goes the alarm in the next room, and I must quit and go to work.

185

The foregoing was written a year or more ago. Since then I have lost that job, through circumstances not unconnected with the fact that I was late three very busy mornings running. Therefore the paper in which it was to appear had to be abandoned. I have had to give up my room and hang out wherever expedient, the present item being written in the municipal lodging house on old envelope and scraps of paper from waste receptacles, the pen having been filled in the post-office when no one was looking.

How this little booklet came into being is an interesting item. An acquaintance of mine had in some way come into possession of a copy of *Driftwind*, a unique little magazine published by Walter J. Coates of North Montpelier, Vt., and unbeknown to me sent him one of my protest pieces written in what I prefer to call staggered prose. Their literary medium is something awful, but I have tried to put into them some real facts and vigorous protest. Before I lost my job Coates had gotten into communication with me and actually had the supreme nerve to print one or two of my outbursts in his magazine, introducing the author in the following note, written by the acquaintance who introduced my stuff to him:

> Willis T. Crossman—"A peripatetic laborer working wherever work may be found. At present in Boston, employed part of time. In winter may be found on sunniest benches around the Frog Pond; in summer on the shadiest behind the Shaw Memorial. When in funds may be seen coming out of the Volunteers of America One Cent Cafeteria on Brattle Street. Has at times pawned everything he ever owned except his fountain pen."

I know of no other poetry magazine of any degree of standing that would have dared to do anything so radical and antagonistic to the general run of poetry readers. Most poetry editors are ultra-conservative by training, anyway, besides being timid and sheeplike by nature, afraid to antagonize their special clique or friends, and with an ear cocked and a weather eye open in the direction of various "patrons," or at least subscribers, whose susceptibilities must not be offended of financial support will be withdrawn. But Coates seems to consider his own inclinations first and the acquiring of a large but staid and conservative and namby-pamby list of subscribers a poor second.

And he will have none of "patrons"—these being people of standing whose names are well known or folks of no standing but with money; both classes paying in one way or another for having their names in the sheet, preferably and usually on the cover. Now Coates, besides publishing some of my stuff in *Driftwind*, acquired the entirely crazy idea of issuing a few of my pieces as a "Chapbook," one of a series of pink or red radical booklets he is publishing. So it came about that I met him—with possibly disastrous results to any reputation he may have in Vermont for being a substantial citizen. And I am responsible.

I hitch-hiked up to Barre, on this occasion there being more hitching than hiking, and arrived in that city some hours before I had expected. From there I called Coates and he drove over the ten miles or so from North Montpelier, meeting me in the park or common or whatever they call it near that horrible monstrosity, a product of the granite-cutter's chisel, which is the most conspicuous object for many miles. While waiting for Coates, however, I strolled around the town a bit, and not far from the abomination in question I found a decidedly compensating attraction in a statue of Bobby Burns standing in front of the high school, a masterpiece of the sculptor's art. Returning to the park I found Coates seated on the designated bench reading Aeschines in the original Greek or whatever the language is whose alphabet looks like chicken tracks or the w. k. Greeley chirography. It was a hot day and that was Coates' idea of hammock reading, I suppose. Coates wanted to take me home with him, but I was hardly presentable enough to be introduced in the bosom of his family. My pants, it is true, bore no obvious holes, having been patched and strongly sewed up before I started, but the rest of my habiliments were somewhat ragged, which combined with a most distressing growth of hair to render me an unattractive object. I *had* shaved, doing it that morning by a mountain brook beside which I had slept the night before and in which I had bathed that morning. It developed that the brook was part of the water supply of a nearby city, and thereby hangs a tale which must await another time and place for the telling. Coates also wanted to take me in a restaurant and buy me a feed, but I did not want to disgrace him by doing even this, and when I saw the Ritz-Carlton prices they were charging in Barre for very ordinary grub I would not let him do it anyway. So going into a chain store I got some cold ham and some biscuits and adjourned to a bench in the park, foolishly imagining that all frequenters of the place would be of the depressed classes. Sitting on the bench with the brown-paper parcel between us, we were eating out lunch (Coates proving very democratic and joining in) when who should stroll by but Coates' banker! He spoke to Coates, then looked me up and down, his back stiffened and he marched along. As I said, I don't know what was done to Coates' reputation. I am almost sorry I ever went up there, for his sake; but for my own it proved a happy event, as he is printing this paper for me for distribution to a limited number of old-time friends.

Do you know of any job in South America or some other *warm* section of the world?

Boston, January 1, 1934

Third bench from Park Street
Behind the Shaw Memorial

Protest Stuff

by Willis T. Crossman

"The needy shall not always be forgotten, the expectation of the poor shall not perish forever."

Psalms IX:18

Introduction

On the evening of March 12, 1934, a man who had sought shelter in the Municipal Lodging House in Boston was siezed with convulsions and fell to the floor, where he lay writhing in paroxysms of agony. The police were at once telephoned and after a wait of two hours appeared with the doctor who is supposed to have charge of such cases. By this time the man was quiet, and many of the more nerve-shattered inmates of the lodging house had left the institution, some unable to witness the spasms, others later thinking him dead and preferring to brave the elements rather than be with a corpse. He was pronounced alive, however, and was removed to the Relief Hospital, where emergency aid was given, and from there to the City Hospital, one of the very best institutions of its kind in the world. Here everything possible was done for him, but the apparently inexcusable delay and lackadaisical attitude of the police made it too late. The patient died early in the morning without regaining consciousness, causes being given as exhaustion superinduced by exposure and malnutrition.

The only possessions of the derelict found in his rags were a fountain pen, a pen-knife, many newspaper clippings, all relating the plight of the down-and-outs, sheets from *Driftwind* containing pieces of "flat–verse" signed "Willis T. Crossman", and scraps of paper, all scribbled over with what were evidently first drafts or suggestions for similar pieces. The address of *Driftwind* was found with the usual thoroughness of the hospital, and this matter was all sent to it as being the "nearest of kin" of the deceased. The editor promptly notified me, and this was my first knowledge of what had become of Crossman, whom I had not seen since cold weather came on the fall before. The last I knew he had gotten out of work again and had expressed an intention of going to New York and seeing what the chances were there. At the best I knew him but casually, he never spoke of his family of relatives, if any, and my acquaintance with him was confined to mutual commiseration on hard luck. I had induced him to put some of his thoughts into printable form and had introduced him to the editor of *Driftwind*, who had printed some of his stuff.

Having nothing but time on my hands myself, I at once, on hearing of his death, went around to the rooming house in the South End where I knew Crossman at one time had a room and which was his last known address. Quite unexpectedly, I found that the landlord was one of that not rare species, a man with something of a heart. Though barely keeping his own head above water during the apparently chronic hard times, he yet would do favors whenever possible. I may say parenthetically that land*lords* as a rule have more heart than land*ladies*. Not at all a gallant or a nice thing to say, but I have had ample enough experience to write $Q.E.D.$ to this proposition. The landlord at Crossman's request had kept for him a shoe-box, strongly tied with cord, and jammed full of papers. These were miscellaneous scraps, ranging from full sheets of regular writing paper down through various gradations to edges torn from newspapers. These were all written over with various things, from attempts at rhythm and rhyme, through what Crossman preferred to call "staggered prose", to prose itself. Much of this matter is undecipherable, not because it cannot be read, but because it would require an intimate knowledge of the author to make any sense from stray and disjointed sentences, obscure allusions, casual remarks, and references to this event or that. Probably most of these would have been worked into some coherent and intelligible narrative if the author had lived and better times had come.

Crossman had often expressed an intention, when and if he ever was in funds, to issue a few of his "pieces" in pamphlet form for distribution to his friends and acquaintances. With the hearty cooperation of the Driftwind Press this brochure is the answer to that urge. His own title as selected by him is used, and the format is one with which he had expressed pleasure. I am sure he will appreciate it and understand the motives prompting its issuance. I prefer to believe this in spite of the fact that he and I differed widely in our opinions of such things.

As what may be termed his literary executor, I am sorry not to be able to say more about the author. As a matter of fact, I know nothing about him. I met him first lying on the grass on the Common. That day I was out of money and without resources of any kind for raising any. Crossman had a quarter and we had supper and breakfast on it. Later the circumstances were reversed. We met fairly constantly after that over a period of some months, but never exchanged intimacies. The man had evidently had his ups and downs, had been up toward the crest of the wave once or twice, but had seen more than his share of hard knocks. One source of exasperation to me was his quiescent, devil-may-care, even fatalistic acceptance of the blows dealt by our social order. It appeared to me that he showed no ambition to fight against the pricks, to strike back, but that his sense of humor was so abnormally developed, warped and twisted that he actually got a kick out of being down and laughed at and with himself for it. Some of the apparently finished pieces in these MSS. would seem to indicate that his supineness was vanishing with the gradual lessening of his vitality, (a strange anomaly this), and that his attitude was getting to be that of the worm that turns—or that of the cornered rat. He actually becomes revolutionary at times, and if he had not succumbed to economic stress, pressed to death by the millstone above, would apparently have become an active Anarchist. I say Anarchist advisedly, for his political or economic philosophy was not complete, he entertained no Utopian dreams of a possible perfect social order, had expressed his opinion of the futility of Socialism as represented by that gentleman and scholar, Norman Thomas, and had repeatedly asserted that under Communism personal liberty would utterly vanish. In short, he was approaching a state of utter revolt at things as they are, but lacked a program or well-defined ideas as to what plan to pursue for their betterment.

The pieces collected here are but a small portion of the "finished" work of the author in my possession. Some of these have appeared in *Driftwind* and some are from MS. Even with the extremely liberal policy of the editor of *Driftwind*, some of these things could not by any conceivable method of reasoning be printed in that magazine. A mass of matter has been held back which I am sure the author would not want used at this time, being of such a character as to appear unsuitable for use for several years—if ever. If I may use such a term, it is too far advanced in its social views for present use. This matter being deliberately held back includes both prose and "staggered prose", much of it of an extremely radical and revolutionary nature. There are in particular one short and two more lengthy MSS. which can be classed only as esoterica or curiosa, and in spite of the care evidently bestowed on them by the author, he must have known their publication would be impossible.

There has been no "editing" done on this brochure, beyond selection of material. Everything is printed as written, including the punctuation. Whether the author would have made corrections and revisions or not we do not know, therefore it stands as he left it—*stet*.

W. P. C.

April 3, 1934

"And there is the usual crowd of hungry unemployed persons hanging outside the back doors of the restaurants for the refuse barrels to be put out. They manage to salvage quite a number of 'delicacies' in the way of fruit and vegetables, which are taken up to the Common to be divided."

"The Observant Citizen"
in *The Boston Post*

Rhyme

Can I speak in rhyme?
I have been asked.
At one time I wrote rhymes—
They were merely rhymes!
I had no message,
No thought to put over,
No one to convince.
I have now, I think, a message,
A message from the under-dog.
My rhyming dictionary seems obsolete.
I think anyone can write a jingle—
Everyone is doing it!
I *can* amuse myself making my stuff rhyme,
I *can*, if I will, write a sonnet
On my lady's eyebrow
Or on the varied aspects of nature.
Let the cloistered student thus amuse himself.
I am living the life of which I write.
I try to write naturally, forcefully,
To picture these things in the raw,
As they are.
If I fail, it is because even this medium
Is too artificial.
In the Boston Museum of Fine Arts
Is a futuristic "Portrait of a Man"
Done in straight lines
And unrecognizable as a portrait—
A sheer absurdity.
Our rhymesters of today
Are burning the midnight oil
Making their dreams rhyme.
The thought they had in the beginning
Is lost when they are done—
Is hidden under verbiage
When they have considered

Accents, measures, rhythms, rhymes,
When they have counted their feet,
When they have emphasized on their fingers
The beat of their verse.
Verse, verse, and more verse,
Most of it *good* verse—
We are overwhelmed with *verse*.
May the shade of Pope forgive me
For parodying the Iliad in my younger days
And thus making rhyming too facile.
Can one think deeply and rhyme,
And stick to a set form?
Perhaps.
But the mechanism is too often evident,
And it is at a cost—
The cost of convincingness.

Futility

All reigns must end,
Civilizations of necessity must crash.
Hyperborean, Atlantean, Lemurian,
Idumean, Chaldean, Babylonian,
Kushite, Phoenician, Egyptian,
Grecian, Roman, Nordic,
American, Antipodean,
And back again to the East,
They have passed or are passing,
Or are coming to power
Only to fail dismally—
Perhaps cataclysmally,
Perhaps by slow decay.
Futility?
Of course.
With history behind us,
Why advocate a revolution?
Why ask for changes in our social order?
We aspire to something
We foolishly think an improvement?
I cannot answer these questions.
I know there is no Utopia
Facing the human race
So long as the human race
Continues to be a "human" race.
There has never been a perfect state—
There will never be a perfect state.
Why advocate what Plato,
What Aristotle, what Spenser,
What Swift, what Butler,
What Bulwer-Lytton,
What countless others
Dreamed about?
They dreamed—
May *we* not dream?

Paternalism

It is easy to say
On a full stomach,
"We don't want charity—
We want work!"
But when you are hungry, my son,
It doesn't matter
Where the food comes from—
From labor, from charity,
Or from garbage cans.
A well-fed labor leader,
A round-stomached Legion leader,
A salaried Communist,
May with noble gestures
Call for *work*.
That is well and good;
But something to eat—
Work or no work—
Must be furnished the unemployed.
Where it comes from,
How it comes,
Matters not at all.
This is the only governmental problem—
How all our people shall be fed.
This is the first duty of statesmanship—
To feed our people.
Stabilization, inflation, deflation,
Foreign relations, tariff acts,
All our machinery for internal government,
Must coordinate to this one end—
To feed our people.
Paternalism if you wish;
Call it what you like,
Twenty million people
Cannot be kept on the ragged edge
Of starvation.

The Root

When it comes,
I shall welcome Communism.
It will be tough on the poor workingman,
But it will be tougher on the leisure classes.
We cannot work where we will,
But they will have to work;
We cannot eat what we wish,
But neither can they;
We cannot wear what we would like,
But they will be garbed like us.
A great leveling!
We shall come up a peg—
Comparatively only, of course;
They will come down several pegs.
What will it "get us"?
Nothing—or less than we have.
But the high and mighties will be humbled!
Jealousy? Envy?
The confessions of a failure?
Probably.
But, after all, we are human!
What root
Do all revolutions have?
Beware of too great inequality
In the classes!

Extermination

"Kill unemployment
By killing the unemployed."
A League of Nations official
So advocates,
As it is being done—
Consciously on the part of some statesmen,
Unconsciously on the part of others—
With open eyes by some countries,
With averted head by others.
It is unfortunately a slow process;
Germans are condemned to death
By starvation
In seven years;
English are kept alive for a normal period,
But their children
Will pay the penalty of malnutrition
In early death
And there will be fewer grandchildren
To present a labor problem.
In our United States
We are manufacturing homeless men
And abandoned women
By the thousands.
Our hit-and-miss systems of relief,
Without expert or even honest guidance,
Are building trouble for the future,
And making sure the next generation
Will be lacking mentally, physically,
And in all qualities
Making for the good of our body politic.
"After me, the deluge!"

Parasites

I would like to see a Soviet
In the United States
For one reason only—
To put the parasites to work.

Thousands of men
Make up their so–called minds
At an early age
To never work,
To never produce,
But by hook or crook
To live off the fruits
Of the worker's,
Of the producer's,
Toil.
"Those who will not work",
[When work is to be had]
"Must not eat."—
I would make the Jamestown dictum
Universally applicable.

I class as parasites
All types of non–producers—
And our society is top–heavy with them.
The worst of it is,
They consider themselves the upper crust
And look down upon the producer,
Upon the laborer,
As a necessary but degraded
Feature of civilization.

None of the parasitic class
Are ever to be found
Sleeping on the Common,
Seeking shelter in an abandoned subway,

Utilizing a packing case as a home,
Pawing over garbage cans
In search of a morsel of food
Only partly spoiled,
Freezing, starving, homeless, naked—
It is the workers
Who are in this plight.

After all, who blames the parasites?
They get away with it
In our present social order.
But there have been such things
As change in the social order.

The Plan

A banquet of directors,
Executives and representatives
Of a great industrial concern.
A workman unfortunately present
In a borrowed dinner jacket—
A guest of a minor official
And unknown as a workman.
Wine, liqueurs, rich foods,
Seven courses and then some,
Service, service, and more service.
Expansion under the influence of alcohol,
A confidentiality due to congenial company,
Hearts opened because of good fellowship,
Lips usually tightly sealed
Now uttering thoughts
Taboo to be given voice.

Our workmen must not be allowed beer.
Luxuries make them harder to handle.
Lack of docility is most annoying.
Their standards of living must be lowered.
Tendency to band together and organize
Must be combatted.
We need another slogan
Like the present successful ballyhoo
Of the "American Plan."

Finally the post-prandial speeches,
And talking became more then ever frank.
The big man of the company
Summed up the matter and the plan
In these exact words:
"Workmen are pampered;
Wages are too high.
Close our factories if necessary

To bring our workers to their senses.
We can live during a lengthy shut-down.
We must make the toiler
Come to us on his knees
Begging for work—
For bread."

This happened a few years ago,
During the inflation.
The plan has been put into effect
Splendidly!

"Night Worker" writes: "Benches about the Parkman Bandstand on Boston Common are a premium these early summer nights.

"On my way home in the early morning, I see practically every bench taken up by 'lodgers,' men who apparently have no homes. Their winter haunts near Scollay square and Adams square, where some of them slept in packing cases, are now deserted except when used as places of refuge on rainy nights."

"The Observant Citizen"
in *The Boston Post*

Mission

Six-thirty o'clock.
Doors open at seven-thirty, they say.
A long line of men
Huddled in ragged overcoats,
Or without overcoats,
Hunched, with hands in trouser pockets—
Those who should be rebellious,
But are merely hopeless.
Fourteen degrees above zero,
With an east wind,
But little shivering in the crowd—
They are beyond shivering.
Numb, comatose, almost the last stage—
Some of them.
The door is opened,
The men pass quietly in
Without jostling, sheeplike, docile!
Warmth, lights, the music of a fairly good piano,
Rows of benches, with backs—
One can lean back and doze and bask
In the thawing heat.

The slum missionary who speaks
Imagines he is bringing help and cheer
To these unfortunates.
He is sincere, and thinks he is consecrated,
But he should be highly salaried by big business,
By the bankers, by the dominant party
In our democracy.
His message is that of the Christ—
But exaggerated—
Patience, resignation, non-resistance,
With a reward of eventual residence
In our Father's house
Of many mansions.

Did Jesus not hunger and thirst?
Did he not suffer from the elements?
Was he not despised and down-trodden of men?
Did he not wear a crown of thorns
And suffer ultimate agony on the cross
Should we rebel at *our* fate?
The address is a soporific, a bromide,
A shot in the arm to ease quivering nerves.

Here, my brothers, is a cup of hot coffee,
With milk,
A bowl of hot soup, with crackers;
Come back in twenty-four hours for more.
Now back to your park benches,
Or, perhaps more sheltered, your alleyways.
A newspaper for a coverlet
Aids in keeping the blood in circulation.
There may be jobs in the future
When you will be needed;
So please keep alive until then.
The taxpayers can hardly afford to bury you.
Have you not been told
That patience is a virtue?

Confidence

"Have confidence!"
Cries and echoes and re-echoes
Official propaganda.
"Have confidence in the soundness
Of our institutions;
Have confidence in the integrity
Of our officials;
Have confidence in our 'democracy'."
We are frequently perplexed
Whether to laugh openly,
To smile quietly and sardonically,
To sneer bitterly,
Or to take action!
The latter will some day be done,
And then God help our rulers—
God help the four percent of our population
Who hold ninety percent of the wealth
Of the country.
Have confidence!
A poor soul who has scrimped a whole year
To have a fifty-dollar Christmas Club
And then is refused the money,
Must have confidence!
When twenty years' savings are wiped out
After a "banking holiday"
We must have confidence!
When our wages are further reduced
By a government ukase
We must continue to have confidence!
When prices of articles purchased
Advance fifty percent on government order,
Coincident with the reduction of wages,
We must kow-tow and praise the government
And keep on having confidence!
Confidence in what—

In the innate honesty of purpose of our officials?
In the basic soundness of our system of government?
In anything else of which you can think?
We know only the conditions as they exist,
And in answer to the demand
"Have confidence!"
Can reply merely—
Bah!

Boomerang

The fools!
Can they not see what they are doing?
They have made these men homeless;
They have compelled these workers to starve;
They have exposed these laborers
To the rigorous extremes of our climate
Without shelter, without protection
From the elements;
They have dulled the intellects of these mechanics
With hardships;
All with a far–reaching purpose—
To be able to hire workers cheaper,
To have labor come fawning, cringing.
Begging to work for room and board.
The plan has worked—
"Help" can be gotten at a pittance,
Men are begging for work,
Factories can be filled in a moment
With a working crew
At incredibly small wages.
But the employers, the fools,
Failed to see
That these men will not be as they were.
Hardship has taken its toll
In dulling intellects, wrecking mentalities,
Ruining the cunning skill of the hands,
Sapping endurance.
The workers have paid and paid and paid
For the criminal greed of the capitalist.
Now the capitalist must pay and pay and pay
For deliberately destroying
The finest body of workmen
Ever existent
In the history of the world.
The fools!

The Butt

"Will you give me the butt, buddy,
If I follow you a ways?
Don't throw it away.
I just walked in from Worcester
And need a drag.
We get used to going without food,
But a smoke is harder to go without
And harder to get.
Gawd! we had cigarettes in the trenches,
Occasionally—
But during peace and in the U.S.A.!"

Yes, you may have the butt—
If there is a butt;
You may have the core—
If there is a core.
We would like to give you some skimmed milk,
Which is somewhat nourishing,
But after the cream is removed
The calves need the milk remaining.
Calves will give us food later;
But even if put to work
You wouldn't produce many dividends—
You are pretty well run-down—
And there are plenty of workers.
As to luxuries in the trenches—
You will never have them again;
We have a crowd of younger workers
Whom we must kill off or incapacitate soon.
A war seems the only solution
Of the labor problem,
Of the starvation problem,
And of the dividend problem—
Especially of the dividend problem.

"Will you give me the butt, buddy?"
What a comment on our democracy!

Fealty

"In spite of the fact
That I lost sixty thousand dollars
When the banks were 'regulated',
I continued to pay him
Forty dollars a month
To keep my lawns and hedges in shape,
And then the ungrateful fellow
Actually wanted a two–weeks' vacation
To visit his mother,
Whom he had not seen in five years,
And who he claimed was ill,
When I needed him most.
I expected people of importance
And social standing
Every week-end
With company at other times.
How *could* I let him go?
It would appear his mother died;
And immediately on getting his month's pay,
The day after,
He left me with no notice—
Said he was going to the funeral.
I was ashamed to have my guests
See my lawns unshaven—
They thought I had poor control
Over my servants.
Of course I had to replace him
As soon as possible—
Apparently he thought more of his mother
Than of his job.
I do not see how I can find a place for him
After he has humiliated me so.
The man I have now
Says that he has no mother
Nor other distractions.

I picked him from one hundred applicants
On that account.
I hope he told the truth."

Vacation

Back and forth, back and forth;
First toes, then heels
Dug into earth,
Sweat streaming down their faces,
Obscuring their vision;
Muscles of arms and back
Bulging under the strain,
Pushing then hauling a heavy roller,
For two dollars a day;
Leveling, smoothing, hardening
A dirt tennis court
That there may be no inequalities
To deflect a ball from a true bounce
When the sons and daughters
Of the well–to–do
Amuse themselves.
"It gives work,"
Says the director of operations,
"To many men who need it.
We are necessary in this town.
Without us the summer months—
The vacation months—
Would be a period
Of great hardship."
Oh noble philanthropists!
Oh soft–hearted altruists!
Were it not that you can give these men work
During the vacation season
They would starve!
When is their vacation season?

Tabloid

A mother fainting at the grave of her first–born—
Snapshot in the tabloid.
A condemned on the march to the death–chair—
Picture in the tabloid:
An especial spread at one time, and a reason
For self–laudation and ballyhoo—
A pin-hole camera picture of the victim
In the death agony
As the juice was applied.
Woman having a baby in a taxicab;
The tabloid showed the world how it was done—
A useful lesson.
Indecent exposure at the beaches—
More indecency for the tabloid.
Imported actress with million–dollar legs—
Not looking so hot
When smeared in the tabloid.
Notorious female character, repentant,
Home, and kissing her mother,
(Her boy-friend and meal-ticket
Having met his deserts)—
Picture in tabloid,
With consequent vaudeville engagement.
Underworld character dies,
With photographer inexcusably absent
From the death bed—
So the tabloid presents him in his coffin.

This is the new American journalism—
And the tabloid sells!

"Rumbling of cars past their sleeping places seems to have little effect on the many apparently homeless men who seek slumber in Dock square.

"No less than a dozen or more may be observed from about 1:30 in the morning sprawled out on newspapers fast asleep.

"Where a few months ago such men were told by police to 'keep moving', I'm told that at present they are not molested."

"The Observant Citizen"
in *The Boston Post*

"Not Molested"

We thank thee,
Oh kindly guardians of the peace;
We are grateful,
Oh protectors of the well-to-do;
We are deeply touched,
Oh tender-hearted champions of the poor;
For being able to forget,
Even if for only a moment,
Your continual, "Move on—
You can't sleep here!"

"Keep moving!"
Harried from Portland, Oregon to Portland, Maine.
Chivvied out of Los Angeles;
Driven out to the desert from Tucson
To be broiled by day and frozen by night;
Moved on out of Salt Lake City;
Night-sticked out of Philadelphia;
Pistol-butted out of New York;
Kept moving in Boston.
We thank you, and the ones higher up,
Who are allowing us
To snatch a few moments' sleep
On these cement pavings,
And even with a newspaper for mattress.
For you must know,
A little sleep, even on a hard surface,
Allows one to forget—
To forget the pangs of hunger,
To forget the dizziness of the head,
To forget the nausea of the stomach,
To forget the sore and tired feet,
To forget the rags and the dirt,
To forget even the aching bones—
Aching from frequent flops like this,

On cement.
But why so suddenly merciful?
We wonder.
Has it occurred to the powers that be
That there are now so many of us
It might be unwise to continue
The old "move on" too long
And too strenuously?
Have echoes reached the ears
Of those in authority?
Has a lesson been learned
From some fable of cornered rats
Or of "bums" driven too far?
Has a flash in the eyes
Of some of those "moved on"
Indicated anything to you?
We wonder.
But it is a wise move anyway—
There are now a lot of us!

Amusement

Fifty millions for amusement?
By all means!
We need it!
No work, no money, no food,
No clothes, no shelter—
Nothing but leisure—
Please amuse us!
Spend fifty millions to show us movies
Of the Prince of Wales
In his latest outfit of sport clothes;
To furnish radio programs for us
As we sit shivering in the park;
To devise other methods of amusement for us.
A few millions devoted
To a gladiatorial combat—
Which could be staged in a football stadium
Or in a wrestling arena or garden—
Would amuse fifty thousand of us at a time
And would make us forget hunger and squalor
And exclaim:
Oh beneficent government!
Thy largesse is gratefully accepted.
The plan was successfully utilized in Rome
For many centuries
In keeping a starving people contented.
Will it work here?
How many empty stomachs
Would fifty million dollars fill?
How many warm garments
Would fifty million dollars buy?

If I were one of the powers that be,
I would stop and ponder:
How long are our people to be kept quiet
With shows, with pageantry,

With birthday parties,
With multitudes of words over the radio,
With large headlines in the newspapers;
How long?

The Parting

I raise a voice
To exalt the presence of the real,
To teach the average man the glory of his daily walk and trade.
                                                —Walt Whitman

Must I part company with you, Walt?
We have travelled together in some storms
And also in a little sunshine.
Do you remember our meeting in Pfaff's, on Broadway,
Shortly after your book was published
And before your hospital experience had chastened you?
You were an arrogant person then,
And I took your words for the gospel.
But now . . .

I have always known you were a preacher—
Although who ever paid you for sermonizing
I could never understand—
Especially when so many of your preachments
Were of the kind to be safely called unorthodox.
But I have heard you quoted by workingmen,
As a sleeping potion, or perhaps as an exhilarant,
But always as a bromide,
As a duller of the intellect,
As a restrainer of rebellious thoughts,
As a pacifier to make us contented with our lot.
When I say good-bye to churchmen—
High–priests of capital;
To labor–leaders preaching acquiescence—
Feathering their own nests;
To employers patting us on the back—
The hypocrites!
To politicians drawing rosy pictures—
But feeding only themselves;
I fear I must also say farewell to you.

Were your times so different from ours
That there was "glory" in the "daily walk and trade"
Of the average man?
You would join with these others
In trying to make us satisfied—
Or at least resigned to our lot—
Even when starving.
You aid in stifling rebellious thoughts,
In making the workingman convince himself
There is glory in labor,
In drudgery, in slavery for a pittance.
Not by these methods
Not by belief in the glory of the labor
That always enriches others than the laborers,
Will the worker come into his own.

We must part company, Walt—
You to stay where you are
And I to continue on another path—
The road of dissatisfaction, of restlessness,
Of rebellion, of revolution!

Joy Street

"The officer was treated at the hospital
For abrasions on his shins
Where she kicked him
In resisting arrest."—
Thus the report of a suborned or cowed press.
When similar testimony was offered in court
Some of the speculators tittered
And the court of justice was cleared.

The officer, six feet and one-half inch,
Weight one hundred ninety-five;
The prisoner, five feet four,
Weight ninety-seven.
Testimony of eye witnesses
Not allowed in court:
The girl, a "notorious Red",
(She *was* red-headed)
Pushed to the forefront of the crowd
To see her brother carried into the station house
Because of verbal protests
Against proposed repressive measures
Anent free speech and right of assembly.
The guardian of the law
With a snarl
Ordered her back.
Failing to obey instantly
She was grasped by the throat,
Held at arms' length,
A torrent of viturperation unleashed
(Much of it indecent)
And dragged after her brother.

"The officer was treated at the hospital
For abrasions on his shins. . . ."

What perplexes us is—
Why doesn't Communism grow faster?

Church

I have been to church—
In fact, I have been to seven churches.
Lecturers have spoken to me
On the following subjects:
The future of the Austrian Republic;
The economic situation in Russia;
Communism or Socialism—which?
The growth of Anarchy in the United States;
The place of G. B. Shaw in English letters.
In the next place the speaker's subject was "Humanism".
He appeared undecided as to what Humanism was,
But was for it nevertheless.
In the last church there was much ceremony
And considerable genuflection
In honor of a virgin,
And much not understandable praise of her.
I can well understand a virgin being honored—
That being a rare species of the human race—
But there appeared to be some doubt
About this particular one.

But I am moved to inquire,
Where is religion now preached?
Are there ministers any more?
If so, do they any longer speak above a whisper
Of Christ and Him crucified?
Is "old–fashioned religion" entirely extinct?
Is this a satisfactory substitute—
This discussion of world politics and literature?
Is Brimstone Corner changed
To a place of polite discussion of financial problems?
Are ministers of today but public lecturers—
Chautauquans and successors of Stoddard?
Is hell-fire and brimstone taboo?

Where can I go to church
And get religion?
I crave some hard-shelled infant damnation doctrine.
I crave to be scared into the fold
And thus find
Such consolation as religion may afford.

PROTEST STUFF

BY

WILLIS T. CROSSMAN

ISSUED POSTHUMOUSLY
WITH A NOTE
ABOUT THE AUTHOR

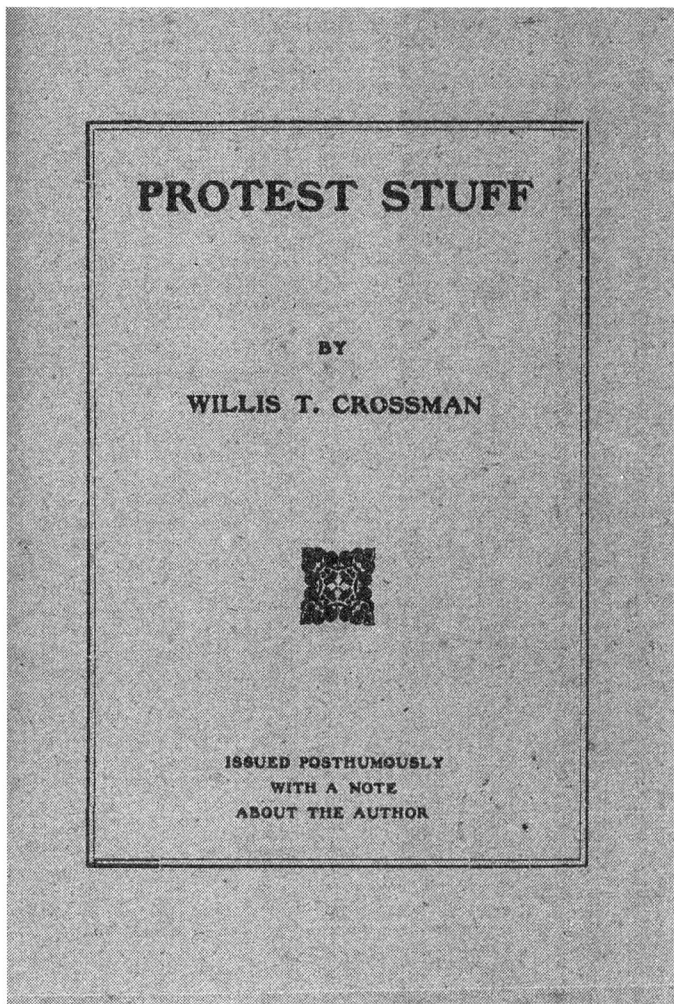

TITLE PAGE OF THE ORIGINAL BOOKLET.

Selections from Contradictions

by Willis T. Crossman

Escape

Death is before me today
Like the recovery of a sick man,
Like going into a garden after a sickness.
— The Book of the Dead

Cribbed, cabined, confined,
Hedged about,
Enclosed by walls, frustrated,
Sick at heart, irked by the limitations
Of this small habitation,
With its frailties, weaknesses, insecurity,
Tortures of mind and of body.
This shell of mortality a pent house,
A prison, builded to hector, to tantalize,
To give an occasional glimpse
Through nearly opaque windows
Into the great Beyond,
Then to restrain one from venturing.
An oubliette with rarely a ray of light from above,
Or a dungeon with never a ray.
In a sick-room, struggling for breath to live—
To live—what a misnomer;
We live only when we have ceased to live.
Under the control of an Inquisition;
The sport of a power
With a devilish sense of humor;
Toys of a huge but childish mind;
Playthings of a cruel—how cruel!—Nature;
Negligible atoms in a Cosmos.

And we endure all this
When there is a way of escape,
A broad avenue leading to freedom
But the other side of that little black door,
Which is always almost ajar.
Beyond that portal lie all the illimitable reaches.
Why do not more of us open it?

Rootless

I do not take root—
My people have never taken root.
A restless lot—
Never contented, never satisfied,
Never close to the soil.
They have never had a home,
Never known such things as home ties.
Family homesteads were not for them.
Large families were scattered,
Brothers and sisters were ignorant
Of each other's whereabouts.
They never came home—
There was no home to come to.

This is the grudge
I hold against my people—
I cannot say:
My ancestors are buried here;
Or, my great-grandfather lived in this house;
Or, this is my great-aunt Syrintha's wedding dress;
Or, this county, or this town, or this village,
Or even this street,
Was named for my folks.

We never left no landmarks,
No achievements, no upbuildings,
No scars, and no traditions.
Why, in these three hundred years,
Have we not?
I do not know—
Unless it be for the same reason
That I, now, at once,
Am moving on from here—
Must move on,
As I have done so many times before.

I left a town once
Because the architecture
Of the Methodist church steeple
Displeased me.

Why do not *I*
Found a new order of things,
Establish a permanence,
Take root,
Become attached to a place,
Be the founder of a line
To start from me?
Perhaps I will—
But I think the next town,
Or some other state,
Would be a better place than this.
And so—
I move on.

Easter

When Jesus walked the shores of Galilee
But small crowds gathered. They heard his voice,
Felt his presence, saw him face to face
And wot not what he would mean to future men.
Clad in flowing white, head bared to burning sun,
He spoke in simple language known to all,
Even the meanest of the gathering.
He spoke simple words,
In the perfect church of all outdoors.
Love was his theme, with Hope for all mankind,
Hope for this life, and Hope for an hereafter.

But he passed on. His name was made a cult.
And this for Easter, 1933:
"A colorful procession," say the prints,
Marched up the aisles of the great cathedral.
Pompous leaders of a sect clothed in gold and purple
Moved ponderously amid the odors of incense,
The strains of a mighty organ,
The chanting of a vested choir;
Basked in the adoration of a throng filling the edifice
Until doors were locked to prevent others entering.
Adoration for what or for whom?—
For the leaders of the sect?
For the mighty spectacle?
For the grandeur of the music?
No one knew.
Certainly not for this Jesus whose name the religion bears.
Prayers intoned, the language foreign to this congregation
As it was to Jesus—
Yet we are told he gave "the gift of tongues"
This his apostles might converse with all peoples in their language.
Of love, of Hope, no word—or no work understood.
The religion of a Christ? Perhaps.
But not the religion of that Jesus whom men knew.

Awakening

Blessed is he who lives and dies
Without awakening—
Without awakening from his smugness,
From his self-sufficiency,
From his conceit,
From his Phariseeism—
Who can to the end of his days
Pat himself on the back,
And say,
"I am not as other men."

But some of us wake up,
Little by little,
And discern here and there
What is hidden—
What *has* been hidden—
In some dark corner
Of our being.
We begin
To understand ourselves a little.
And every small understanding
Lessens the high regard
We have had
For our infinitesimal souls.
Luckily indeed
We do not live long enough
To awake fully!

I am beginning
To open my eyes—
Not very much,
Not very wide,
But enough to see dimly—
Enough to make me think.
Hitherto I have done little thinking

About myself.
I have taken the me as I found it
And have put the best construction
On what I found.
Self-searching has never been.
It is something of a shock
To peer into an unopened chamber
In your soul,
To open a musty closer
In your mind.

I have never quarrelled
With anyone's belief.
The proselytizing spirit
Has been lacking in me.
All creeds have been alike to me—
So long as they did not become violent,
Shake their fists in my face,
Or tread on my toes.
"Ah," I have said
With great complacency,
"I am tolerant.
I ask no one to believe with me.
They are privileged to go their way.
They are probably as right as I."

But suddenly I find
That I am *not* tolerant,
That I have never been tolerant.
I have been indifferent.
Worse yet,
I am still indifferent.
Just go on
And be damned in your own way
And I'll be damned in mine.

Agnosticism

. . . a mind which cannot find God;
and a heart which cannot live without Him.
– said of John Stuart Mill

The outer light we have
Comes from a central,
Yes, a hidden, source.
We call it sun;
And some pretend to know
Something about it.
The inner light we have
Comes from a central,
And a hidden, source.
We call it soul,
Or spirit, or god;
And some profess to know
Something about it.

Certain it is,
There is a source of outer light;
Certain it is,
There is a source of inner light.
Turning from the sun,
We are in an outer darkness;
Turning from spiritual urgings,
We are in the inner darkness:
We cannot live without the one
And the other.
Blinded without the physical light;
Groping without the spiritual brightness.

We do not know—
We can *never* know.
We can but take the light and warmth
Of the sun
As it comes to us;
We can but be receptive to an inner glow
When it manifests itself.

Waters of Lethe

Fill up the glass !
Here's to merry laughter.
Empty the glass !
Let regret come after.
Life holds enough of sadness;
Let's grasp an hour of madness.

Brim full the cup !
See if we can forget it.
Tip up the cup !
Though we may live to regret it.
Black out yesterday's sorrow
And think not of the morrow.

Dip deep in the bowl !
These moments come not often.
Leave but the lees in the bowl !
This will fate's rigors soften.
Why be a slave forever
When the bond easily sever ?

Lower the beads in the bottle !
We will live for the minute.
Bottom up with the bottle !
There is joy if we but win it.
For surcease we are striving
While life is driving, driving.

First published in the *Ghost* No. 1 (Spring 1943): 30 (under the author's
nom de plume, Willis T. Crossman).

About the Editor

Sean Donnelly is assistant to the director of the University of Tampa Press, where he is editorial assistant on the literary journal *Tampa Review*, a co-editor of the series Insistent Visions, and an associate of the Tampa Book Arts Studio. He also collects and deals in fantastic literature and mystery/detective fiction from the late 1900s to the 1950s, with a special interest in the pulp field. His previous book on Cook, *Willis T. Crossman's Vermont: Stories by W. Paul Cook,* was published in 2005. He is also the author, with J. B. Dobkin, of *The Peter Pauper Press of Peter and Edna Beilenson.* He is active in the American Amateur Press Association and occasionally publishes a journal called *from the Wild Hills.* Sean lives in St. Petersburg, Florida, with Michael, Psyche, and Mr. Church (two of whom are cats).

The book was typeset and designed by
Sean Donnelly at the office of the
University of Tampa Press
Tampa, Florida.